MW00986986

Island People:
Deep
Water
Dreams

Henry R. Danielson

Illustrated by

Julie C. Danielson

ISBN-13:
978-1719585590

ISBN-10:
1719585598

Cover photo:
Frank Adshead, *Alcid*

DEDICATION

This book is dedicated to the wonderful people who helped us find our way from the Virgin Islands to Bermuda, the Azores, England, Morocco, Spain, France, Italy and on to Turkey. You were smart, kind and always caring and helpful, and for that we thank you.
This book is dedicated to you.

Contents

Dedication.................................3

Introduction...............................10

Preface...................................11

Part 1   Crossing the Sea.....................12

  1 Preparing our Girl.........................14

  2 Finding Crew............................19

  3 The Launch.............................27

  4 Crown Bay..............................31

  5 Installations.............................36

  6 Some Troubles...........................48

  7 FinishingTouches.........................52

  8 St. Croix...............................55

  9 ChristmasWinds.........................61

  10 St. Lucia..............................66

  11 Betsy's Visit

      and on to Bequia.......................71

  12 Heading North, Mustique..................82

  13 Adventure in Martinique..................87

  14 Smooth Sailing,

      The French Islands......................98

  15 On to St. Eustatius......................100

  16 Magical Saba...........................103

  17 Saint Martin: The Dutch and

      the French...................,.........112

  18 On to Antigua..........................123

  19 Parties and Last Minute Fixes..............131

  20 The Start!.............................139

  21 Dorado!..............................144

  22 Bermuda, Poetry and

      Song!...............................151

  23 Off to the Mid

      Atlantic: Wild Weather! 158

24 After the Storm A.Poetry
   Competition!............................168

25 Horta...................................175

26 Terceria............................. 182

27 Volcanic Cooking,
   Narrow Roads and
   Gales.................................. 186

28 England! Success!.....................202

29 A Warm Pub, An
   English View, Poole...................205

30 The South Coast of
   England...............................218

31 Biscay and La Coruna.................229

32 Camarinas............................236

33 Rota, Spain..........................240

Part 2   Exploring the Med................246

34 Eastward.............................247

35 Gibraltar.............................251

36 Morocco..............................255

37 The Costa Del Sol...................258

38 Cartagena............................262

39 The Balearics, Ibiza.................265

40 Mallorca.............................267

41 Cabrera..............................270

42 Porto Cristo.........................272

43 Menorca..............................274

44 Ciutadella...........................276

45 Sardinia.............................279

46 Cala di Volpe........................290

47 Corsica..............................292

48 Elba.................................301

49 Giglio...............................306

50 Fiumicino and Constellation Nautica..307

51 Fire!................................311

52 Loose Ends.............................313
53 Learning................................ 317

Part 3   A Return to Italy and East..............319
54 Good News............................320
55 Anzio...................................323
56 Messina and Taormina..................326
57 Siracusa and Return to
      Italy...................................331
58 Greece..................................335
59 Delphi..................................340
60 The Corinth Canal
      Naousa,Amorgos and Symi.............344
61 Marmaris,Turkey.......................352
62 Istanbul................................357

Part 4   Island People: The
      Middle East, EMYR...................360
63 Back to Turkey........................361
64 Bozu Buku.............................365
65 Knidos, Gumusluk
      and Turgut Reis.......................367
66 The EMYR.............................372
67 Alanya Surprise........................374
68 Recovery...............................379
69 Rehabilitation...........................383
Glossary....................................387
Acknowledgements.........................398
About the Author...........................399

Illustrations
Paintings and Drawings by Julie Danielson
Photos by Henry Danielson

Page
12 Painting of *Tapestry*
13 Map of the Caribbean
26 View from Gemini House, Tortola, B.V.I., painting
54 *Tapestry* in Crown Bay, U.S.V.I.
111 The Road that Could Not be Built, Saba
111 Julie on the Peak, Saba
138 Map of the crossing, Bermuda to Rota, Spain
150 *Tapestry* in St. Georges Bermuda
181 We left our Mark on Horta
246 Map of Spain to Italy
254 Gibraltar, painting
257 Smir, Morocco, painting
261 Alhambra Gate, Spain, painting
266 Ibiza, Balearics,
269 Port D Andratx, painting
271 Cala di Volpe, painting
273 Porto Cristo, painting
275 Menorca, painting
281 Stintino, Sardinia, painting
283 A Pink House, painting
289 Sardinia
296 Bonifacio, Corsica, painting
305 Marina di Campo, Italy, painting
310 Fiumicino, painting
319 Sardinia to Syria, map
351 Hozovoiotissa Monestary, Amorgos, Greece
356 *Tapestry* on hard standing in Marmaris, Turkey

Poems
by Henry Danielson

14	*Tapestry*
29	Virginalia
35	Tickles Bar
41	It's Hot
53	They'll Miss Us
59	The Caribbean
64	St. Croix to St. Lucia
83	Imagine
180	Horto Ho
248	Rota
251	The Rock
252	Gibraltar
255	Tetauon
259	Almerimar
262	Cartagena Afternoon
263	Siesta
279	Stintino
280	Pressure
281	Alghero
282	Artista
284	Fourth of July at Porto Pozzo
288	Sardinia Morning Coffee
292	City of the Strait
295	Bonifacio
296	Calvi
303	Exile
315	The Bridge
328	Taormina
329	Domed Freight
329	Taormina Tribute
333	Rocella Ionica
333	Delle Grazie Marina

336   Ithaca

337   Happy 39th Anniversary

338   Missalongi

342   Greecian Sunday

345   Naousa

346   Blue and White

347   Fourth of July on Amorgos

365   Bozo Buku

Introduction

"You've got to write a book", he said. "You sailed your boat across the sea, and now you have to write a book!" So I wrote the book. "But you're not coming from any place," he said, after I had written the book. "You have to tell us who you are and where you came from. We don't know anything about you." So I wrote that book and I published it and I called it *Island People: Finding Our Way.* That is my first book and it is available in some bookstores and from Amazon.com. It deals with our Peace Corps training in segregated schools in Macon County, Alabama, our teaching school on Likoma Island, Malawi, Central Africa, teaching in Western New York, and our daunting experiences learning to sail and cruise on the Great Lakes.

But this book, *Island People: Deep Water Dreams,* is about crossing the Atlantic Ocean! We had the boat, a Nauticat 35, pilothouse cruising sailboat, built in Finland, with a short keel and spade rudder, built to cruise anywhere. We had bought it used, fixed it up a little and sailed it from Annapolis to Florida, the Bahamas and then, the big step, on to the Caribbean. That's when we met him, an older guy tied to the dock in a second hand boat. "I'm gonna sail across the Atlantic" he had said. "You could too." Us? Bermuda? The Azores? England? Europe? He said his dad had been in Croatia in World War II, and it was the most beautiful place he had ever seen. That's where he was going, and he bought a used charter boat to get him there. *World Cruising*, that was the website. We could do it too. All we need do was fill out the application and write the check. That would make us prepare the boat and do the deed. After all, when Jimmy Buffett wanted to learn to fly, what did he do? He bought an airplane! A dear friend of my parents, Hank Granger, after whom I was named, had been in the Azores during World War II. He loved that place. Always wanted to go back; never did.

You get the picture, Gibraltar, Morocco, Spain, the Spanish Islands, Sardinia, Corsica, Italy, Greece, Turkey. But first we would have to ready the boat. We would have to make a nine year old used sailboat ready to cross the Atlantic. How would we do that? What if something happened? Who would we call? What about food and water? What about storms and pirates, and collisions with ships. We would sleep in shifts. watch the radar, navigate.

After all, we were retired, we indeed were *Island People* having *Deep Water Dreams* and we would soon again be *Finding Our Way.* This book is a sequel; dare I say "sea quell," Could we quell those seas, to sail over them and find what kinds of people lived on the other side? You're holding the answer in your hands.

Preface

Where are we when this book begins?
Hank and Julie Danielson, retired high school teachers, have sailed their boat, *Tapestry,* a Nauticat 35 pilothouse sailboat, from their home in Englewood, Florida, to the British Virgin Islands, where they met a man who was preparing to sail a second hnd sloop to Europe. He would go with the Atlantic Rally for Cruisers. The book begins as the Danielson's first learn of the man's intended cruise and consider the notion of following.

Prior to that time, this retired couple had spent summers exploring all five of the Great Lakes in various small yachts from the 22 to 31 foot range. They made several passages to the East Coast, including one voyage out the St. Lawrence and down the Eastern Seaboard, across the Bay of Fundy to Maine and eventually New England and New York City, where they headed up the Hudson to Albany, the Erie Barge Canal and back to Buffalo and Western New York, from where they had started. On their 25th anniversary, they had sailed to Bermuda and returned to Lake Erie. In retirement, they explored the Intra-Coastal Waterway and the Abaco and Exuma Islands in the Bahamas.

It wasn't until they purchased the Nauticat 35, a larger boat with more fuel and water capacity, that they seriously thought of venturing farther. There was the voyage to the Caribbean, eleven days off-shore, that showed they could. After that, it was a chance encounter with a gentleman preparing his boat for a trans-Atlantic voyage that set things in motion.

This is the story of crossing an ocean, but more than that, it is the story of those they met as they traveled. There is courage here, there is great beauty. Join Hank and Julie as they venture forth to explore the world. Meet those who sailed with them, who got to know them on the other side. You need not know how to sail to enjoy the ride.

The story starts out with a poem describing their boat, *Tapestry*. She is, indeed, a gem and like them she is from different countries and is ready, in her relatively old age, to explore our world.

Part 1

Crossing The Sea

Tapestry

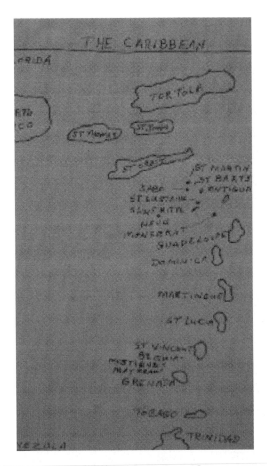

Caribbean Islands

Chapter 1

Preparing our Girl

Tapestry

So civilized, the dark Teak,
The perfectly even steps
The ship's wheel, polished brass
And varnished wood.
True symmetry.
Her sole, glowing
Varnished teak
Spaced with holly.
Orderly and efficient,
With a Japanese engine and American sails,
She is *Tapestry*, an American sloop that
Sails the clear blue waters of the Caribbean...
White sails among struggling
Black men and women, shy and gentle, bright and capable,
But largely unable to sail their own crystal seas.
Hung up by slavery and punished by
Lingering prejudice, they buy gas and
Race the human race over bumpy paths,
Keeping left on narrow roads, crashing
Over speed bumps and chasing the European Dream in circles
On a tiny island.
We are *Tapestry*
Denizens of a northern land;
Hoping to
Avert tropical storms and sail smoothly
In shimmering tropical waters.

H.R.D.
January 9, 2004

Screaming roosters. There were screaming roosters and a
hint of wood smoke in the air. There was a gentle breeze that

rippled the water. We were in Soper's Hole on the Island of Tortola in the British Virgin Islands. It was early morning. The sun glittered on the water and small sailboats painted bright red and green and blue, tugged at their moorings nearby. *Tapestry*, our thirty-five foot sailboat was anchored very near the top of the harbor. Astern, a marina and the pastel colored shops of the Pussers Rum complex shone in the morning sun. It was hot. It was always hot in April in Tortola. Julie was pulling on her running shoes and I was lowering the dinghy from the davits on the stern. I would row her past the smaller anchored sailboats, the wrecked tug washed up on shore to the dock of a second marina where several larger boats were stored and where a Jenneau 37 had just taken a slip.

Julie climbed out of our seven-foot fiberglass dinghy onto the metal pier, waved and jogged off toward the road. I sat for a moment and then got ready to push off to row back to *Tapestry*. Julie would be gone 40 minutes, not really long enough for me to go to breakfast, but too long to hang around old boats in a marina.

"Good morning" said a voice that came from the cockpit of the Jenneau.

"Oh, hi," I said, slightly startled. I hadn't expected anyone to be around so early. "Nice boat." I said, trying to be agreeable. It was nothing special, similar to hundreds of charter boats in the area.

"Thanks. Just got her. I bought her from a fellow over the internet. We had her surveyed last week, and I'll sail her over to St. Thomas to pick up my life raft later today." The man paused and looked at me to see if I wanted him to continue. I nodded and then he said: "We had to have the raft inspected. We'll be sailing to Europe next month."

"Wow," I said, suddenly quite interested. "You been planning the trip for a long time?"

"Yes. I'm going to Croatia. I have friends there, but it's also the most beautiful sailing in the world. It's just beyond Italy in the Mediterranean, Adriatic, really. Ever been there?"

"No, no. My wife and I just bought our boat last fall". We've talked about crossing an ocean some time. We sailed her off shore from the Bahamas to the Caribbean, to St. John, actually." I said, eager to share our voyage. "Took us twelve days sailing nonstop. We loved it, really. It was a great trip."

"We're going with the ARC," he said, as if he thought I should know what the ARC was.

"The ARC?" I echoed.

"Right, the Atlantic Rally for Cruisers. We leave from Antigua in early May. There will be about 20 boats. We go to Bermuda, the Azores and then some of us go on to Lagos in Portugal, and others go to Plymouth, England. There is also a start in St. Augustine, Florida."

"I suppose you need three people?"

"No, just two. Actually any two man crew with a well found boat 27 feet or more can go. It's a cruising race, and the ARC people check out your boat before you leave, but the requirements are well spelled out and not a really big deal. I needed to add a tricolor light to the masthead, and attach lights to all my life jackets. I'll need a man overboard pole and a lifesling. Of course you need a life raft which has passed inspection within a year from the date of the end of the event. Like I told you, I'll pick mine up later today."

"That is really exciting."

"Yes. They've been doing it for years; it's an English company. Hundreds of boats come west every year, but only a handful return to Europe in the spring. Most stay in the Caribbean or sail on around the world. I guess they sank one boat that lost its rudder and had to be scuttled, and someone died of a heart attack one time, but they really have an amazing safety record. You know the secret to that, don't you?"

"I guess not."

"They go at the right time. They sail east in early May, after the winter storms and before the hurricane season. They come back in November, after the hurricanes. It works. There is a web site, www.worldcrusing.com. Just remember, 'World Cruising,' that will take you right to the ARC. Costs about a thousand dollars. Let me write that web site down for you."

"I'd really appreciate that. Thanks. Good luck to you," I said.

With that I took the bit of paper, pushed the dinghy off the dock and rowed quickly back to our boat. I paused, realizing I hadn't even asked the man his name. When I glanced back, he had disappeared below.

I tied the dinghy to the stern ladder and climbed up into the cockpit. *Tapestry,* our 35 foot Nauticat sailboat, suddenly took on a new significance. Could we take her to Europe? What an idea. What an exciting idea! I closed my eyes and visualized our boat surging through huge seas as she had earlier in the winter on our passage from Staniel Cay, in the Bahamas, to Saint John, in the U.S. Virgin Islands. I remembered talking on the radio to a giant freighter as we sailed through large swells a day or so before landfall. The ship would literally disappear when we entered the trough between waves and come back into view on the crests. Thrilling! We were fifty-eight years old, Julie and me, and retired. If we were ever to do such a thing as cross an ocean in a small sailboat, this would have to be the time.

I looked up from my seat behind the wheel and there was Julie waving from the shore. I glanced at my watch and sure enough forty minutes had passed. I climbed back down the ladder, stepped gingerly into our dinghy, and rowed quickly toward shore. We had something to talk about.

That was in late April of 2003. A few days later we sailed the boat around to Nanny Cay on Tortola, and moved her into the marina there. We wanted the boat out of the water by the beginning of the hurricane season, secured and stored on land. The weather was hot, the winds had died, and mosquitoes were finding their way into the boat at night. It was not what we had signed up for. We changed oil, spread roach and rat poison around, added bleach to the water system, sealed the boat as best we could, packed our things, and caught a ride to the airport. It was not easy leaving the most expensive thing we had ever bought in a strange yard in a foreign country, but that had been our plan all along. It is just too far to sail back and forth between the Caribbean and Florida. Next winter we would pick up where we had left off, perhaps with a very exciting destination in mind.

Chapter 2.

Finding Crew

Our condominium in Englewood, Florida, is located on Manasota Key. It is a modest two-bedroom apartment in a 14 condo association. We had never lived there over a winter, but we had purchased it for retirement during the last years of our working life as school teachers from Western New York State. It had a dock and was a short walk from the beach. It was just right for Julie and me. Our good friends, Bob and Carol Markus lived next door. Julie and Carol enjoyed running together along the roads and beaches of Manasota Key. We had become close friends. Although we had been neighbors for several years, we actually met the Markuses in Highborne Cay, in the Bahamas. I remember we were anchored in Highborne harbor and their 35 foot Hunter sloop *Irie* was tied up in the marina. When we went to shore in our dinghy, I noticed their boat and I was sure I had seen it somewhere before. After a brief conversation we realized we were both from the same Florida town, Englewood.   Not only that, we lived in condominiums that were right next door to each other. What a way to meet our neighbors. We have laughed about that ever since. We visited for a few minutes while we were there and became fast friends once we got back home.

The Markuses were the first people on whom we tried the idea of going transatlantic. Bob was thoughtful, but admitted that, though he would enjoy the racing, he had never had any desire to cross an ocean. Carol was frank.

"Cross an ocean," she said, "I never even wanted to sail over night." Besides, Carol's father was old and ill, she told us, and they were caring for him. That was that.

In the meantime, however, we had contacted "World Cruising". There was a sophisticated web site available with pages of stories and communications from those involved in the crossing. Wow! It was great. We were excited. We downloaded the rules and there on the last page was an application form. We were pretty sure we would end up sailing across alone, just the two of us. It would take a big commitment of time for anyone to join us; more than most people would be able to give.

Our boat, *Tapestry*, was capable, but only marginally ready for such a journey. Although we had owned her for less than a year, she was nine years old, with well under a thousand hours on her four-cylinder diesel engine. Her sails were like new, but she had been somewhat neglected by her previous owners. She had been basically a dock ornament in her other life. *Tapestry* had some very good points and some not so good ones.

Nauticats are heavy sea going boats, built for the demanding conditions of the North Sea. In her pilothouse, there is a dry place to steer inside regardless of the weather outside. With her feathering propeller and modern fin keel, skeg rudder design, she sailed well, even in moderate wind. Those were her principal strengths. Ours had an in-boom roller furling mainsail that always worked, but that seemed to require tremendous power to raise or lower the sail. That power came from electric winches. I had never seen electric winches on a sailboat before *Tapestry*. I hadn't even wanted them. Although they were powerful, they required lots of electricity to operate, and even with the addition of solar panels, the fifty-five amp hour alternator on our engine was simply not up to the job. We had discovered that the refrigeration and lights quickly overwhelmed the electrical supply even without the use of the winches. We would definitely have to find a way to generate more electricity and resolve her other shortcomings before we attempted the crossing.

We began to compile a list. We would need a man overboard pole, and serious emergency flares. We would need an array of automatic lights for life jackets and man overboard equipment. Of course, there was the tricolor light for the masthead, and a fire blanket. What is a fire blanket? Our lifejackets would also need "crotch straps." We might need a water maker.

Somebody once said, "The best way to learn to fly is to buy a plane." Julie wrote the check, and we filled out the application, and sent it in. We would simply have to finish equipping our boat. We were going to cross an ocean. Before long we received a reply that our application had been accepted.

At the end of May that year, we returned to our little home in Ashville, N.Y. We raced on, Ed Will's, 24 foot Shark sailboat on Lake Erie, and enjoyed our 14 foot West Wight Potter, *Tinker*, sailing her in nice weather.

On the fifth of July we rose early and headed for Buffalo where we flew to Seattle. There, my cousin, Ann, was having a family reunion. She had worked for over 20 years as a cook for an outfitter who took pack trips into the mountains. As a thank you to her, the owner of the business had outfitted a trip for her whole family. This was to be her last trip. We would ride horseback from 3,500 to 7,000 feet into the Cascade Mountains of Washington. As Julie and I had only a passing acquaintance with horses, we were cautiously excited. There were as many as twenty-five of us in the party, and a wonderful party it was. Ann's children and grandchildren were there along with other relatives. We rode for hours up narrow trails to a beautiful mountain valley with a pond, streams and snow in the shadows. Mules carried tents, food, and a complete kitchen, as well as our personal gear.

Trouble was, once we got there Julie couldn't breathe. When she reclined in her sleeping bag at night her lungs became congested and she was unable to sleep. We were terribly concerned at first, but Cindy, Ann's daughter, and an E.M.T., was able to help with some medication, and after a day or so of rest, Julie was able to join us on hikes to the nine thousand foot level. It was not a big deal, she had endured similar symptoms several years before. We would look into it back home. As it turned out, an inhaler was prescribed for her asthma and she was diagnosed with Graves Disease, a thyroid hormone excess, which was treated with medication. Julie is a survivor. She had been afflicted with polio as a child and breast cancer as an adult. Of course, this was not a reason to change our plans. Quite the contrary, it served as a reminder that every day in our lives is precious.

On several occasions over the summer we mentioned our impending trip. The reaction of friends and family was skeptical. They sometimes thought we were kidding. Other times they thought we were crazy. A few people, usually after a beer or two, were enthusiastic and confided that they, too, had shared our dream. When we wondered if they would like to join us, they would often pause and then begin to think of reasons they couldn't. There might be weddings, graduations, birthdays, births, golf tournaments, whatever, but the idea of taking May to July to cross an ocean was not likely. By the end of summer, we knew we would be going it alone. That was really not a problem for us; we had always cruised by ourselves. Because Julie and I had been school teachers, we had lots of free time in summer. Unlike many other "yachtsmen" however, we didn't have much money.

Our boats were always on the small side, crowded for more than two people. Our first, a Pearson 22, named *Twiga,* carried us to various ports on the eastern end of Lake Ontario. Our second, *Temerity,* a Morgan 27, added Lakes Erie, Huron, and Michigan as well as a wonderful trip to Maine and New Brunswick via the Erie Canal. Our third boat, *Trilogy,* which we had purchased new in 1988, was a Tartan 31. We sailed her twice to Lake Superior. In 1990 we took her to the Maritime Provinces of Canada. We explored the Saint Lawrence River, past Gaspe to Isle Magdalena. We continued to Cape Breton, and Prince Edward Island. We sailed through the Straits of Canso to Nova Scotia, where we ducked into Halifax Harbor just ahead of Hurricane Bertha. We carried a spinnaker across the Bay of Fundy, to Northeast Maine and then wound our way back to New York, and Lake Erie via the Hudson River and the Erie Canal. That was truly a summer to remember. To help celebrate our 25th anniversary, in 1992, we sailed *Trilogy* to Bermuda. Finally, when we retired in 2000, she carried us safely to Florida and the Bahamas. The point here is that we had lots of experience sailing by ourselves. We were capable enough so that we felt we wouldn't need additional crew.

In October of 2003, we headed for Annapolis and the Annapolis International Sailboat show. There we made several purchases that would significantly change *Tapestry* and make her better equipped for long distance cruising. The first was a small engine driven alternator. Rather than add a large alternator to our main engine, which is not recommended by Yanmar, the manufacturer, we opted to purchase a 6 horsepower diesel engine attached to a 160 amp alternator. The system was simple and cheap, and it would not waste energy converting power from 12 to 120 volts and back again. It would simply top up our three 4D batteries quickly and efficiently. A Balmar electronic "smart" regulator and a Link 10 monitor would help us maintain and keep track of our battery bank. We would also add a separate Absorbed Glass Mat, (AGM) starting battery to the boat. That way we could use either the starting battery or the house bank to start either engine. Of course we would have to rewire a good portion of the boat's electrical system to make all this work, but that didn't worry us at the time. We also purchased a popular brand water maker at the boat show. Both items were purchased from Jack Rabbit Energy Systems. They would be shipped to Crown Bay Marina at St. Thomas in the U.S. Virgin Islands. We would move the boat to Crown Bay from Tortola and do the installations at the marina there.

In November we headed south. Englewood is beautiful in November and we enjoyed the beach and the bay. Most of all, however, we were focused on outfitting our boat. There were automatic lights for life jackets, harnesses and "throwable devices" to be purchased. "Crotch straps" were required on life jackets, but in the U.S. they didn't come that way. We bought nylon webbing for crotch straps for our life jackets, which Julie stitched in place on her sewing machine. Certain things, however, were not so easy. We had to special order an oversized radar reflector that met the specifications of the ARC; there was a page of instructions on non-verbal communications with a rescue ship or plane. We found where to send for it on the internet, and had to pay over twenty dollars to have it sent to us. At the boat show we had learned about new LED. tricolor lights, which took less power and gave off much more light than conventional models. We were on the list for the first one to become available. It would be sent to us right before departure. A life sling and a new horseshoe life buoy were needed along with appropriate lights and a man overboard pole. We purchased a DSC, Digital Selective Calling, radio with a cockpit remote to replace the old unit in the pilothouse. We spent a day in Fort Lauderdale purchasing charts and pilots and almanacs and other books that would be useful and necessary on the cruise. We would need courtesy flags for each country we would visit. There were many filters, belts and spares for the engine that we needed to buy. We bought a clock and barometer for the pilothouse. We would need a specially graduated cup for the ditch bag and "non thirst-provoking" food in case we had to abandon ship. (This turned out to be hard candy.) We also had to carry a second drogue for the life raft and several can openers for the ditch bag. In addition to those items specified on the list, we knew that we wouldn't be able to eat from plates at sea. Food would slide off onto the table. Julie bought some bowls with non-skid bottoms. We purchased a "high lift muffler" for the new generator, and several "thru-hulls" for the new equipment. We took along our sextant and its almanac as well.

By the time December rolled around our spare bedroom in the condo was pretty well filled with gear. There were even blankets and hats and scarves and gloves as we were going to the North Atlantic. England is often cold even in summer. Still, we hadn't been able to find a fire blanket. Finally, our friend Bob, a life-long fireman, found one in a catalogue used by the fire department. It would cost about a hundred dollars, but we sent right out for it. The fire blanket came in a heavy round plastic container. It was a sheet of plastic coated with slippery gel and designed to be opened and placed around a person who had been burned in a fire. (It wasn't until we arrived in England that we learned that a fire blanket was actually just a fireproof sheet used to extinguish a blaze.) Julie and I both took courses in CPR, Cardio Pulmonary Resuscitation and First Aid. We dusted off certificates from "Safety at Sea" seminars along with our United States Power Squadrons certificates.

Months earlier, we had signed up to take a three day, four night Carnival cruise with Bob and Carol and their friends, Barb and Terry, to Key West and Cozumel. It was a benefit for the local Red Cross. Unfortunately, Carol's father had become so ill the two of them were unable to go. While we were gone, Carol's father passed away. When we got back, Bob and Carol met us at the bus station in Englewood.

"We've changed our minds," Carol said. "We want to go with you guys." Carol who never wanted to sail through the night and Bob, who never cared to cross an ocean, were going with us. What a surprise. I would have to write to the ARC and send an application with their names on it. We would need a couple more bowls for eating while at sea. They would take care of their personal needs and safety gear. They would also pay for their passage to Saint Martin in the Caribbean and home from Europe. Wow.

By the time we had all our gear loaded into boxes and unloaded into the Fed Ex office, we wondered whether we had made a huge mistake. It cost over seven hundred dollars to ship our things. But there was no turning back now. When we arrived home from the shipping office, there was a message on the answering machine. Someone had hacked into our credit card company computer and stole our credit information. We would be issued a new card in two weeks or so. Help! Fortunately, we had several hundred dollars in cash. It was too late to change our reservations. The next day, we left for Tortola.

From Gemini House, Tortola, B.V.I.

Chapter 3

The Launch

From the moment we arrived in Tortola, the tension resulting from a missing credit card began to mount. Perhaps for others, the Caribbean is laid back and easy. That was not true for us. We were greeted at the airport by a good friend, Hastings Desant. He was a dark skinned mechanic with a delightful sense of humor and a wonderful way with engines and all things maritime and mechanical. Our good friends Ed and Joan Will had met Hastings years before, and they made sure we met him, too. The Will's had rented a house in Tortola for several weeks and would be there while we were doing the refit. What a wonderful thing that turned out to be.

Hastings had greased the ways for us, and when we arrived, *Tapestry* was already moved to a work area without us having to request the move. If the yard moves the boat it is free. If they move it at your request, you pay. He had also found a man to sand and paint the bottom for us. The price was right and included paint, which at local marine supply stores was twice the cost of similar bottom paint in the States. It sounded wonderful, until we were told by the marina foreman that we had to hire a man employed by the yard to do the work. Hastings assured us there was no problem. His man would paint on Sunday when the yard was closed. As an old school teacher, and one who is not accustomed to bending the rules, I found myself very uncomfortable. But the paint appeared on Saturday and the painter appeared on Sunday, right on schedule. Of course, he wanted to be paid in cash. Unfortunately, the pin number on our replacement credit card didn't work. We could charge with it, but cash machines didn't know us. A check was worthless. Fortunately, Ed's card worked in the machines. We could write Ed a check. He would get us the cash. Whew!

On Monday, Hastings and Ed crawled under the boat and

helped drill the thru-hulls for the motor charger and water maker. They were properly located in the bilge in positions where there would be room to route houses and lead them properly. With these in place, we were set to launch.

The following morning the travel lift picked *Tapestry* up from her "jack stand" cradle and moved her toward the sea. I went to the office to pay my bill, expecting to hear that because I had broken yard rules there would be some terrible penalty. But the young lady had the bill ready and when she charged it to our new credit card, it went through. Victory! Things were better.

From Tortola, we motored *Tapestry* directly to Saint John, in the U.S. Virgin Islands, where we hoped to find that our boxes of materials had arrived at the local shipping office. We motored into the tiny harbor at Cruz Bay where we had first entered the Virgin Islands, a little less than a year before. When we dropped the anchor we were dismayed to find a sign, "No overnight anchoring." We lowered the dinghy and rowed to shore where we checked in with U.S. Customs.

It was just a short walk, past the rib joint with sputtering pork ribs on a barbecue, past the street-side bar, through the traffic light and down the shaded street to the Fed Ex office. Good news! Our huge boxes had arrived. The kind lady behind the desk lent us a hand truck and we moved our heavy load, box by box, down the street toward the pier. A lady inside the tourist office by the pier agreed to watch our pile of goods as we returned for the next load. It was obvious that we would not be able to fit the huge boxes into our tiny dinghy, even one at a time. We would have to bring *Tapestry* to the pier.

The "No Docking" signs on the wharf were conspicuous, but as it is easier to ask forgiveness than beg permission, I rowed out to the boat, raised the anchor, and motored our girl into the pier. Julie caught our lines and we set to work muscling the heavy cardboard crates onto the boat. About half way through, a uniformed attendant approached looking serious and angry. He was certain that we could not stay there even a moment longer. We would have to leave immediately! We tipped the last of the boxes aboard. The indignant official would stand no more. I climbed aboard and started the engine. *Tapestry* motored slowly toward the anchorage where I again dropped anchor.

Julie, in the meantime, returned to the Fed Ex office where, at her request, the attendant searched for a missing package, a box of containing two all important storm sails. Finally, another large box was located. Julie lugged the box to our dinghy on the hand truck and then pulled the truck back to the office. Finally, with the box of sails balanced on the aft end of the dinghy, Julie rowed back to the boat. We struggled to hoist the heavy box onto the boat, pulled up anchor and chain on our hand powered windlass, and motored to nearby Caneel Bay where we picked up a mooring. Before, the moorings had always been free. This year they charged fifteen dollars per night. We could pay on shore in the morning we were told by a man in a small rubber boat. He maintained his "free" status by passing out forms to visitors and instructing them where and how to make payment. The good news was, we had our packages. In spite of numerous administrative roadblocks, we had prevailed. Was our luck changing? The next morning the outboard motor on the dinghy wouldn't start. I rowed two miles against a strong wind to pay our mooring bill.

Virginalia

"Fifteen men in a dead man's
    chest" wrote Stevenson.
This is Robert Louis land in
    warm, sunny, showery
    Virginalia.
Place of left hand drivers,
    uniformed children, hot
Winds and deep woeful

smells of decomposition;
Sweat and procreation,
    of black *belongers* and white
Guests growing darker
    under a hot tropical sun.
Where sparkling waves chase each
    other to the shore.
Here, averted glances define
    citizenship, and children play freely
Among discarded beer bottles
    and crushed cans.
Tortola, the turtles are few,
    but green volcanic peaks jut skyward,
White buoys dance on crystal
    waters, and a virgin land is violated by greed.
Here is soft brown skin,
    and the flowing music of
Brown eyed black men and women,
    Who have found paradise and
Plan to keep it.

H.R.D.

Chapter 4

Crown Bay

The Virgin Islands are tall and dramatically beautiful Islands nestled in the warm tropical waters of the Caribbean. Saint John is, with the exception of Cruz Bay and Coral Bay, mostly a national park. St. Thomas is commercial and residential. The next morning we powered *Tapestry* from her mooring in Saint John, past Cruz Bay, past Red Hook on St. Thomas, and around toward Crown Bay. We wended our way through a narrow pass with a wrecked sailboat on one side, past lovely houses on the hills and finally, past several small islands.

Around noon, we came to Crown Bay Marina. Here we were pleasantly surprised to find a modern facility with wide floating docks, a chandlery nearby, and a small restaurant right off the docks. Huge, beautiful mega-yachts were moored nearby and there was internet service and an exceptional deli right at the marina. The staff was most accommodating and when we contacted them on the radio that first afternoon, they promptly assigned us a slip. We had been told by Jackrabbit Energy, when we purchased our motor charger and water maker, that this was the best place in the Caribbean to find knowledgeable craftsmen, materials and convenient shipping. Hence this was where our motor charger and water maker had been shipped.

Once we had secured the boat and made arrangements with the marina for a week's stay, we headed for the "Tropical Shipping" depot. They were the ones who had our two pallets of goods. Just two blocks down the street from the marina was the home of Tropical Shipping. We found an African American woman behind the counter. She smiled pleasantly and peered at me over the top of her reading glasses. I told her my name and that we were expecting a shipment.

"Danielson, is that right?" She tilted her head and pressed her lips together. "Yes, your order arrived on the *Tropic*

Tide earlier today."

"Wonderful," I said. "Perfect timing."

"Mr. Danielson, I hope you are in a good mood." She said.

I could feel my stomach begin to tighten.

"Well, we've just passed a new law, January first, in fact, on shipments over ten thousand dollars, there is a tax of four per cent." she said. I could smell her perfume, and suddenly the room was very warm.

"Your order has a value of just over ten thousand dollars. You will have to get customs clearance before we can release it to you, and you will have to pay. Sorry."

"Oh," I said.

"Customs is right next door," she said. She gave me a sympathetic smile and pushed several papers toward me.

Julie and I picked up our papers and walked to the door.

"Did you notice," I said to my wife,

"What's that?" said Julie, enthusiasm disappearing from her voice.

"They never even asked for identification."

"Right," she said. "I'll get in line at customs, you get the checkbook."

After an hour's wait it was our turn. We wrote our check, filled out several more forms, listened to the thump of rubber stamps and watched endless entries being penned into journals by tired black men wearing visors. Finally we were cleared to return to the warehouse to pick up our goods.

There, on the concrete loading dock, were our two pallets. Each weighed well over 150 pounds, too much for us to carry or drag back to the boat, even though the marina was less than a quarter mile away.

"I'll deliver 'em for a hundred dollars," said a black man leaning against the warehouse wall. He laughed and then he looked at several other black men who stood nearby and smiled, showing a row of bright white teeth. He had to be kidding. Another man was engaged in conversation near a battered flatbed truck. As I approached he turned to me.

"Twenty dollars an hour. I don't think it'll take an hour, will it? "

I heaved a sigh of relief. A fork lift loaded the pallets onto the bed of his truck and I climbed aboard as Julie slid into the cab. After lurching over uneven streets for a short distance, we arrived at the marina. I helped slide the pallets from the back of the truck and struggled to lower them to the pavement.

"I'll lend you a dolly to move them to your boat," the friendly driver said. "I got to make some deliveries, but I'll be back in half an hour to pick it up, okay?"

"Thank you so much" was all I could say. I paid him his twenty dollars, tipped him, and shook his hand. We were left in a cloud of oily blue smoke as he roared away in his squeaking truck. Perspiration was running from my forehead into my eyes. It was hot!

Julie slid the dolly under the first pallet as I rocked it up on its side. Together we pushed the load over the sidewalk to the docks. It was there we discovered where Crown Bay might have gotten its name. The docks were concrete and very much crowned. If we let up for even a moment as we pushed the pallets toward our boat, the casters on the dolly would turn toward the dock's edge and our goods would roll off, splash into the water and be lost forever! We had just unloaded the second pallet when the driver came back in search of his dolly.

Loading the goods from the dock to the boat was another matter. The water maker was easy. We cut the plastic wrap and passed the modules onto the boat with relative ease. But the motor charger, or MC 160, for short, was a real challenge. It was heavy and awkward and there was no way one of us could hand its heavy diesel engine, steel frame, and alternator over the side of the boat to the other.

We loosened the main sheet and swung the boom over

the side of the boat above the dock, and then attached the motor charger to the main halyard. We ran the halyard through a block (pulley) on the boom and then used the genoa winch to carefully lift the heavy motor charger into the air. The electric assist might be too difficult to control, so we turned the winch manually. We lifted and struggled and finally we pushed the boom with its heavy load over the coaming and above the cockpit floor. We eased the line on the winch and lowered the motor charger, first to the cockpit floor, and finally into the pilothouse companionway, down five steps and onto the teak pilothouse sole.

While we were struggling with our heavy burden, the clientele of Tickles Bar, at the end of the dock, paused momentarily in their drinking and eating and watched. No doubt there were plenty of opinions about what we were doing, but fortunately, we succeeded with neither a loud crash nor a scratch on teak or fiberglass. We had made it.

The heat in the boat was oppressive, but we had succeeded, so far, and there was nothing to do but walk down the dock and join the folks having drinks and dinner. It had been a long day. It was almost dark. We were exhausted.

We had just selected a table, ordered and gotten our drinks, when there was a tremendous roar in the air. Rain was pounding on the metal roof, bouncing off the dock, pocking the water. And *Tapestry* was wide open. I dashed out onto the docks and ran for the boat. I fumbled with my keys, removed the companionway boards and descended the wet, slippery pilothouse steps. I stepped over the various items scattered on the pilothouse floor, closed the windows and the three hatches, and wiped off the laptop computer, which was, fortunately, closed at the inside helm. Ascending the steps I stepped back into the roaring rain and walked back toward Tickles, soaked to the skin. When I got back to the little bar, our table was covered with water, my wife and my drink were gone and I was momentarily stunned. But Julie was smiling from a nearby dry table.

No doubt about it, this crossing an ocean business wasn't easy!

Tickles Bar

Music issues from Tickles Bar,
 A siren song to sailors.
    Tied to docks
    Working bailers
    Retired sailors
    Beer and alers
    Whiskey drinkers
    Heavy thinkers
    Social drinkers
Music issues from Tickles Bar.

H.R.D.

Chapter 5

Installations

We awoke early the next morning and stared, dumbfounded by the clutter. The several large boxes we had brought were yet to be unpacked as was the motor charger which sat in the middle of the pilothouse floor. Water maker parts were everywhere and the smell of damp cardboard filled the air. We had lots of work ahead of us. Before long we had cut the boxes open and stored their precious cargo as best we could. That left the motor charger, or MC-160, underfoot and staring at us.

Part of the base of the pallet under the machine was three quarter inch plywood. We removed the rest of the wood, leaving the solid plywood base. Then we opened the hatch to the space below the floor that we called the engine room. There our trusty diesel main engine occupied most of the cramped quarters. It was immediately obvious to us that if we placed the new MC-160 where we had planned, centered just ahead of the engine, we would have no access to the bilge pump. Obviously, we couldn't isolate such an important part of our vessel. We measured and thought and talked and the perspiration began to flow. Although it was early morning, the air in the bilge was thick with the smell of diesel fuel and old oil. Even though the windows and hatches were open, *Tapestry* baked in the hot Caribbean sun. To say that working conditions were uncomfortable is an understatement.

After more than due consideration, we decided to place the machine slightly off-center to port at the forward end of the engine room. That would crowd the autopilot servo and fresh water pump, but still have access to them, and we would have just enough room to service the bilge pump if need be. We would also be able to service the belts and drive wheels of the

MC-160. With that decided, Julie set to work making a pattern for the mounting board to support the unit. After lunch, we walked to a nearby hardware store to purchase a saw and heavy stainless steel bolts with nuts and washers. We were amazed at the security. Heavy steel doors guarded the place. Inside, clerks filled our order. After we paid for our purchase, our receipt was checked against our goods before we could leave. We accepted the slow service and tedious routine and returned to the boat with our goods.

I hand sawed the plywood board to shape in *Tapestry's* cockpit and we fastened it securely to the floor of the engine room. Then we struggled to lower the heavy machinery onto its platform and wiggled it into place. There was just enough clearance. I drilled holes and pushed heavy bolts through as Julie held nuts and washers in place underneath, squeezing her tiny hands under the floorboards. We gritted our teeth, groaned and leaned on wrenches, tightening bolts, wary of finger jamming mistakes. But in the end, the machine was securely mounted in its new home under the pilothouse floor.

But now what? We would need to plumb it into the boat's fuel system. We would have to install cooling water intake and exhaust hoses, and worst of all, we would have to wire the alternator. But, aside from some promotional material we received when we made the purchase, there were no instructions to tell us how to do any of it.

We walked to the office of Crown Bay Marina and explained our problem to an attractive, neatly dressed young lady behind the desk. She gave us a phone number.

The next morning, when Les arrived, we were a little taken aback. He had long graying blonde hair, ragged cutoff shorts and no shoes. He hadn't shaved since the weekend. He had a nasty cut on his arm for which Julie offered hydrogen peroxide, but he refused. He said he preferred bottom paint. He claimed it kept away infection. But it was immediately evident that he understood what we were doing and knew how it should be done. There was hope. He looked around, complemented us on our clean and orderly bilge, and said that he would send a man later in the day to do the work. Les was the owner of the company.

In the meantime, we contacted an outfit whose specialty was inspecting and repacking life rafts. The lady on the phone was sure our Plastimo, four man, double floor raft could be inspected and repacked in just a few days. She suggested we take it to a nearby marina where they would pick it up at the end of the day. Julie and I lugged the heavy raft out of a locker under the seat in the pilothouse and onto the dock where we lashed it to our dock cart and began the long trek to the marina. The road was rough and dusty in the heat of the day, and the lady at the marina knew nothing of our plan, but agreed we could leave the raft.

Back at the boat, someone named Marvin appeared in jeans and a tank top. His specialty was motorcycles, but he wasn't afraid of anything mechanical. He quickly analyzed the fuel system of our boat and explained it well enough so that I felt confident that he could do the work. He didn't mind our working with him and he clearly understood mechanics. When I asked him whether he had read *Zen and the Art of Motorcycle Maintenance*, he got a strange look on his face.

"No." he said, "but I've heard of it." With that he climbed out of the engine room and headed for his motorcycle. "Gotta get some parts", he said, "I'll be back in a while." As it was late afternoon, that was the last we saw of him that day.

Evenings at Crown Bay varied little. The showers had no hot water, but the air was so warm that wasn't really a problem. In fact the splash of cold water was refreshing. Tickles Bar, just down the dock, was open to the air and filled with the sounds of pleasant conversation and music. Sometimes we went there for dinner, but most nights Julie would prepare dinner aboard. I would enjoy a cocktail or two while she made a delightful meal in the galley. There was a wonderful delicatessen behind

Tickles. We enjoyed all manner of fresh vegetables, cold, crisp salads and deli meats and cheeses.

Afterwards, we would walk the docks and acquaint ourselves with the sumptuous mega-yachts docked there. These were huge vessels in the 100 to 200 foot range, some sailboats, but mostly giant motor yachts. Their fiberglass hulls were carefully polished and gleamed in the evening light. The drone of whispering generators and the faint smell of diesel exhaust always surrounded them. Cockpits, lighted indirectly, revealed beautiful polished woods, and instrument lights glowed red at magnificent helms. Through glass doors one might see beautiful paintings and elegant furniture. An open port would reveal an engine room sparkling in white and chrome. To their owners, these yachts were the stuff of dreams, a very expensive pursuit of perfection. For the most part, they were vacant. Occasionally a puddle of shoes outside the boarding ramp of one of these giants would indicate guests were aboard. As in a sacred place, one removed his shoes before entering. Most of the time, however, only the crew, dressed in white uniforms, could be seen going about their business. To them, Julie and I simply did not exist. One night, however, there was an exception.

"Hello" I said to a middle-aged man dressed in white standing on a hardwood cockpit sole. He looked at us for a moment and then said, "Are you a Christian?"

I was taken aback by his question, and amazed he had answered me at all. As Julie and I had irregularly attended the Presbyterian Church, I muttered, "Yes."

"For God so loved the world that he gave his only begotten son that whosoever believeth in him should not perish but have everlasting life."

"John," I said, but for the life of me I couldn't remember the number.

"Yes," he said and he looked at me with large wide eyes. I wasn't sure where this conversation was going, but I had a pretty good idea we wouldn't be invited aboard for a drink.

"Most of these people aren't Christians," he said, "Oh, the man who owns this yacht, he's a pretty good man, but most of 'em, na, not even close." He looked at me with those large unblinking eyes. "Drink, women, drugs, gambling, greed, the ways of the devil. Do you know the way to salvation?"

Julie had the presence of mind to keep quiet, but he had me momentarily in his grasp. I mumbled something about thinking I did, but I knew my lack of conviction would spur him on. He handed me a paper with some biblical quotations on it. We thanked him and said good night, thankful to get away so easily, and headed back to the boat.

There were just six boats between Tickles Bar, and us and several nights each week the little bar had entertainment. Occasionally it was country, often it was a small band, but whatever the genre or volume, it was never enough to prevent us from falling quickly to sleep.

The next day, Marvin appeared right on schedule. He had parts with him and went to work at once. He cut fuel lines and installed a valve that would direct fuel either to the main engine or to the motor charger.

"Wait a minute," I said. "I'm not sure I like the one valve idea."

"Why's that? Marvin said.

"What if we're anchored some night and a storm comes up. I start the main engine, but the valve is in the wrong position. Then what?"

"You throw the valve and everything's fine. I told you. I don't think there's enough fuel to run it both ways. Anyway, I got these parts, you want me to put' em in or not?" Perspiration ran down Marvin's face,

"Go ahead," I answered. Frankly, I was glad to have the help, but I didn't want to compromise the safety of the vessel. Even with help, this job wasn't going to be an easy one.

Marvin ran return fuel lines, necessary on all diesel engines, and then set to work on the cooling system and exhaust. As we had already installed the thru-hull for the water intake, he snaked the hose from that fitting, through a bulkhead to the intake side of the engine.

"You'll need some kind of a tank for the coolant overflow," he told me. "We can use an old pop can or something like that." As I was quite sure "an old pop can" would cause any marine surveyor to look skeptically at the rest of the installation, I made an alternate suggestion.

"What do you say we plumb the overflow into the main engine overflow tank? Since both engines would be using the same antifreeze solution, it should pose no problem."

Marvin agreed and we set it up that way. It was a good addition to a neat installation. With the floorboards taken up in the pilothouse, the gleaming little white diesel M.C.160 shone beside the large gray Yanmar main engine. They virtually filled the engine compartment. That was interesting because, tomorrow, Larry, the electrician, would join us to rewire the boat to include the motor charger. There would be four of us working in a very small space in the suffocating heat of Crown Bay.

It's Hot

It's hot at Crown Bay
Hot breezes in January...
Sunburn on white skin
Bilges stink and diesels pant.

It's hot at Crown Bay
Short shorts
Reggae music
Green hills
Unshaven men
Shapely women

Sudden showers
 Lovely yachts...
With cut flowers.
It's hot at Crown Bay
But folks mellow
Black and white
Old and young
Talk and laugh
And enjoy
    And be cool, man,
        And it's hot!

H.R.D.

When Larry arrived the following morning, he was as different from Marvin as could be. He was an older man, who was both neatly groomed and articulate. He had been a marine electrician and had lived on his own yacht for a number of years. Almost immediately, I found out that he knew just what he was doing and I listened carefully to whatever he said.

"Henry, decide just where you want the Link 10 and drill a two inch hole in the console for it. Be sure you don't drill into any other wires. Locate where you will want the Balmar voltage regulator as well. You locate them and I'll wire them. We'll put the starting battery here against this bulkhead, if it's all right with you, and I'll use it to start both the main engine and the MC-160. We can use the switch there by the companionway to access the house bank to start the engines if the starting battery fails. That way you'll have a back up. Is that about what you had in mind?"

"Yes, Larry, that's just what I was thinking," I managed to reply.

"Now, the bigger wire we use, the better the system will be. Understand?"

"Uh huh."

"Right, so I'll measure the length we need and you go over there to the store and cut some wire for me. Swage end fittings on it and we'll fit it into place. Remember, the bigger the better. First thing we'll need is a buss, a big heavy buss. We'll use that for the negative. We'll run all three negatives to it, and then we will connect the positive sides together and run them through to the panel. It will give you 12 volts and power like you've never seen, but only if we do it right."

There was no doubt about it; he was a master of wire and electricity. He connected wires to the MC-160 in places I never had imagined a wire belonged. He hooked up the Link 10 and the Voltage regulator with hardly a peek at the pages of instructions, and he kept Julie and me running to the store for more and more wire. Number 1, number 2, even double zero wire we pulled off the rolls, clamped on end fittings and brought back to the boat. As he carefully ran lines from place to place in the bilge, he supported them, and neatly secured them in place.

Meanwhile, Marvin was working just inches away. He had arrived with a heavy, stiff exhaust hose. I searched, but did not find a Coast Guard stamp of approval for marine exhaust on the hose, but Marvin, a bit indignant that I should question his choice, assured me that it was rated for marine engine exhaust. We decided on a place in the side of the boat where it would pass through, and I carefully measured inside and out before I pushed the hole saw into the fiberglass. I dreaded the thought of a solid stream of water gushing inward when I had finished, but it was only sunlight that cast a bright ray in the bilge. We were a good foot above the waterline, right where we wanted to be. Marvin wrestled the hose through apertures in bulkheads, to the high lift muffler, up to deck level and back down to the hole in the side of the boat. We sealed the exposed balsa core within the side of the boat with fiberglass, slathered the bronze exhaust flange with marine sealant, placed it in the hole and drew the nut tight on the back of the flange. Then we attached the hose from the muffler and double clamped it.

There was nothing more to do but add oil and antifreeze to the engine and twist the key to see if it started. After carefully measuring oil and anti-freeze we poured them into the engine. Then we opened the thru-hull in the bottom of the boat and water gurgled through the hoses into the engine. Both Marvin and Larry looked at me and nodded. I twisted the key and there was a "wa wa wa wa wa wa, click thump," and that was it.

"Don't forget the glow plug," Larry said, a smile on his face.

I twisted the key backwards and heard a click, click, click, click, click, and then I moved it clockwise and the wa, wa, wa, wa, wa, evolved to a thum, thum, thum, and then became a steady roar.

"Hooray!" we all called out, as the engine caught and settled into a smooth rhythm.

"Check cooling water," said Marvin.

I raced up the companionway ladder and leaned over the side. Water was spraying out our bright new exhaust flange on the port side of the boat and filling Larry's dinghy, which had drifted beneath it. After pulling the dinghy away from the deluge, I returned to the engine room where both men were looking at the Link 10 charging monitor. There was no movement of the numbers at first, but then quite suddenly the numbers leaped upward until we were putting nearly 30 amps into the battery bank.

"Shut it off," said Larry. We had been running the electric battery charger on shore power since we had arrived in the marina and the batteries didn't need a charge. We reluctantly turned off our new charger.

"Everything appears to work fine," he said.

Julie and I smiled. Finally, our world was beginning to look better. We paid both men and they went their separate ways. Larry began bailing his dinghy, started his small outboard and motored off into the night. The roar of a motorcycle engine signaled Marvin's departure.

44

It was Friday night. Tonight we would celebrate with dinner at Tickles Bar. On the way to dinner we called the life raft company.

"They've had some problems with that model and year of life raft at Plastimo, you know," the nice lady said over the phone. "The seams burst sometimes when they are inflated. We probably won't be able to certify it. I've got a call into Plastimo in France now, but it doesn't look good at all. Perhaps you would want to begin thinking about a different one. Call me back in a few days and I'll have a more definite answer."

It sounded like another three thousand dollars. Would this torture never stop? I hung up the pay phone and Julie and I walked to the bar, determined to celebrate the good and shut out the other. It was a beautiful, warm night in the Caribbean in the middle of January. Besides, it was our birthday weekend. Mine was the sixteenth, Julie's the eighteenth. What could be better than that?

The next morning we turned our attention to the water maker. I had determined that we would place it under the pull out baskets that we called the pantry of our boat. There was a space there that was easily accessible from the galley, and any heat generated by the unit would help keep our crackers and cereal dry.

Julie immediately took out the instruction book, and I mean book, and began to try to decipher the instructions. We identified the various parts and were dismayed to find that there were parts in the kit that were never mentioned in the instructions. Search as we did, there was simply no mention of them. Our book, it turned out, was not only obsolete instructions for our water maker, but instructions for other models as well. Just trying to get an overview of how to set up the unit, we found ourselves flipping from one part of the book to another and then back again. Julie, who is by nature organized, was terribly frustrated. The illustrations in the book showed the unit spread out in a large locker beneath a bunk. No serious cruiser in his/her right mind would waste so much space for such a device. The instructions pointed out that it was important that the various parts be near each other, but it did not state how near. We found we could mount most everything in the chosen locker, but the membrane itself simply would not fit. We wanted to mount it in the forward head, or bathroom, and we felt it would be best if it were mounted vertically rather than horizontally, as was pictured in the instructions. Finally, we decided to call the company in California with our concerns.

The lady who answered the phone was pleasant and easy going, but didn't have her computer up and couldn't find her glasses. When she was finally up to speed she told us that our system included a "fresh water flush" and that was the part omitted from the instructions. She offered to mail us a new book, but that would take weeks and we feared we would not receive it until we picked up our mail in several months. We finally gave her a fax number and she said she would fax the required pages. Once they had arrived, things were still not clear, but we hoped that we could complete the assembly. We mounted the various pieces of hardware and Julie began stringing hoses and wires from one component to the next. We began with the sea water inlet and carried the lines through the first filter, the fresh water pump, the primary filter, the high pressure pump, the diaphragm, and finally to the sea water discharge and, for the fresh water, to the fresh water tank in the boat. We also hooked up the fresh water flush system, which pumped fresh water from our tanks backwards through the system to clean it. There was also a console with start/stop buttons, gauges, and indicator lights. We had mounted that in a cabinet in the head. The instructions for connecting the console were as vague as we had come to expect. Julie who usually is confident with complex tasks assured me that she was terribly frustrated.

"It was one of the hardest things I've ever done," she said. When we finally were nearly finished with the installation, days later, we were both quite exhausted. It was obvious to us that we needed more time, but other matters beckoned. Even though our water maker was not installed and our life raft was in limbo, we would have to leave this place and return to Tortola. Had we made the boat better, or had we just cluttered her with marginal gear that might lead to eternal frustration or much worse? Maybe an interim shakedown cruise was a really good idea. At any rate, we would check out of Crown Bay and head back to Tortola

Our friends Joanie and Ed Will, back on Tortola, would not be able to stay in the house they had rented the whole time they would be on island. We had looked forward to having them as guests for the few days that remained before their flight. What a good idea that turned out to be.

Chapter 6

Some Troubles

We bid good-bye to our friends at Crown Bay and headed for Tortola. We knew we would have to return to resolve the life raft question and finish the water maker. Before long we noticed that our diesel engine was coughing and running poorly. We shut down and let the boat drift. Julie squeezed into a small space beside the engine and removed the fuel filter from the Racor water separator. We had changed it shortly after launching the boat and the filter didn't look dirty enough to cause the engine to stall. We looked with suspicion at the new valve installation. Had we set the valve in the correct position for the main engine? It wasn't marked. We moved the valve setting and the engine ran better. Before long we had landed in Tortola, cleared customs, and were back together with our friends. It was wonderful to see these good people again. Eddy, an electrician in his own right, climbed right into the bilge and inspected the installation of the M.C. 160. Methodically, he went over every connection while tugging on and puzzling over the reason for every wire, he found a few loose ones.

"Henry, give me a wrench." He checked each of the bolts to be sure they were tight. "Shrink wrap, he said. Is there a reason you didn't use shrink wrap on these connections?" It was a long while before he emerged from the bilge. .

It had dawned on me that people don't generally come to the Virgin Islands because they want to work real hard. At the same time the work we were having done was deadly serious. It is a long way across the Atlantic.

Winds were strong when we headed out the next morning. We raised sail right outside Soper's Hole and beat our way along the Sir Francis Drake Channel. A long, sleek racing sloop, several times *Tapestry's* length, gushed by us on a port tack. She was just a couple of boat lengths below us. Her huge bronze bottom glowed as she momentarily heeled far over in the afternoon sun. We sailed through the Islands to Norman's Cay where we picked up a mooring and stopped for a drink at a little bar on shore. It was filled with couples from charter boats relaxing after their day's sail. We had a drink and after a bit, we headed for the *Willie T* an old fishing boat anchored in the harbor and converted to a bar.

The place was noisy as vacationers drank and laughed. There was a tradition that any lady who would climb to the top deck, take all her clothes off and then jump from the top deck, past the bar, into the water below, would get a free tee shirt. When we got there a young woman had just made the plunge, much to the delight of the sharp-eyed revelers at the bar. While she was in the water she had struggled back into her bathing suit, but her eyes belied a kind of panic and she was beckoning to her girlfriends to help her onto the boarding platform. She seemed to have hurt her back. Her friends pulled her onto the ship and then helped her into a dinghy. The noisy bar was suddenly quiet. The crowd gathered round and stared at this rather voluptuous woman in distress. There was something very unpleasant about the whole scene. The magic of the evening faded. In our seven-foot dinghy, I took Joanie and Julie back to the boat then returned for Ed. The girls cooked a fine dinner for us, and that evening we enjoyed *Tapestry* as she swung at her mooring. We were buffeted by gusty winds as we watched the warm tropical sun settle behind the steep hills of Norman's Cay.

The next morning the batteries were down a bit and I decided it would be a good idea to charge them up. I moved the valve to the proper position and confidently started up our little motor charger. It roared to life just as it should have and I directed Ed's attention to the Link 10 charge meter. After the MC 160 had warmed up for a minute or so, we watched the amps begin to climb and then, inexplicably, drop to zero. Ed dropped right to the floor and lifted the floorboards. We found the problem right away. Although the engine was turning normally, the shaft was not turning the pulleys connected to the drive belts for the alternator. We shut down the system and Eddie struggled to remedy the problem, but with no success.

Frustrated, we dropped the mooring and headed for Marina Cay. There were no empty moorings there so we motored across to Trellis Bay, near the airport. We dropped anchor and prepared to go for lunch to the little bar called "The Last Resort," where we would be greeted by Vanilla, the friendly mule, and a pack of tail wagging dogs.

But it was Eddie who suggested that we forget about lunch and head back for Nanny Cay, where we could get the boat repaired properly. Our installations were clearly not ready to cross an ocean. Neither of us could relax until we had them working, as they should. Our original plan had been to have our parts shipped to Tortola in the first place so that the work could be done there rather than at Crown Bay. But customs formalities on Tortola could tie up materials for weeks or even months and we could not get a straight answer about time or costs. Hence, we had gone to Crown Bay in the U.S. Virgin Islands.

A few hours later we pulled into a slip at Nanny Cay. Ed located Hastings right away and he came over to the boat. Hastings, who had helped us so much when we stored the boat over the past summer, had come to the rescue again. We felt he was an old friend. We had met his wife, Sylvia and his son Kyle. He confidently assessed the situation and said he would fix our motor charger and replace the single fuel supply valve with two valves, so that we could run the motor charger and the engine independent of each other. Hastings' confidence and easy sense of humor broke the tension. Things would be all right. We had a beer and laughed with Hastings as he told wonderful stories about his experiences at the marina. We spent the next several nights in the Nanny Cay marina, while Hastings expertly serviced our boat. When he was finished, the motor charger worked perfectly, and we no longer had to choose between running the engine or the M.C. 160. Hastings had done beautiful work. He looked carefully at the whole boat and, found several problems we had missed. For one, a block in the system for hoisting the main sail was jamming under load. Our electric winches could overcome the problem, but that block added serious strain to the rig. Hastings lubricated and repaired the stuck block. There was other good news as well. When I contacted J.R. Energy systems and told them about the problem with the motor charger, they sent a check both to pay for repairs and for the time we stayed in the marina. Good people; I was impressed.

By the time Ed and Joan were ready to depart for the airport, and we had said good-bye to Hastings, we felt the boat was on the road to being ready for her transatlantic crossing. Later that day, when we checked out of customs, we learned that we had used all of our allowed time in the British Virgin Islands.

Chapter 7

Finishing Touches?

Back at Crown Bay we disassembled the electrical installation one wire at a time and added shrink-wrap to each terminal. Then, using a cigarette lighter, we heated the plastic material and sealed each connection. A call to the life raft people revealed that Plastimo, in France, thought our raft should be fine. It had been repacked by the firm in Charlotte Amalie, and they would be happy to deliver it to our marina. That was the good news. Back on the boat we noticed that the gooseneck, the place where the boom attaches to the mast, had a small crack in it. This junction is critical on a sailboat. The boom was loose and creaked ominously when it moved. We had to do something. The lady at the marina gave us another phone number.

The man who stepped smiling onto the boat later that afternoon attached a jeweler's loop to his glasses. He looked at me and said

"Now, where is it you think you found a crack?"

"It's right there," I said. pointing to a crack in the aluminum about a half-inch long.

"Oh, my," the man said. "I think I have to go back to the office. I don't think I am prepared to deal with this. I'll talk to Bill. He'll know what do."

An hour or so later Bill appeared. He was tall and lean and very pleasant. He understood the problem and with the help of our old manuals told me who to call for support and exactly what parts to order. On the phone I was surprised that the people at Pro-Furl wanted me to return the boat to Tortola where they had a representative. Unfortunately, that was not possible. We had used up our time in the B.V.I.'s and there was no going back for us. They would "overnight" our parts. But overnight takes several days in the Caribbean and it was several days before our new parts arrived. We were alarmed to see Bill drill out rivets in our furling boom and completely disassemble it, but he obviously knew what he was doing. He entertained us with stories of his own transatlantic sail and time spent in Europe. He had raced on famous Maxi boats. He seemed totally competent. Everything went back together smoothly except he had difficulty securing one cotter key that held a clevis pin in place right at the gooseneck. Finally he got it to fit, the job was done and the boom worked better than ever before.

In the meantime we had been working on the water maker. Because we had installed the "fresh water flush" feature incorrectly, it had flushed an entire tank of water, over fifty gallons, over our membrane. After another call and more redundant installation, we finally got the system set up right. It had taken several more calls to California and by the time I was done I had become so frustrated with the installation instructions that I had rewritten them and faxed the company a copy of my rewrite. However, once it was installed, it worked beautifully. We watched the Super Bowl on the television at Tickle*s*. The heat was stifling at night. It was too hot for closed ports and mosquitoes made it nearly impossible to sleep with them open. We were tired of this place.

It was time to go sailing.

They'll Miss Us

They'll miss us when we go.
All those who greet us on the dock,
Those who seat us at the bar,
And those who serve us round the clock.
They'll miss us when we go.
But not as much, I fear to tell
As one who needs to go to Hell!
Red bellied, screaming in the night.
I slap my face,
Horror bright!

Mosquito'll miss us.
Serves him right.

H.R.D.
2/03/04

Tapestry in Crown Bay

Chapter 8

St. Croix

The following day we got an early start and eased out of the Marina to greet another beautiful February morning. Things were looking up. The engine growled strongly. There was a breeze. It would be little more than a 40-mile sail to Christiansted in Saint Croix. We raised sail and fairly raced along. I turned on our Single Side Band/ham radio and was able to faintly hear the Waterway Cruising Club, a ham radio organization that keeps track of cruisers as they travel, mostly in the Bahamas, but also in the Caribbean and along the Intra-coastal waterway on the Eastern U.S. coast. When I tried to call, there was clearly something wrong. A closer look confirmed it. Sure enough, in all of our enthusiasm to upgrade, someone had damaged the connector that attaches the microphone to the console. It was badly distorted. I couldn't talk over the radio. Would we be able to find a part on St. Croix? We might have to order new and wait for it to be shipped. Another setback.

Meanwhile, the weather was changing as we got away from the Island. We knew there had been a small craft advisory posted for the afternoon, but we hoped the morning would be reasonably calm. Still, steep waves and gusty winds caused us to shorten sail. These were the lingering Christmas Winds, strong breezes that make boating in the Caribbean challenging. Because we had worked right up to the last minute, we hadn't stowed everything quite as we should have. Various items began crashing to the floor and Julie raced below to put things away as I sailed the boat. The previous year had been nothing like this. Waves broke over the foredeck and spray flew back into the cockpit. Of course, the wind was right on the nose. With the boat closed up the pilothouse was stifling hot in the midday sun. That was some shakedown sail.

When we arrived at the nearby island of Saint Croix, we headed right for the yacht club. The people there had been so kind to us the year before, we looked forward to a reunion. They had included us in their Easter Brunch, found a place for us in their fleet of Rhodes 19's on race day, and exchanged burgees with us for our Dunkirk, NY, Yacht Club. We motored through the opening in the reef and then down toward the beautiful clubhouse. I brought the boat into the anchorage area between the club docks and the reef and Julie went forward to drop the anchor. The wind was screaming across the deck and although we were protected from the ocean waves by the shallow water of the reef, small waves were forcefully striking the bow of the boat as it swayed back and fourth in the strong breeze. Next to us was a boat with a "bimini," or cockpit awning, which had broken loose, was whipping in the wind, and was being destroyed. Once we were sure the anchor was set, we went to work taking our bimini down. With that safely stowed, Julie reached for the cockpit instrument covers. Immediately, one of the plastic lids was torn from her hand by a particularly nasty gust. It went over the side, but landed right side up in the water. I leaped to the davits and quickly lowered our dinghy, climbed aboard, and rowed downwind for all I was worth. But it was too late. The cover had sunk. I turned the little rowboat around and began rowing back toward *Tapestry*. It was all I could do to row into that wind. Spume flew from oar tips and the bow of the boat; I found myself soaked and nearly exhausted when I finally got back to our boat. What a wind!

We had looked forward to going into the club for dinner that evening, but by the time we had mounted the motor on the plunging dinghy, and climbed aboard ourselves, in that wind and chop, it clearly would have been unsafe. Even as the sun set in the western sky, there was no sight of let up.

Although the boat was secure, held in place as she was with her 45 pound plow anchor and seven to one scope of 5/8-inch chain; worry about a dragging anchor is a serious problem.

It is difficult to sleep in such conditions and one wakes frequently to check the boat. Weather radio offered no reprieve from the wind for the foreseeable future, so we decided one night at the club was enough. I called a marina at Christiansted where they promised us a place at the dock.

Docking a 35-foot boat with a fairly high profile in 20 to 25 knots of wind can be challenging. The marina found a spot for us where we could tie to the downwind side of the pier. As no one was there to help with the landing, I made several practice passes to check wind and current, and then brought *Tapestry* right up to the side of the dock. In the few seconds one has in such conditions, Julie stepped onto the dock, secured a spring line and then made up lines on bow and stern. It was neat and quick. I love a plan when it works.

At the marina, I asked about the microphone connection.

"Definitely not available here," was all the attendant could say.

"Have him go over and see George at the hardware," said a man also behind the counter. "He is a ham, maybe he can help him out."

The Christiansted hardware was loaded with goods and was very busy. Behind a desk at one of the checkouts an old white haired man sat in a swivel chair. He was answering the telephone and making transactions and obviously he had little time to spare.

"Hello," I said.

He looked at me with bright blue eyes.

"Hello there, what can I do for you?"

"Well, I'm on a sailboat and I discovered that the microphone connection on my S.S.B. is broken. It's an ICOM 710. I wonder if you know where I can get a new one around here." I pulled the microphone with its cord from a bag and I handed it over to him.

"These things are generally well made. Somebody must have really clunked it one. You can't get anything from ICOM here. We could send away for a new one and it would probably be here in about a week. Maybe we could find an address on the Internet. You be around a few days?"

"Yeah, Julie and I want to sail down to St. Lucia, but I'd like this wind to let up some before we head out."

"Looks like you'll be around a while. Mind if I take this home. I've done a little work with radios, myself. Maybe I can fix it."

"Oh, that would be great. I hate to head out without an S.S.B.; besides, Julie and I will be heading for Europe in the spring. We'll sure need it then."

"Ah, yes, I did that trip myself back in the 60's. It was wonderful. When we came home I talked to an old man up on the hill on the radio. I knew he was a ham. It was at night and I told him to look out the window and he could see our lights as we entered the harbor. We were so excited about our landfall. Learned years later the old guy was blind. Couldn't have seen us anyway. Well, drop by tomorrow; I'll let you know whether I can fix it."

With that the phone rang, the old man answered it, and Julie and I made our way out of the store and back to the boat.

The following morning I gave Dan and Nancy Putnam a call. The Putnam's had shown us part of the Island the previous year and had been so gracious; we really looked forward to seeing them again. They lived on the shores of Lake Erie near Dunkirk in the summer and were members of the Dunkirk Yacht Club. For the next week and a half, our lives began to sparkle again. We went to dinner and to lunch at various clubs and restaurants. We saw a pig that drank beer and we enjoyed St. Croix from every vantage point. We even took a house tour of some of the lovely homes on the island.

When we went back to George at the hardware store, he produced our microphone. He had rewired the plug, set the connections in silicone and wrapped them in tape. He had done a beautiful job. When I offered to pay him for his work, he absolutely refused. No way. He finally agreed I could give a small contribution to the local animal shelter. What a true gentleman he was. We had similar experience years before when our ICOM 735 radio broke down near Halifax, Nova Scotia. The ham, who fixed it, though he was in the radio repair trade, would not accept a cent in payment. That speaks volumes about ham radio operators. This group of individuals is bound by a common love of radio, technology and proper radio operating techniques. The services they provide in time of need are priceless and always on a volunteer basis.

With the repaired microphone the radio worked like a charm. Even the water maker hummed quietly in its place by the galley, and, in spite of our difficulty installing it, we were able to make clean, delicious water from the sea, just as advertised.

Finally there was a break in the forecast. The weathermen predicted a period of decreasing winds of from 18 to 24 hours. We had a good-bye dinner aboard *Tapestry* for the Putnam's and early the next morning we were off to St. Lucia.

The Caribbean

When the sweat collects in the creases of your neck,
And you wake to sour sheets,
It's hot in the Caribbean.
When it is hot every day,
And the screaming wind kindles fire,
It's hot in the Caribbean.
When ocean spray is to be avoided
Because it is sticky, not cold,
You have arrived in the Caribbean.

But when the wind blows gently,
And the warm and fragrant air wafts over the
Island and through the boat,
That is when you know why you came to the Caribbean.
That is when you understand why so many others have come,
Why so many wish to come to the Caribbean.

Why the roadsides are sometimes littered with trash,
Why the streets are crowded with cars.
Why the locals talk of how nice it used to be.

When the sweat gathers in the creases of your neck,
When you wake to sour sheets and a wet pillow,
When mosquitoes ring in your ears and the boat heaves
With the waves,
That is the Caribbean.

    H.R.D.

Island People: Deep Water Dreams

Chapter 9

Christmas Winds

Some people say the most dangerous thing on a boat is a calendar. Weather, not time should determine when you decide to leave port. On the other hand, we were going to cross an ocean. Why should we worry about a little 30 or 35 knots of wind? The answer should be obvious. The prudent mariner understands that no boat is stronger than the sea. A yacht may be able to survive a storm or two, but when things fail at sea, it is usually in heavy weather, and when that happens, the short-handed sailor has his hands full.

But Julie had arranged with her sister, Betsy, to meet us in Saint Lucia on the fourteenth of February. The reservations had been made and cancellation was out of the question. We certainly didn't want Betsy to arrive without us there to greet her! We pushed off the dock at St. Croix in gusty, but less intense winds, and headed on a rhumb line almost due south from St. Croix to St. Lucia. As it was February, we hoped these "Christmas Winds" would soon abate.

Rather than sail back toward Saint Martin and follow the island chain south, we elected to sail straight toward our destination. For the first day or so the wind was just off the nose and sailing was reasonable. We were not quite making the rhumb line, that is the line between our starting point and destination, we were falling off a bit because the wind was so much on our nose, but we were sailing and that was wonderful. The winds were warm day and night and our bodies were always covered with a thin layer of perspiration. We would plunge ahead through the waves, often taking heavy, green water over the bow, sending sheets of spray back over the boat. We found ourselves almost always in the pilothouse. It was hot there, but we were protected from the spray and able to use our

61

navigation instruments and steer the boat from there when we weren't using the autopilot.

From time to time a dark cloud would appear on the horizon. As it passed over us it might drench us with a rain squall or buffet the boat with short-lived strong winds. The rain was of no concern, but often the wind would cause excessive heel and we would scramble to the cockpit to shorten sail. It was a relatively easy operation, and consisted of simply releasing the sheet, easing the halyard on the main and then taking up slack on the reefing line. When we trimmed the sheet we would be ready to go again, but with a much less powerful sail. What we had done was to roll the main into the boom and thus present less sail to the wind. Similarly, to reef the jib we would ease the sheet and trim the furling line. It wasn't hard work under normal circumstances but, especially at night, after being awakened from a fitful sleep by the person on watch, strapping on a harness and climbing into the wind and rain, it all seemed terribly difficult and confusing. Our safety was foremost on our minds and we always wore harnesses on deck at night. These harnesses had inflatable life preservers attached with strobe lights should we somehow be washed overboard.

By any standard, that passage was rough. It was necessary to hold on all the time to keep from being hurt by the plunging boat. Sleeping was very difficult. As the boat plunged and rolled our bodies would roll around on the bed. If one assumed a pre-natal position some stability could be found; stretching out was most always a mistake. Most offshore yachts use lee cloths to hold the sleeper in a narrow birth. Unfortunately, *Tapestry* had no narrow berths. There was a double bed forward and another aft. Because the berths went all the way from one side of the boat to the other, it was not possible to fall out of bed, but one couldn't be strapped in place either. In fact we experimented and found that when the boat was heeling most severely it was more comfortable to sleep athwart ships, crosswise to the keel, with one's head on the high side and one's feet to leeward. In this blow, sound sleep was a rare commodity. We took three-hour shifts through the night. Our watches were often interrupted by the need to go on deck. It was during the day that we managed to get most of our sleep. Catnaps are a wonderful friend of the sailor.

Julie, as always, was a real hero on this cruise. She did the cooking. At times the wind was up around thirty knots or so. Waves were huge and we were plunging right through them. Two mornings of the three, the coffee pot tipped over on the stove, sending its grounds mixed with the hot coffee onto the cabin sole and down into the bilge. This wasn't just your average coffee pot either. This was a coffee pot on a gimbaled stove and clamped in place with metal arms. After the spill, Julie would lift the floorboards, mop up the mess with a sponge and go on preparing breakfast. I don't know how she did it, but she made three meals each day. We ate fresh fruits, salads and some canned goods, and for our main meal, we always had something hot. Of course, when we are off shore we don't drink alcohol. Julie doesn't drink anyway, but in those circumstances I don't either. It may sound corny but things change quickly at sea; I feel I need all the resources I can muster.

It had been a rough trip, but on the morning of the third day, we spotted St. Lucia on the horizon. By then the wind was right on the nose, and we had started the engine rather than try to tack back and forth. We were north of the Island and we turned to starboard to head up to the entrance to Rodney Bay. It was about 8 in the morning. Just before we reached the end of the island, and were about to turn into the entrance, we found ourselves broadside to the waves. At that moment a huge breaking wave came crashing down on us. I saw the green wall outside the port pilothouse window and yelled,

"Julie, look out!"

She was sitting at the settee, reading just inches from the large port. She glanced to the left and actually let out a scream.

In thirty-seven years of marriage, it was the first yell I had ever heard from her.

There was a loud thump and then a crash as the wave smashed into the port side of the boat. The wave struck the pilothouse windows squarely with what must have been tons of water and literally body slammed *Tapestry* onto her beam's ends. It came from nowhere. Our binoculars flew from one side of the boat to the other, dishes and pans slammed into the sides of their cupboards, and several pans forced the oven door open and landed on the floor, but as we immediately righted, we could tell there had been no real damage, at least not inside. Outside, water was still draining from the cockpit. The leeward man overboard horseshoe was gone and on the weather side a quarter inch bolt that had held the solar panel in place, had sheared off. Within minutes we rounded the bend and entered the bay. We made radio contact with Rodney Bay marina and found our way to a safe slip next to a boat called *Hello World*. It was owned by a British couple, a husband and wife team who had just sailed from England. We really wanted to talk with them.

St. Croix to St. Lucia

She drives into walls of water
That pummel the bow and roar over the hatches,
    The dorades,
    Slide up the windshield and
    Drain from the cabin top.
Lee side down, breaking
    Waves dance with our bow wave,
    Lapping deck and stanchions,
    Stressing drains,
    Making heaped puddles in corners,

Dammed by the wind.
We hold on to keep still;
    Bounding through waves,
    Heeling far over.
    Hoping that strained shrouds.. .

Out here where there is no rescue,
Just warm rolling ocean
    Playful with waves.
The big kids
Playing rough.
    Out here
    Where the water is warm,
    But filled with sleek menace.
    Out here
It is beautiful,
    Dangerous,
        Wonderful,
            Exciting,
                Bountiful.
It is the West Indies,
 A little bit of Africa,
    A little danger
In the Western Hemisphere.

        H.R.D.
        2/17/04

Chapter 10

St. Lucia

Rodney Bay proved to be a simply beautiful marina. We had power and water at our slip, and were surrounded by magnificent yachts from all over the world. Unlike some of those at Crown Bay, these weren't simply polished showpieces, but real yachts of all sizes that hailed from ports in Europe, Asia and elsewhere.

As soon as the boat was secure, we grabbed our passports and boat papers and then we headed for Customs, located in an office above several attractive shops and restaurants near the entrance to the docks. Check-in was routine, the officials polite and efficient. Immigration was not so simple. There was no one in the office.

"She's probably at the airport," said the Customs officer. "Check back later today or tomorrow, you'll catch her."

With that good news Julie and I descended the stairs to a quiet little restaurant on the ground floor, below the Customs office. It was open to sea breezes and overlooked the docks. The pace was relaxed and the smiling waitress was pleasant and helpful. This was the real Caribbean, I thought. Our new dock neighbor was there with his wife and we joined them for a cool drink. He had been a photographer who made his name by taking photos from perilous places. He had climbed mountains and explored jungles. It was exciting to hear stories of his adventures. *Hello World* was the beginning of his and his wife's cruising life.

As soon as our new friends left, a smiling Rastafarian appeared, with numerous dreadlocks hanging from his head. He was selling baskets, which he made of bright green palm fronds. We watched as he began with a piece of wire.

Julie looked at him and said, "That looks like telephone wire. Is that what it is?"

"I don't know ma'am, just wire."

"Is that why some of the phones don't work so well?"

"I don't know ma'am."

We were fascinated as his fingers flew and the basket took shape. It was beautiful bright green.

"I'm Jumbo. You buy the basket?"

"Well, I don't know, it certainly is colorful." I answered.

His hands took off again and as palm fronds twisted and hissed, a bird appeared, attached to the edge of the basket.

"You buy now or basket fly away! Five E.C."

"How about three?"

"Hey, mon, I buy the wire, I need food, Mon. Five E.C."

I bought the basket. It wasn't something we needed, but I bought it anyway.

E-mail is an important part of a cruiser's life. It is reliable way to communicate with friends and family. Since our retirement in 2000, Julie and I had used "Pocket Mail" to stay in touch. Pocket Mail was a miniature keyboard and computer in a pocket sized device that could be used to write e-mails then held to a phone anywhere in the world to send and receive e-mail. Well, I accidentally left my device in St. Croix. I had been able to contact our friends Dan and Nancy by cell phone after we left and they promised to send our device by courier to St Lucia. We hoped we could pick it up at the airport. Besides, we would want to meet Julie's sister, Betsy, at the airport when she arrived in a couple of days. Picking up the Pocket Mail would be good practice for locating the airport.

So we walked outside the marina gate and waited for the dollar bus. In St. Lucia, the dollar bus was a three-seat minivan; in the Virgin Islands it was a pickup truck with seats where the cargo box would normally be. Often the dollar bus and the taxi are the same. If you ask "how much?" it is a taxi and you pay accordingly. If you pay the driver a dollar, it is a dollar bus. Cultural sensitivity is important when visiting foreign countries;

Julie and I learned that years ago in Central Africa while we were in the Peace Corps.

We learned several lessons right away when we climbed aboard the dollar bus. People were squeezed in three to a seat. One passenger sat next to the driver. Whoever sat by the door opened it and closed it when others wanted to enter or leave. Also, whenever someone entered, he or she always said "Hello." It was a courtesy. When they left, they said "good-bye." It was standard behavior, and everybody did it whether he or she knew anyone aboard or not and whether he or she was an attractive young lady or a dirt covered construction worker. We learned the trick and though it felt awkward at first, we got used to it quickly. I told the driver we wanted to go to the airport and he nodded. Loud music played from tinny speakers as the bus bounced and lurched over the streets. As we drew nearer the city, traffic was heavier. The driver frequently stopped to pick up or discharge passengers. Finally, the driver pulled over to the side of the road, looked back at us and said, "airport."

There was no airport, but, as I was sitting next to the door, I pulled on the handle and slid the door back and Julie and I climbed out on to the shoulder. We understood that if we waited for a few minutes another dollar bus would come along and take us the rest of the way. As we were at the end of the runway and the terminal was visible in the distance, we decided to walk. Besides, the runway ran right along the beach. There were shade trees along the way, and it would be a beautiful stroll.

I wish I could remember the name of the Rastafarian we met beside the road. We took a little detour toward a particularly attractive beach and passed a small settlement nestled in the trees. A young man saw us coming and introduced himself. He was smiling and had magnificent dreadlocks hanging from his head. He was selling necklaces. They had seashells on them and he was sure they were pretty special. I bought one. He was funny and pleasant and non-threatening. He hung it around my neck and smiled and told me now I looked like I belonged in St. Lucia. Then he looked at me.

"How you get high, Mon?"

"What do you mean?" I answered.

"You just drink that liquid? I got some good stuff here, Mon. It real sweet. You like it?"

"I don't think so," I answered, and Julie and I said good-bye, turned and begin to walk toward the road to the airport. We had no desire to have anything to do with drugs.

We picked up the Pocket Mail at the airport, and searched for the immigration lady who, we understood might be at the airport. Unfortunately, she wasn't there. We walked back to the bus stop and quickly caught another dollar bus to Rodney Bay. On the way home we stopped at a market and picked up a few groceries. Success. We felt a little more at home in St. Lucia.

The next day we were introduced to Taka and Jun. They were aboard their Amel ketch, *Ben Kai*, a beautiful 52 footer, made in France. They were the first Japanese we had met while cruising. Taka had a strong command of English and we got along well from the start. As we had visited Japan years before on our return from Peace Corps service in the sixties, we had a common thread from the beginning. We had been in Kyoto while they were there in the fall of 1969. They had been dating then. We were, of course, only tourists. It turned out that Taka's father had worked at a military base during the American occupation of Japan after World War II. Taka had learned English as a kid while on the base with his father. Later he had attended school in the U.K. He had begun working with an American soft drink manufacturer but ended up as the head of a brewing company in Japan and then in all of Asia. His wife, Jun, was an attractive, but quiet woman. She spoke a little English, so her conversation was limited. They had sailed from Europe with the Atlantic Rally for Cruisers, the same people we had signed up with for our crossing, and we were anxious to hear about their adventure. They showed us pictures of their boat crossing the finish line and shared the notebook of instructions they had received prior to embarking on the trip. They had had a positive experience with the ARC, so they strongly reinforced our plans. They intended to sail to the States, but did not have the necessary charts; Julie quickly offered ours. We had purchased charts all the way from the Bahamas, through the Turks and Caicos, to the Dominican Republic, Puerto Rico and on to the Virgin Islands. Taka and Jun were very grateful. We felt we had made new friends.

That afternoon we again climbed the steps to the Immigration office. This time the lady in charge was there, just beginning to eat her lunch of tropical fruit. She was not impressed that we had stopped by her office several times during the past three days when she was not there. She thought we had waited too long to check in.

"I think you've been having too much fun on your vacation," she said with a lilt typical of the Caribbean.

"But we went all the way to the airport to find you."

"I don't work at the airport; even if I did, you came in at the sea port. I couldn't have checked you in at the airport."

Julie broke the tension easily.

"What is that you're eating?" she asked.

"Why, it's a guava, she said, putting her frown aside." At Julie's prompting, she began showing us the fruit and how to eat it. After she finished eating she processed our paperwork and everything was fine.

Chapter 11

Betsy's Visit and on to Bequia

We met Betsy at the airport the following day. Of course it was great to see Julie's sister, and we were relieved to see her luggage. It was just a duffle bag, but it held   everything she needed. Other cruisers had told us stories of relatives showing up with suitcases, ready for life on a yacht. If the truth were told, life on our boat is much closer to wilderness camping. There is hot water, but no room for suitcases, or much else. We anchored the boat off Pigeon Island, which shelters Rodney Bay, and explored the old fortifications there. We swam in the warm waters, drank a beer in a stone walled pub that was older than the United States, and enjoyed beautiful February weather in the Caribbean. Later we went to shore and purchased a permit to visit the Pitons, a national park featuring a unique "drive in" active volcano and the beautiful volcanic peaks that jut from the water up thousands of feet into the air. The botanical gardens were to be part of the package as well. We were excited about the visit.

Next morning we hoisted sail and headed for Soufriere. It was a beautiful morning for a sail and *Tapestry* heeled just a bit and slid along in calm water. We were excited when we first spotted the Pitons, volcanic "plugs" which stretch from the water skyward almost to the clouds.

While we were still miles from the mooring area, a small runabout raced out to meet us. Francis introduced himself and said he wanted to help us with our lines at the mooring. It is standard practice to hire someone who will help you tie to a mooring and then carry a long line from the stern of your boat to shore. That way your boat stays headed off shore and is less likely to roll in a swell during the night.   The usual price, according to our cruising guide, was about four dollars U.S. Before he touched the lines, I called to him.

"Four dollars, okay?" But Francis didn't answer.

I knew there was something unusual about Francis's accent. After we were tied to the mooring ball, he motored his runabout back to the boat. I asked him about his accent and he hesitated and then admitted that he was actually a recent immigrant, from Brooklyn! We visited for a few minutes. Meanwhile, Francis's assistant walked out of the trees to the shore behind our boat. He stripped off his shorts and, naked, entered the water, swimming the fifty yards or so to *Tapestry*. I handed him the end of a new 300-foot coil of braided line and watched him swim back to shore, make the line fast to a palm tree, pull on his shorts, and disappear back into the trees.

"We don't do the lines stuff anymore, man," Francis said, a new edge to his voice. "We sell package deals, $100 U.S. Tie you up, take you to town, take you to the volcano, the botanical gardens and untie you when you're ready to leave. It's a good deal, you'll find out. We have two hours left today. Let's go."

"No, Francis, I don't think so," I said in my strongest voice. But Francis was not easily deterred.

"They charge you a hundred bucks just for the taxi ride, man. You're crazy to pass this up."

I held up the four dollars.

"No way man, a hundred dollars for the package."

"I offered four dollars before you touched my lines, Francis. Four dollars it is." With that he snatched the four dollars from my hand, started his Evinrude and roared off. I had a feeling that wouldn't be the last we would hear from Francis. Julie and Betsy looked uncomfortable. What had I gotten us into? We had dealt with local people before, but we had never felt such hostility. Besides, Francis wasn't local at all, he was from Brooklyn, N.Y. He was intimidating us and no doubt had intimidated others ashore. No one else had offered to help us tie up. That night I locked the companionway, shut and secured the hatches, something we had felt unnecessary in the past.

The next morning another "boat boy" approached and negotiated for a "round trip" ride to town and back later in the day. We knew we could take our dinghy to shore, but kids on the docks would insist they be paid to watch it. What chance would there be of its being there when we got back if we didn't go along? I was angry with myself for my insecurity, but felt the threat was real. We climbed in his boat. On shore we wandered around for a while in this colorful tropical city. We looked at restaurants and shops, but soon began looking for a taxi. The town of Soufriere is nestled in a valley between several volcanic peaks. Should there be another eruption, not rare in this part of the world, this town would be right in the path of the lava flow. It seemed a natural setting for a natural disaster. Before long we found the tourist office, which arranged a taxi and driver whom we hired for the day. He agreed to take us to the three attractions plus to the "Bang between the Pitons," a restaurant recommended by friends back home.

The "drive in volcano" was our first stop and it was just what its name implied. We drove up a winding mountain road to a parking area and then walked a short way to a small crater. Below, boiling mud rolled and bubbled and plumes of noxious hydrogen sulfide gasses, to which our guide seemed immune, filled the air and made us think of things other than lunch. The landscape was alien and rugged. We had no desire to linger there.

A few miles from the volcano we stopped at a magnificent waterfall that dropped several hundred feet into a small pool. Nearby were "the baths." As we had brought our bathing suits, we found a restroom and changed. The water was hot and soothing as it swirled around us. The clerk had assured us, as we paid our fee, that we would feel younger when we emerged. Napoleon had built these baths for the well being of his troops during one of the French occupations of the island.

"The Bang" a quaint restaurant between the Pitons had been taken over by a resort and the majesty of the place reported by our friends from home had somehow been compromised. Sure enough, the two towering peaks were visible on either side of us as we sat at our table in the restaurant, and we were, indeed, "bang between the pitons." Perhaps it was the helicopter that hovered overhead as it landed and took off with passengers, offering them a closer look at the peaks; perhaps it was the water skiers and jet skies that buzzed by in front of us; perhaps it was mediocre food at gourmet prices, but somehow the bang came off as a kind of pop.

We spent the afternoon in the beautiful botanical gardens. We walked every path and were engulfed by sweet fragrances, gigantic philodendrons, red and white crab claws, hibiscus and other tropical flora amid streams fountains and pools. Betsy, an enthusiastic gardener, could name many of the plants and we were delighted at the vivid and fragrant blossoms. After we had nearly exhausted ourselves in the gardens, our taxi driver returned us to the dock at Soufriere. He insisted that our lunch stop was farther away and longer than he had expected, so the previously negotiated fare was insufficient. We paid him. Of course, the young man who had sold us the "round trip from the boat to town and back," in the morning was nowhere to be found that afternoon. Instead we found ourselves on the pier, surrounded by little boys loudly clamoring for money. They didn't want to dive for coins or do anything for money, they just thought we should give it to them. Soon another "boat boy" came along and sold us one-way passage back to *Tapestry*. Frankly, I was surprised to find everything intact when we got there. We enjoyed dinner aboard and the next morning headed back toward Rodney Bay. Did Francis show up to help us with the lines? Not a chance. Betsy swam ashore, untied our stern line from the palm tree and then swam back to the boat. In one regard, Francis was right, we did spend all of a hundred dollars on our day's entertainment. The difference was, we didn't squeeze our tour into the two hours at the end of the day as he had suggested. We had a full day to enjoy the attractions.

The winds were light on the return; we stopped at Margot Bay for lunch and a swim. There was plenty of room to anchor at Margot because the week before armed men had boarded a yacht there in the night and attacked the crew. The yachting community no longer considered Margot Bay to be a safe place to stay, hence it was pretty empty.

The next day found us back at Rodney Bay at a celebration of the 25th anniversary of the independence of St. Lucia. Marina slips were free for us, and there was a huge party at the park adjacent to the marina. It was wonderful to see the local population mingle with the sailors and expatriate community. There were steel drum bands, political speeches, even a fashion show. There was a chicken barbecue, a beer tent, and popcorn and cotton candy concessions. There was a lighthearted carnival atmosphere, complete with giant speakers and stage. Kids were running around; everyone was dressed up. It was a good time. Loud music rang through the park and marina until the wee hours of the morning.

We took Betsy to the city of Castries and showed her the local market as well as the "mall" that had been built for visitors aboard cruise ships. We could hardly believe that tourists in large numbers would visit this mall or collection of "discount" jewelry shops and liquor stores and then think they had visited St. Lucia. We had found these discount malls to be much the same wherever cruise ships landed in the Caribbean.

After Betsy left, I had one more thing to accomplish before we left St. Lucia. I had purchased a "Winlink" system to install on *Tapestry*. It worked in conjunction with both the computer and the ham radio, and allowed us to send e-mail, via amateur radio, anywhere in the world from our boat. It would be essential during the Atlantic crossing. Although I had purchased the right components, there were no instructions to make them all work together. So, knowing that this was a system much enjoyed by sailors everywhere, I began to search for someone who used it. Right away, I got lucky. I met a Spaniard, Atilo, as he was busy tying his boat to the dock.

"Excuse me." I said. "I wonder if you use Winlink aboard. Are you familiar with the system?"

"Please," he said as he looked at me with tired eyes. "I have this very moment arrived single handed from the Canary Islands. I am very tired. I will help you with your Winlink later today and we will make it work. But now I must check in to customs, then I must rest. Which boat is yours?"

"We are on *Tapestry* the Nauticat 35, just five boats down from here." I said, both thrilled to have found him and eager to talk to him, but at the same time not wanting to antagonize him.

"The Nauticat 35, yes, I know the boat. I'll work with you later, but please, I am very tired."

"Thank you." I said. "We'll see you later." Here was a man who had sailed single-handed across the ocean. I was profoundly impressed.

Early that evening, Atilo joined us on *Tapestry.* We had the Winlink up and working in less than an hour. I was amazed at his competence. He showed us the installation aboard his boat and then he hooked ours up the same way. It worked beautifully. I was very grateful. We enjoyed dinner together in one of the restaurants at the marina. He told us about his crossing. He had begun with a friend who, the first day out, had suffered a detached retina. As Atilo was a physician, he knew he had to return to the islands as soon as possible to get medical attention for his friend. But then, hardly giving it another thought, he set off again, by himself. What a courageous man. He told us that at night he had used his radar alarm to tell him when he was in the vicinity of a ship. It would wake him when he was fifteen miles away and he would have to make appropriate maneuvers. I truly admired this man for what he had done. Atilo had the perfect excuse to quit. What had driven him, instead, to forge ahead through the cold dark ocean alone?

What caused him to leave his wife and family and comfortable surroundings and venture into the unknown? I didn't know the answer, but somehow I understood. Whatever the force it is that makes us want to cross an ocean, there is another force even stronger that makes us not want to turn back. Sometimes it seems that even common sense doesn't prevail against our desire to press onward. I thought about some of the difficulties we had encountered while preparing *Tapestry* for the journey, and I shivered a little. We exchanged e-mail addresses and promised to keep in touch. Atilo is the kind of man we often find sailing. He is a man of true integrity, and willingness to help others.

The following day we said good-bye to Rodney Bay, and headed south to Bequia. part of the island group St. Vincent and the Grenadines. To get to Bequia, however, we had to pass St. Vincent. Friends back home had named their boat after a delightful town on St. Vincent, Wallylabou. We had looked forward to visiting this port, but other sailors had warned us that the boat boys there were far more aggressive than any on St. Lucia, and that the hassle just wasn't worth the visit. We bypassed the island altogether.

But Bequia was wonderful. We anchored in the large harbor there and took the dinghy to shore. It was hassle free. There were kids around, but they did not beg for money. Ashore, there were interesting shops, bookstores, restaurants, bars, coffee shops, and grocery stores, but there was no pressure. Carvings and trinkets were available along the beach, but the prices were marked and definitely negotiable. It was our kind of place.

One thing that set Bequia apart was Daffodils. Daffodils was a fuel service that would bring fuel to your boat on a barge, and pump it into your tanks. The cost was two dollars per gallon of diesel. In other words, rather than five dollars per gallon, as it was in town, diesel was seven dollars from Daffodils. Rather than face the prospect of filling our five gallon plastic jerry can in town, lugging it to the dinghy, taking it to the boat, hauling it aboard and then, without spilling, pouring the fuel into the tank, and doing that ten times over, we called Daffodils on the radio. In a matter of minutes the bright yellow outboard powered barge was docked alongside. Half an hour later fifty gallons of fuel was transferred from the tanks on the barge to those on *Tapestry*. It was a good deal, even at that price.

Ashore on Bequia, we met several fascinating people. The first was Brother King who had made it his personal ambition to save as many sea turtles as he could. He built a turtle orphanage where he raised turtles that he collected from the shores of nearby islands soon after they hatched from their eggs. At his "orphanage" we could look at hundreds of sea turtles of all ages, each in its separate seawater tank. He was horrified at the way the turtle population had declined due to turtles being eaten and their shells being sold. His goal was to collect as many young as he could, raise them in captivity and release them as young adults in the sea. Exactly how many turtles he had saved is not clear, but there is no faulting his effort. He was one of the more dedicated naturalists that we met.

There was a French woman who painted on silk. We walked to her home. Flowing down the hillside, a stream gurgled along, spanned by a lovely wooden bridge and a path that lead to her place. A hand made fence outlined the limits of her home but was in no way imposing. It was low and beautiful. Her studio was open to the sea on one side and was a simple, beautiful room adorned with her work while being very close to nature. She greeted us when we appeared and showed us around. Her home was similar to her studio. We didn't see it all, of course, but I especially remember her bedroom. It appeared to be a regular room with bedroom furniture. On the ocean side, however, there was no wall. In fact the floor of the bedroom simply dropped away in the middle of the room, and suspended over the shrubbery below was a hammock. That was her bed. It was covered by a roof, but open to the foliage below and the sea in the distance. It was unique and charming.

She was a lovely person who appeared to be totally at peace with herself and the world around her. I tried to imagine what it would be like waking in the morning suspended in that hammock-like bed over her beautiful garden, protected from the rain, but buffeted by the warm winds from the sea. Her place was so small in scale, so open to the elements, and so enchanting. It seemed the home of a nymph or a goddess, hardly a regular human woman. She spent her day painting on silk. She showed no fear of strangers, her heart was as open as her home. There was something alien about it all. We were so American; she was so French. Shouldn't she lock up her valuable work, shut herself in from the dark night? After all, businesses here had steel bars over their windows and doors. It pleased me, but it troubled me all the same.

But everything on Bequia wasn't perfect. One morning a Swedish couple with a baby on board their boat, which was anchored right behind *Tapestry,* began hauling up their anchor.

"What are you doing?" I called to him over the roaring wind.

"Hauling anchor," the man said. We must have dragged twenty meters last night in that squall. Didn't you hear it?

"No," I confessed, "We didn't hear a thing. Doesn't look like you're any farther away from us than you were yesterday," I said, without thinking.

"Right. You dragged, too, you know. There was a gust near forty knots. Probably be a good idea for you to reset, as well," he said, after hesitating briefly.

I checked our bearings, and sure enough, *Tapestry* had moved a good distance astern. We, too, then hauled anchor and searched for another spot in the harbor. In response to all of this I sent my first Winlink e-mail:

At the moment Julie and I are in Bequia harbor watching the lights on shore flicker on as the sun sets. It is Saturday night. We will spend the night on the boat as we most always do. We generally go out for lunch, but we like to be aboard the boat after dark. It has been warm and windy here all week; windy with a big "W." The breeze topped out at 38 knots on Thursday and actually moved the boat, anchor and all, about ten feet. Last night with violent windy squalls, the anchor went for another walk, and this morning at first light we were hauling it up and re-anchoring between raindrops. For the moment, all is well. We have been here a week and hope to move south for the last time tomorrow. Then we will be moving back to Saint Martin, where we will store the boat in April while we return to the States to make final arrangements for the trip across to England. The boat is in good shape. The water maker and generator work properly and finally I got the e-mail to work with the ham radio. Please feel free to reply to this address at any time. We love hearing from you. There is always a list, but the boat is coming along fine. We hope all is well with you. Hank and Julie

But time was fleeting. We would have to move on if we wanted to venture farther south and return to Saint Martin in time to meet the Markuses and make final preparations for the crossing. In good weather we sailed south to Union Island, but our attempt to land in the main harbor there was frustrated by the number of boats already at anchor and boat boys who darted about in runabouts, shouted at us and insisted we employ them to help anchor. Frustrated, we sailed around behind the island and anchored in a quiet cove where a young man wanted to sell us lobsters. We bought them, but thought they were rather small. We learned later that they were indeed, too small, and could not be sold legally. How disappointing.

At The Tobago Cays, we anchored among literally hundreds of boats, most of them part of the charter fleet. Here was a fascinating reef where the wide Atlantic meets the Caribbean. The reef absorbs the huge Atlantic swell and there is a calm area to anchor when the weather is moderate. There were dozens of boats anchored behind the reef. Boat boys were busy bringing everything from fresh bread to tee shirts, jewelry, and food items to the boat to sell. After enjoying the roaring surf for a while we raised anchor and explored several smaller islands in the vicinity and went to Mayreau where we anchored for the night, and the next morning enjoyed an English breakfast on stone furniture secluded among palms, jungle fauna, and quiet lagoons. There were several small islands in the area and we hiked up mountains and explored villages on several of them. Views were spectacular. Granada was visible in the distance, but, it was time to head north for the final shakedown. So far things had gone well. We reached northward and found ourselves on Mustique, an exclusive island known for being home to many rich and famous people. We picked up a mooring and the man in charge offered us a deal, three nights for the price of two. We took his offer and moored the boat to a float in this shimmering blue bay.

Chapter 12

Heading North, Mustique

Mustique in some ways was different from all the other islands we had found. It was steep and covered with foliage, thick and green. But it was home to royalty and rock stars, and that made it different. Palm trees leaned against the wind along the shores. Colorful boats, red, yellow, and green were pulled up on the beaches. Fish nets dried in the sun. Old men sat around and smoked and visited after their day on the water. We walked every road on Mustique. There were large, contemporary homes, most of them invisible from the road, but handsome gates and out buildings were in clear view.

On the second day, while walking near the peak, we found a restaurant recommended by a construction worker who gave us a ride up the road. We were ready for lunch and it seemed like a wonderful place. From the door we were escorted past the bar to a table in the front. It was in a corner of the building, and from the precipitous height of this cliff-side restaurant, the view of the deep blue, white-specked sea was spectacular. Our green salads covered with fresh tuna were delicious as a warm breeze bathed us in our shady nook. We were alone in the place and the staff left us alone to enjoy our food and ambiance. It was a memorable afternoon.

The next day we had lunch in another restaurant, closer to the sea. We were about the only guests this time too, but service was mediocre and we felt ignored rather than left alone.

The fishermen and the store where they sold their fresh fish was an intriguing feature of the island.

We bought a fresh snapper from the fishermen on the beach and took it back to *Tapestry*. Julie, crouched on our aft deck and used a very sharp knife to slit the belly remove the entrails, head and skin and carefully filleted the delicate fish.

Later she sautéed it and we enjoyed eating it aboard the boat. There is nothing like a meal of truly fresh fish.

But there is another side to this island as well. Those who are indigenous live in a small enclave on one end. It is a steep rocky settlement, with huts crowded together along the streets. Perhaps it is not poorer than other Caribbean towns, but next to the opulence we had seen on Mustique, it surely seemed to be.

Imagine

Imagine an island,
A tall island with swaying palm trees
And aromatic gardenia bushes,
Gardenia bushes, tall ones, with pungent,
Sweet smelling blossoms.
Imagine that!

Imagine a warm night.
Not hot, but just right.
The moon is rising over the hills on the island,
And you are watching it from a small yacht in the harbor.
The boat sways back and forth on its mooring
And rolls in the seaway.
The breeze carries the pungent tropical scents
Of the jungle after rain.

There is a little bar on stilts over the bay.
It has a thatched roof and open sides.
Inside a band is playing music that sways with
The rhythm of the rolling boat.
The men in the band are playing drums and singing.
The rhythm is soothing and pleasant.

The wind is changeable as it carries the rhythm of the band.
Mostly it is gentle,
But sometimes there is a gust that causes the boat
To tug on her mooring.

The moon is clear and bright, just past full,
But occasionally a cloud pushes in front of the moon
And hides it completely.
That cloud might bring rushing rain,
Causing us to dash from the cockpit of the boat,
To shut the hatches and ports,
Closing out the music and the bouquet of the tropical night,
Leaving only the odors of recently cooked fish,
Or a warm diesel engine.

Sometimes life is simply wonderful,
But give us a dark cloud and though things
May not really change greatly,
They seem to.

And the boat rolls, and the music plays,
And the moon shines and it is sweet and warm and beautiful.

H.R.D.
March 10, 2004 Mustique ,W.I

From Mustique we headed back to Bequia. We dropped anchor on the opposite side of Bequia harbor this time, next to the yacht of a friendly Canadian couple. Once our anchor was set, we lowered the dinghy and headed off to shore and on to a restaurant we wanted to try.

We had just ordered our salads when it started to rain. We looked out the open window and saw the boats in the harbor all straining on their anchor rodes and pointing due east into the wind. White caps spread over the harbor. The trouble was, *Tapestry* was heading in a different direction from the rest, obviously dragging her anchor. I was horrified. What could we do? I knew we had set the anchor, but I also knew the holding was only fair. We were half an hour away by dinghy! Fortunately, the squall was short lived and when the wind dropped the anchor reset. Although I stood up to dash after our nautical home, it would have been a futile chase. I was relieved to see that we had dragged but a short distance.

We enjoyed our lunches, and later that afternoon, we returned to customs and checked out of St. Vincent and the Grenadines, of which Bequia was a part. We had happy memories of this tropical paradise, tempered only by a footnote: fair holding here in Bequia. Early the next morning, we made our departure.

As soon as we left the harbor, we knew we would have our hands full that day. Winds shrieked in the rigging and we struggled to reef both main and jib. *Tapestry* was heeled far over as large waves slopped over the coaming and slammed into the pilot house. We were steering from the cockpit and holding on for all we were worth. We bounded up and down waves and in spite of the strong winds the boat definitely felt sluggish. Something was wrong with our girl. Several charter boats approached from astern and overtook us. We tried shortening sail and easing our sheets. We tried moving the main traveler to leeward and moving jib leads forward and outboard. Nothing seemed to work. When we slipped into the lee of St. Vincent, we were nearly becalmed. We headed farther off shore and found more wind. The day proved to be one of those too much or too little conundrums. It was well after ten at night when we finally dropped the hook in the shadow of Pigeon Island at Rodney Bay in St. Lucia. We had difficulty finding the right spot in the dark, but there was a show at the resort on shore and lights from there gave us a bearing. We fell asleep to steel drum music that night.

Early the next morning we were off again. We rounded Pigeon Island and headed for Martinique, just to the north. Around the time of the American Revolution, there had been nearly constant warfare between the English fleet based on St. Lucia and the French ships on Martinique. The two islands were within sight of one another and one could imagine the terrible pitched battles that must have regularly ensued. As we sailed, again in winds on the plus side of twenty-five knots, we began to overtake a sail ahead of us. Finally! But when we caught up with them, we found it was a boat of little more than twenty five feet. There was something wrong with our rig! We had heard good things about the marina facilities at Marin on Martinique. Perhaps there would be a rigger there who could check things out. We seemed to have too much head stay sag. Marin was our destination that day. We were running out of time to get things right.

Chapter 13

Adventure in Martinique

When the city of Marin appeared at the head of the bay on Martinique, we found a busy sailing center with hundreds of sailboats tied to its marina docks, and many more anchored in the harbor. We dropped our hook in a well-protected area not far from the marina. Holding was excellent and the anchorage was filled with small boats, many of them from France. When we spoke to those aboard, we struggled with our French. Most folks appreciated our efforts and generally responded in English. We had expected to find people with an arrogant, perhaps even anti-American attitude here, but what we found was quite the opposite. Everyone we had to deal with was warm and friendly. Customs and Immigration were casual and cooperative. There were restaurants and bars everywhere. Markets were modern and clean. It was a wonderful place, we thought.

Early the next morning, we entered the large marina and climbed the stairs to the chandlery. What a well-stocked store. The shelves were loaded with all sorts of hardware, electronics and other marine goods. At a desk in the front of the room a tall very slender young woman was entering figures into a ledger. A cigarette burned in the ash tray beside her.

"Do you do rigging?" I asked. She looked up at me with a wrinkled brow, her large brown eyes intent, but not quite focused on me.

"Ah," she began, and then she raised her voice, "Filipe!" she yelled. Then she pointed to a door on the left side of the shop.

In the back room a young man was working on cutting rigging wire. He was slim and tall with dark hair, apparently from France.

"Filipe?" I said as I entered the room. "Ah, excuse me. Do you speak English?" Filipe looked up from his work.

"*Oui,*" he said; and he smiled.

"We have a boat out there in the harbor and I think it needs some rigging work done. I wonder if you could have a look at it," I said, not wanting to waste time.

"Is the boat in the marina?" asked Filipe, assuring me he actually did speak English.

"No," I said, "it is at anchor in the harbor."

"Bring it to the fuel dock tomorrow morning," he said. "Tell them Filipe needs to look at your boat."

"Ok, I said." In my mind I could already hear the objections of the busy fuel dock attendant as I moved *Tapestry* into his space.

"About nine?" I said

"Nine at the gas dock," said Filipe," he smiled and continued carefully measuring   a length of thick stainless steel wire.

"*Merc*i", I said,

"Not at all," Filipe replied. I knew I was going to like this place.

Below the ship's store there was a restaurant built on the dock right over the water. We had lunch there and enjoyed our first taste of French cooking.

French cooking?. But this is the Island of Martinique, not France. Not so, we were surprised to find. To the citizens of this island, this is France. License plates say France. As far as the residents are concerned, it might as well be France.

We had another surprise later that day. As we walked the marina docks, while checking out the fleet, we found our Japanese friends aboard their boat, *Ben Kai*. Taka and June were eager to see us. We decided to find a nice restaurant and have dinner that night.

Later that evening, we found a quiet little place not far from the marina, and enjoyed dinner at a table on the street.

"I've been working with a man," said Taka," who has

gone to great lengths to find a printer for me, one that will print Japanese characters. He took me in his car. He was wonderful. You see I have a manuscript I need printed… his name is Ed…. Ah. Calls himself the Minister of Rum…"

"Ed, Ed. You don't mean Ed…?" I muttered. "I can't remember his last name, but I think I know who you mean," I said.

"You know him?" Taka replied. He looked right at me.

"Yes, I know Ed." I said. Last year Julie and I were anchored off the Dutch side of Saint Marten. This man came by in a rowboat. He misread the hail port on our transom as Asheville, North Carolina, rather than Ashville, New York. Anyway, we got to talking and as I was having my evening cocktail, I asked him aboard for a drink. When I told him all I had was rum, he said that was fine. He said they called him 'The Minister of Rum.' Then he asked me what kind of rum I was drinking. I said Mount Gay. 'Oh,' he said, 'bring me a glass of water.' He went on about how he had fallen asleep at the helm of his boat one night and had run it up on an island and lost it. People had come together and gotten him another boat. He was working on his new boat's rigging then. Interesting guy. He drank the water, too. Said he drank nothing but imported rum at least ten years old that sold for less than ten dollars a bottle. Said it was wonderful and that it was plentiful in the Caribbean."

"That's Ed," said Taka.

"I thought it was all a line until I saw an article about him in the local paper. Then, when I got home, I found another article about him in *Cruising World.*"

"Ed is coming to our boat tomorrow night for dinner," said Taka, along with another couple I don't think you have met. Why don't you and Julie join us."

"That would be great," I said. "We'll look forward to it! What can we bring?"

"What do you mean you don't want fuel?" the   line

handler said as we bumped *Tapestry* on the dock at the Marin Marina. He grabbed our bow line and made it fast to a cleat. Filipe was nowhere in sight so Julie dropped to the deck and sprinted down the dock toward the marine store. It was a long dock and it seemed forever until the lean frame of Filipe appeared.

One look at our sagging forestay and Filipe turned to me.

"I see your problem," he said. "Bring your boat around to the slip nearest shore. I'll take a closer look."

Once we were secure in the slip, Filipe attached himself to a boson's chair and attached that to our sturdy jib halyard. His assistant stood by the halyard winch, but he had little work to do other than keep the line taught. After checking the forestay and backstay Filipe almost leaped into the rigging, pulling himself up the mast and checking for chafe or bad connections on the two spreaders as he went up. At the masthead he dropped one end of a tape measure for his assistant to record shroud length. He carefully looked at every wire and every connection. Frankly, I was impressed. We had never had such a careful rig survey.

"I think your backstay is six inches too long," he said. "I checked the turnbuckle at the deck and the threads are galled. It was junk to begin with and now it is ruined. We will shorten the wire by six inches and add a new turnbuckle, one with a bronze screw. That should last for years."

I was stunned. Just two years before, when we bought the boat in Annapolis, we had ordered a new insulated backstay for her. At the advice of a rigger we had the new backstay shortened by six inches. Obviously, the man who cut the wire ignored our instructions and cut it to the same length as the original and then added a cheap turnbuckle as well!

"What about using a hydraulic backstay adjuster," I suggested.

"Not good for in-boom furling," replied Filipe. "You need a fixed angle between the boom and the mast for that system. Besides, with the external track you have added to the mast, the mast would not bend well. You need a shorter backstay and then more tension on the rig will remove much of the headstay sag."

I couldn't fault anything that Filipe had said. His assessment was much the same as mine.

"So when can you do the work, and what do you think it will cost?" I asked, hesitantly.

"It depends," said Filipe, lighting up a cigarette. "We can replace the backstay, no problem, but I wonder about your forestay. It has been hiding under the jib roller furling extrusion all these years. What do we know about its condition? Before I can tell you what it will cost to repair your rig, we will have to remove the forestay and check that system. The roller furling you have on there looks small to me. Honestly, I don't think it was designed for boats as long and heavy as this one is. Your shrouds are all right, but we must look at the forestay." He blew a puff of smoke into the wind and flicked the ash from his cigarette.

"When can we get started?" I said,

"Bring your boat here next Monday." said Filipe. "Make a reservation and tell them that I will be working on her. They will assign you a slip as close to our office as possible. That will save us time. It is a long way across the Atlantic, Henri, believe me; we want to do this right."

I thanked Filipe, made the appropriate reservation, backed the boat from the slip and returned to the anchorage behind the marina.

That night it was spitting rain as Julie and I climbed down the ladder on *Tapestry's* stern and started our little Honda outboard. The motor hummed quietly, Julie balanced a salad bowl on her lap and a bottle of wine vibrated in the bottom of the boat as *Triplet*, our seven foot long fiberglass dinghy, splashed through a mild chop and scattered raindrops, past the huge marina, toward the dock next to Taka and Jun's beautiful Amel

52, *Ben Kai*.

It was wet in the cockpit, so we went below right away. The Amel is an elegant French boat designed for a couple to sail around the world safely and in luxury. Inside the warm woods and cream colored upholstery, illuminated with indirect lighting, made the boat glow. We had just found seats around a comfortable table when the other couple and Ed, the Minister of Rum, appeared. Their names are not important, but they were interesting folks who were sailing a sixty plus foot Sundeer yacht, the first one I had ever seen. He was a tall and strong and obviously a very capable man. She was quite short, but very attractive and lively, and, like Jun, she was Japanese.

Ed had a small case with him. He opened it and inside were several decanters of very special rum. We had begun the evening with a glass of wine, but soon we were introduced to "tea punch." For the remainder of the evening, we enjoyed one new rum drink after another. It was delightful, wonderful. Of course we had all contributed a bottle of wine to the meal, and they were all open before us, sitting right on the table. The food was great and the conversation never lingered. At the end of the meal ramekins appeared. Then someone took a small blow torch from a pouch and he lit it with a match and next thing I knew the *crème brulee* was being crisped with the torch. Wonderful. When the night finally ended and we ventured to the stern of the boat, I remember noticing that the boat and the floating dock were moving, but not in unison. There was a rubber fender on the stern of *Ben Kai*. When we entered the boat earlier in the evening I noticed that fender, and it appeared to be firmly attached to the stern. As we left I saw that fender again and I thought that if I could use it as a step to the dock…

Wrong!

Suddenly I was suspended in a warm dark world watching bubbles drift upward toward the light. The fender wasn't attached at all, and I had slipped between the dock and the boat into the warm Caribbean water. I was not panicked, comfortable as I am in the water, and I knew what waited for me on the dock would be less pleasant than my current predicament. Then I was treading water right next to the dock. The fender had been a step to the wet. With a little assistance from Taka, I pulled myself with my heavy clothes back onto the dock and found myself apologizing profusely. Julie was, as I had anticipated, not pleased. We said our final good-byes and walked to the dinghy. My shoes squished as I walked, and I left a watery trail on the dock. With some difficulty, I climbed aboard our tiny dinghy, *Triplet,* and we motored back to *Tapestry.*

The next morning my head ached and I had only vague memories of the night before. After a little breakfast and coffee, I felt a bit better, only to see Ed approaching in his dinghy. He had a small bag with him. I had rushing 'demon rum,' thoughts, but quickly put them aside.

"Hi, Ed," I said as I squinted in the sun and grabbed his dinghy painter.

"You said last night that you had some frozen thru hulls?" Ed said, smiling, as he climbed aboard.

"Oh yes, of course. Did I say that? I…"

" We were going to fix them this morning, remember?"

"Right, yes." I said.   I was definitely having tongue trouble.

"Would you like a cup of coffee?" said Julie.

"Oh, thank you, Julie" said the Minister of Rum as she handed him a steaming cup. There could be no doubt Ed was far too cheerful to have been in the same boat I had been the night before. After a little more coffee we moved aft to Julie's and my stateroom and found the offending thru-hulls under the berth.

At each place where water enters or leaves a boat for a toilet or a sink drain there is a ball valve attached to the hull. Should for any reason the hose fail, the valve allows those aboard the boat to close off the opening quickly and easily. It is a major safety device. Unfortunately, due to salt water corrosion, several of ours had frozen in the open position. Using the tools that Ed had brought along in his bag, we carefully loosened the offending thru-hulls as much as we could and forced grease into the part that was stuck. By carefully working them back and forth, we managed to free them up. In spite of my headache, I had learned a valuable lesson. In fresh water, ball valves rarely need attention, but in the salt water environment, they are as susceptible to corrosion as is any other metal part. In other words, ball valves need to be greased regularly, and they need to be opened and closed frequently to keep them from becoming stuck in one position.

That morning we fixed both of the thru-hulls. I was most grateful for Ed's help. He understood the problem and was good at explaining the fix. Although we had soft wood plugs tied to each thru-hull in the boat, to use as a back up in case of emergency, as long as the valves were working, there would be no emergency.

On Monday morning we returned to the marina. In the mean time, Filipe had looked up the number on our Fulrlex roller furling. It was for boats to 30 feet. In addition, whoever had installed it had also removed the original forestay and replaced it with a 7mm one. The forestay was the smallest diameter wire supporting the mast and arguably it carried the most load. That was a formula for disaster. We agreed to replace the roller furling system with a new Pro Furl model and upsize the forestay. We were talking thousands here for the whole deal, but what are a few thousand dollars when a dismasting at sea hangs in the balance?

Julie got out our English/French dictionary and with a bright marker wrote 'For Sale, US$100' in French on a piece of paper, and taped it to the old furling system and forestay, which we laid out on the pier. Within an hour a gentleman came along and handed me five crisp twenty dollar bills. He gathered up our used gear and disappeared off the dock.

Meanwhile, our rigging work had caught the attention of

an Englishman aboard *Dixi*, a Hallberg Rassy 36, built in Sweden. His name was Chris and he and his wife had sailed from England. He had done a great deal of yacht delivery work, and he was obviously a very experienced sailor.

When Filipe brought the new extrusion and roller furling unit to the dock, we were busy selling the old one.

"Excuse me," said Chris. "It's none of my business, but do you realize he's selling you an older, more obsolete model roller furling?"

I wasn't ready for any trouble. It seemed as if we had finally found someone we could trust. Now this. I had had about enough. " What do you mean, Chris", I said. "What's wrong with it?"

"Well," said Chris, "In the first place the track has room for just one sail. When you sail back from Europe, you will definitely need two tracks, so you can fly two jibs off your forestay. That's what just about everyone does when they sail a sloop, like yours, downwind in the trades. Also, that model is thicker at the base than up the forestay. I have known folks who bought them and found they caused excess wear on the foot of their jibs. There is a newer model without those drawbacks. You might ask him about it."

Meanwhile, Filipe was double-checking his measurements. When he came down from the mast I asked him about the furler he had unpacked and laid out on the dock.

"But I thought you were concerned about the cost." Filipe said.

"Well, I am, but how much difference would there be between this one and the newer model?"

"Not that much, really, maybe a hundred dollars. I have a new one in stock. I'll go get it."

"I would be very grateful," I said.

Several hours later the job was done and we were ready to pay the slender lady smoking a cigarette in the office. She had the bill ready and I gave her my credit card while Julie and I browsed among the gleaming merchandise. I knew things weren't going smoothly. I could see another cigarette near the tips of the first two fingers of her left hand. Her right hand was punching furiously at a number pad on a credit card machine. Her brow was wrinkled and she was shaking her head. It didn't look good. She spied me down the isle and we made eye contact.

"Filipe!" she called. "Filipe! Filipe!"

Rapid fire French spilled out of Filipe's office.

"Oh no" I said to Julie. "It must be something with the card."

"Relax," said my ever so patient wife. "They'll just want your mother's maiden name."

"Henri," Filipe looked at me and said. "Your card has refused to pay. It says to call some number in the States."

"Oh," I said. "Well, can we use your phone?"

"Sure," said Filipe.

I dialed the number for foreign countries on the back of the card.

The man at the U.S. bank asked for the usual information. Then he told me why the transaction was refused.

"Whenever we get a charge as big as this one from the Caribbean we generally challenge it. This one was especially curious."

"Why," I said. "We replaced half the rig on our boat. It cost just over two thousand dollars. It's legit," I said

"But you didn't let me finish," the man said. "They charged it twice. Same amount two times."

"Oh." I said and paused.

"Will you authorize one charge of two thousand fourteen dollars?"

"Yes," I said, somewhat stunned.

"It may have been a mistake. It may have been a mistake from which they could have made a lot of money. Maybe it was an honest mistake. We have turned your card back on and sent a confirmation of the charge. Thanks for the call."

I turned to Filipe and told him the whole story. The slender young lady had smoked her cigarette down to a stub. Filipe jabbered in French and her eyebrows went up. I could not follow the repartee that ensued, but her defense, according to her body language, seemed sincere. She was visibly upset.

"She tells me," said Filipe, "that she made the charge and that there was no response from the machine, no authorization. Thinking she may have made a mistake in her entry, she entered it again." He shrugged and then shook my hand, thanking me for our business. He gave Julie and me each a tee shirt.

Chapter 14

Smooth Sailing, The French Islands

From Marin, we sailed on to Fort de France, the capitol of Martinique. Along the way we passed Diamond Rock, a small, very steep and heavily forested island, which was only a mile or so from the Martinique coast. During the wars between the British Admiral Rodney and Napoleon, the British captured that island for a short time and used it as a base to fire on Martinique. It never came to much, but it shows the level of hostility between the two countries at that time.

Tapestry sailed beautifully after our rig work was completed, and the new furling system worked like a charm. We were very pleased. Although we had found it difficult at times, we will remember Marin as a fine place. We liked it a great deal.

Fort de France was a splendid city. We had our first taste of true European coffee while we were there and we had lunch in a hotel, too. I clearly remember the lunch. For us it was an unusually large meal, served in several courses. The table next to us held a gathering of French business people. The men were dressed in suit and tie, the women in dresses. They began with cocktails; several cocktails. During lunch they drank wine. They had bottles of wine. They were boisterous and talking loudly in French and laughing and obviously having fun. They had come before we got there and they were still going strong when we left. Apparently, they would go back to work later in the day. This lunch time in Fort de France reminded me of something an English cleric had said to me years ago while we were working in the Peace Corps in Malawi.

"To a European a meal is a ceremony to an American it is a biological function."

These Frenchmen must have really had something to celebrate. It was a glimpse of a foreign culture I had not expected here in the Caribbean. The French have different values than

Americans. Rather than politicians, they sometimes put artists and writers on their coins; they think drinking wine is important; they teach their children to imbibe at an early age. We seem to think our children will magically know how to drink when they turn twenty-one. I could feel the puritanical American coming out in me, and something new to think about.

There is a small group of islands just to the south of Guadeloupe, which we visited next. They are called "The Saints" and they are very lovely. There are shops and resorts in the area and they revolve around several especially picturesque towns. There are also a number of fairly remote anchorages and remains of old forts left over from Napoleon's day. Interestingly, Josephine, Napoleon's wife, hailed from one of these French islands. There are trails with magnificent vistas and, wonderful little remote bays.

Tapestry was one of several boats anchored in one such bay one beautiful Sunday afternoon, when a power boat, under twenty feet long, came by and anchored a short distance from us. There was an older man in the boat and several boys around ten or twelve. There was also a young woman, perhaps in her late teens or early twenties. The boys jumped in the water right away and began swimming around their boat. After a while the young woman, who was dressed in a bikini bottom and a tank top, crossed her arms, took hold of the bottom of her tank top and pulled it over her head, revealing her rather large, firm bare breasts. She did not leap into the water, but rather she got out her towel and folded her clothes and then eased herself down the swim ladder on the side of the boat. Of course I understood it was impolite to stare and I tried very hard not to…at least not to appear to be staring…

It is a different culture. I never said it was a bad culture, just different. And it is precisely to explore these different cultures that we go sailing.

Chapter 15

On To St. Eustatius

The Saints were a delightful taste of paradise. We had hiked the trails and enjoyed the bustling towns and villages, but it was time to move on. We raised anchor in the little town of Borge, hoisted sail and headed for Guadeloupe. We sailed past Dominica, and continued on to Guadeloupe where we stopped for a short time in Basseterre, then sailed on to Deshines, where we anchored right off the town. We walked along narrow streets, poked about in quaint shops and enjoyed dinner in an intimate restaurant open to the sea. Candles flickered in the warm breeze. The hostess was charming, the service was excellent. The food and wine were superb. It was a wonderful evening, nothing like what we had expected. It was a soft embrace from a lovely new acquaintance.

On the thirty-first of March we sailed past the smoking volcano at Montserrat. Since its eruption in July of 1995, a portion of the population of the island has either moved away, most of them to England, or resettled on the safe-third of the island. It is eerie indeed to sail past the smoking mountain and see huge boulders scattered among the abandoned dwellings. Some of these rocks are as big as the houses and wrecked havoc as they were tossed helter-skelter by the eruption. Through the binoculars we could see that some of the houses were burned out while others appeared to be intact. Whatever their condition, it is illegal for anyone to cross a line, established by the local government, and venture into the area surrounded by the still active volcano. As we had visited Montserrat once before, we opted not to go ashore and deal with the formalities of customs, but to anchor in the harbor and get an early start the following morning.

Fair winds and blue skies carried us past beautiful Nevis and St. Kitts the following day. The mountains of Nevis reach nearly to the clouds and it is said that Columbus mistakenly thought they were snow covered when he first saw them. As we passed an anchorage on Nevis, we were reminded of the days we had spent there the previous year, in 2003, when we anchored right off the coast. A short time before we arrived, a tidal wave had washed a sloop at anchor far up on the beach. There was nothing left of it but the fiberglass shell. Every bit of metal, from the engine to the steering wheel, had been removed. It was a difficult place to feel comfortable.

We also remembered checking in to St. Kitts customs and immigration. We anchored off a little point near the customs office and took our dinghy to shore. There was no place to properly secure the boat so we fastened it to the rocks and hoped it wouldn't dash itself to pieces before we returned. Customs was slow, followed by a seemingly endless visit to the Port Authority where we learned we would have to dinghy across the harbor to visit the immigration office. Cabs were eager to take us, but we felt we couldn't leave our dinghy banging against the rocks, so we motored our little cockleshell, past huge cruise ships, far out into the rolling waves of the harbor at Basseterre, to a marina where they charged us a hefty fee to moor the dinghy for a short time. At immigration a tall black woman took our passports, stamped them angrily, and when she handed them back to us she loudly said, "Have you killed Saddam Hussein yet?"

It was shortly after the American invasion of Iraq, and I was totally unprepared for the question. It seemed suddenly that everyone in the large office was looking at us. I could think of nothing to say and we simply accepted our passports and left.

St. Kitts, named after Christopher Columbus, had not been a very welcoming place the previous year, and we had no intention of going back. We sailed on to St. Eustatius.

Unlike the other islands we had passed, St. Eustatius was in no way spectacular. We motored into its small harbor and paid ten dollars to a young man for a mooring. We were rather sure it wasn't his to sell as he had no identification, but it was late and we were tired. We had sailed sixty miles from Montserrat that day. There was one other cruising boat in the harbor along with a few fishing boats, but that was all.

According to our cruising guide, St. Eustatius, or Statia, as it is sometimes called, had a very colorful past. It is the first of the islands in the Dutch West Indies. In the Eighteenth Century it was a free port, that is, a place where one could purchase goods without paying duty. Slaves, gold, silver, sugar and other commodities were for sale there. Hundreds of ships might be anchored off the port at any one time. It was a wild and exciting place; the place to be in the Caribbean. In 1778, an American ship entered the port and, flying the American flag, it fired the traditional salute. The Dutch port captain fired the traditional reply. That was the first time an American ship had ever been officially recognized by a European power. When word got to the English Admiral Rodney in St. Lucia, he was so angry, he sent an English ship to take the port. In October of that year, before the English arrived, a terrible hurricane largely destroyed the city. Hence, when the British arrived there was little for them to take. It is said that when Rodney got there he noticed that there were many fresh graves in the cemetery. He was suspicious and exhumed the coffins to find them filled, not with corpses, but with the Dutch merchants' gold. Today, some remains of the old port can be seen at the water's edge, but very little. It was a quiet night at anchor and early the following morning we set off for Saba.

Chapter 16

Magical Saba

A rising breeze early on the morning of April first made it convenient to simply drop the line to the mooring and pull out the jib. *Tapestry* backed down nicely and as I turned her wheel to starboard, her bow eased to port, filling the jib and driving us forward and out of the harbor. Once clear of the island, we headed into the wind and raised the main for the short sail to Saba. It was a beautiful morning for a sail, but there was a problem that had cropped up with the steering.

When we launched the boat in January, the rudder was rock solid. When I tried to wiggle it while standing on the ground beside the boat, there was no movement at all. Now, however, it had somehow become loose. During the night at St. Eustatius, there was little wind, just a gentle swell. While we lay in bed we could hear a thump,…thump as the boat rolled. It sounded as if something heavy was moving back and forth with the motion of the boat. We first heard the sound in the Saints, but had dismissed it as an anchor rocking in its locker or perhaps a partially submerged mooring ball bumping the boat.. The previous night, however, we had checked things out and pretty much isolated the sound. It was coming from the rudder post. The rudder must have somehow loosened on its shaft and made thumping sounds as it moved.

During the sail that day we noticed the autopilot labored more than it should have just keeping the boat on a straight line. Saint Martin, would be our last stop before we headed for Antigua and the beginning of the ARC. We would have the boat there for nearly a month, and the island had a good reputation for reliable service and reasonably priced marine repair. We hoped this would be the last of our problems and we could get it resolved in a timely fashion.

Saba stood out ahead of us in the morning sun. Friends of ours, who had explored the Caribbean for five years, had spent several weeks on this island and raved about it. We decided it was an important stop. Saba appears to be little more than a steep mountain top jutting skyward from the sea. The water is deep right up to the shore and there is no port or marina where one can find safe dockage or marine supplies. There are a few mooring balls a short distance from the steep, rocky shore. The water was so deep, anchoring was out of the question for us. We found an unoccupied ball about two miles from the tiny refuge harbor, tied to it and launched the dinghy. There were whitecaps about and we felt a bit precarious as we lowered ourselves into the tiny dinghy and motored through the wind and waves. We rounded a seawall and tied to a dock in the calm waters behind the break-wall. A short distance up the hill was a tourist and information office. Inside a young lady with blonde hair and bright blue eyes smiled at us as we entered.

"And how can I help you?" she asked,, smiling pleasantly.

"Well, we've just arrived, ah, by boat, and we would like to see the island for a day or two." I said.

"Wonderful," the young lady replied, "I'm sure you'll enjoy your time here. There is a small park fee that covers the use of the moorings. You can pay that here. You will have to stop over at the customs and immigration office as well; formalities, you know. We have pamphlets here. Would you be interested in a snorkeling tour?"

"I don't think so," I said

"Well there are two cities, Bottom and Windwardside. You might want to go up today. You would have time to look around a bit and tomorrow you could go back to Windwardside and then climb to Mt. Scenery. Would you like me to call a taxi for you?"

"Oh, well, we are used to walking and…"

"You might want to taxi up to Windwardside and, perhaps, walk back. I think it might be possible to do that before dark. There is a good road, but it is a long way. Can I call a cab?"

"Yes, of course, but we'll have to check in at customs first. It may take us a while," I finally said.

"Don't worry too much about customs. You have checked in with me and paid your fees. Customs here is quite informal."

Where had we heard that before, I thought to myself.

We thanked the young lady and wandered out of the office. Huge diesel engines silenced by gigantic mufflers rumbled nearby, a sophisticated power plant for the Island. We walked up the steps to the customs office, but it was closed and the door was locked.

In a few minutes, a small cab arrived. It was driven by a man who spoke English well. We climbed aboard.

He dropped into first gear and the boxy little European car rounded a curve and headed up a steep road paved with stone. There were walls on each side and it was narrow, just wide enough for two vehicles to pass. Switchback after switchback lay ahead of us. Our driver shifted from first to second gears, but rarely got any higher. We noticed several things right away. First of all, houses on the island were immaculate cottages painted white with red roofs and green shutters. Gardens and flowers were abundant. Secondly, the road was devoid of litter. We had often been disappointed by the broken glass and litter on the sides of the roads in most of the Caribbean. Here, the roads appeared to have been swept clean. No piece of paper fluttered in the wind. The place was immaculate. Our driver told us a bit of the story of the Saba.

"My father helped build this road," he began. "Up until World War II there was no road. They had tried to design one. In fact they brought in several big-shot engineers to help us design one, but they said it couldn't be done." He paused for a moment.

"There was no road," he said, "just a stairway. In the old days, ships would anchor down by where you moored your boat. They called that place 'Ladder.' They would move the ships as close to shore as they could and then men, standing up to their waists in water, unloaded and then carried everything up a stairway that led first to Bottom and on up the mountain to Windwardside. The steps were carved right into the stone. Everything that came from the outside world came up those steps. Food, pianos, building materials, you name it, it was carried up by the sturdy people who lived here."

"So where did the road come from?" I asked.

"Well, there was a man named Joseph Hassel who lived here. He was head of the local Department of Public Works. After the war, he took a correspondence course from the University of Chicago in Civil Engineering. When he finished, he engineered the road. We called it 'The Road that Could not be Built.'"

"And you built it."

"Yes, pretty much by ourselves. My father worked on it. He wore a back pack and they would load him up with cement or rock or whatever they needed at the construction site and he would walk up to it and drop his load. He was paid per trip. Sometimes he made as many as three trips per day."

"I can't imagine it." I said, as we dropped down into first gear again and rounded another steep curve. "How long did it take?"

"Twenty years" he said. "It was a long time building."

We motored through the town of Bottom and then ascended further until we reached Windwardside, where we paid our fare and set out to explore the city.

There were shops along the streets, much like other cities. They were clean and neat and modern. There was a fresh breeze and the air was cool. It was delightful. One shop we entered sold European style lace. They had especially beautiful tablecloths and napkins and other goods. The lady who worked there making lace asked us whether we had been to Mount Scenery.

"Mount Scenery?" Julie asked.

"Yes" she said. "You start from here and go up the steps. There are 1,064 of them. I try to do it at least once a year," she said.

Julie's eyes lit up. "Just where do you start?'

"There is a little park about a block from here. You can walk over there in no time. You'll see the steps. It is not easy, but not too hard either. Wear good shoes. The view from the top is spectacular."

"Great," said my wife. Julie, being an experienced cross country skier, I knew there would be no holding her back.

We said good-bye to the helpful attendant and began the long walk down "The Road that Could Not be Built" toward our floating home. Along the way we marveled at the construction of the road, the rugged countryside, and the beautiful white homes nestled among the steep hills and cliffs. We stopped briefly at the medical school, a modern facility by any standard. What a beautiful and unique place to get an education. Back at the port we again knocked on the door at customs, but again there was no one at home. Our feet hurt as we climbed aboard *Triplet* and started our reliable little Honda four-stroke engine. We motored through the rolling waves and back to *Tapestry,* where we pulled out lots of slack on the lines from the davits before we connected them to the dinghy, as the stern of the large boat rose and fell with the waves, but not in unison with the small one. Once we had our little boat safely lifted over *Tapestry's* stern we went below where Julie made a hearty spaghetti dinner. It looked as though we would have a full day tomorrow.

The next morning we again knocked on the door at customs and again there was no answer. The lady at the visitor center called a cab for us and we again wound our way to Windwardside. We had our hiking shoes on and walked right to the trail or the "stairway". We knew there were over a thousand steps ahead of us and we thought it important that we get going.

It was truly a challenge. There were flights of stone steps, sometimes a short walk between steps, but there were always more steps ahead. The steps were of varying height as well. We think of climbing a lighthouse with several hundred steps as a daunting task, but those are steps of even height. On Saba, the steps ranged from just a few inches in height to perhaps eighteen inches. They were made of stone. In some places they were carved out of the rock. In others, stones had been set in the soil. In all cases, the trail was trimmed and easy to follow. Obviously, the warm moist climate of the island was conducive to rapid plant growth. We passed a few couples and a family or two who were descending from the summit.

About three quarters of the way up, we passed two men with a weed whacker and a gas can. One carried a rifle over his shoulder and had a large knife in his hand.

"Hello," I said to the man with the rifle. He had been cutting foliage away from the sides of the trail with his machete.

" Is this your job," I asked him.

"No, we volunteer," he said. "We do this for a day every week or so. It is a wonderful way to get out and enjoy the beauty of the island."

"What about the gun?" I asked.

"Well, we use it to hunt wild goats. They escape from the farms down below," he said. "They graze on the fresh foliage up here and they are wonderfully tender to eat."

I looked around. The ocean and the green hillsides were beautiful, but there were also steep cliffs with dense foliage.

"How do you retrieve a goat after you shoot it, I asked."

He looked at me and smiled.

"And you carry it down, along with your weed whacker, gas can, and your gun?"

"Right. And the goats are delicious and absolutely worth it." With that he turned back to his work and Julie and I continued on our way.

Of course I was concerned about Julie. After our last visit to the mountains in Washington, her doctor had said that there would be no more mountain climbing for her. He had prescribed a powerful inhaler and told her to use it twice each day for her attacks of asthma.

"How is your breathing?" I asked her from time to time.

I could tell from the spring in her step and the smile in her voice that she was fine. Julie looked great. It was a wonderful day in an absolutely beautiful place. We had always enjoyed exercising together. We were certainly doing that now.

A short time later we heard a loud, "crack." It was the report of a small caliber rifle. We wondered whether he had got his goat. And if he indeed had got it, how he would get it back to the trail.

After several hours of hard climbing we approached the summit. The mountain had been worn down to little more than boulders and rocks. There was a weathered rope, perhaps an inch thick, which was attached somewhere above and led over the steep rocky trail. We grabbed the line and pulled ourselves up until we came to the top. There we found a monument with a bronze survey mark set in the top of it. We were 2877 feet above sea level. We also found that there were two other peaks. Would we have to climb those as well? Julie had already checked our map and found they, too had trails on them.

We did climb all three, and the scenery there was unforgettable. The cities of Windwardside and Bottom lay below us, colorful foliage surrounded us and the islands of the Caribbean stretched out in the distance. All of this and the great Caribbean Sea and the Southwest North Atlantic in their vast blueness melded with the sky.

On the eastern side of the island, at the level of the sea, there is a small airport with regular airline service from Saint

Martin. While catching our breath on the top of that mountain, we watched a small white cross far below us slip over the sea and roll to a stop on what appeared to be a very short runway.

From the airport we could see another road. Our cab driver told us that road had a name, too. It was called "The Road that Should Not have been Built." Apparently that road was so narrow and steep that it had been the site of a number of accidents.

If it was difficult to walk up the mountain, it was even more difficult to walk back down. Just above Windwardside, we found a trail that led to a lovely restaurant. Inside we enjoyed lunch. The place had high peaked white ceilings and the rafters were carefully painted with patterns of green. It was an eco lodge. Solar panels generated electricity for the place, there were candles for lighting, and vegetables were grown in an organic garden behind the building. After lunch we did a little shopping. Julie found a pair of black corduroy slacks. Obviously, in light of the 90 degree heat in the Caribbean, she was thinking ahead to England. We took a cab all the way back to the port, and we again stopped at customs. No luck. The door was locked and it seemed customs didn't really care whether we had visited or not.

I suppose if I were to write a fairy tale, I would set it on Saba. It is a clean land of white houses with red roofs, green shutters, and spectacular flower gardens.

The Road That Could Not Be Built, on Saba

Julie on the
Peak on Saba

Chapter 17

Saint Martin, the Dutch and the French

Saint Martin, the Dutch part of the island was to be our last port before we headed for Antigua and the start of the ARC. We had made reservations at Simpson Bay Marina months before, and as the island was within sight of Saba, we arrived before lunch. Escorted by inflatable "tug" boats, actually eight foot rubber dinghies, we moved *Tapestry* into the proper row and eased her into the designated slip. The rubber boats were there in the event things got out of control. A strong gust of wind can push a yacht into a position where the helmsman cannot maintain sufficient momentum to steer. When that happens, expensive damage can follow. Consequently, marinas that cater to large, expensive boats make sure there are dinghies around to prevent bad things from happening while the boats are being maneuvered.

Right next to us at Simpson Bay was a celebrity of sorts. It was a 33 foot open sailboat whose Dutch owner had sailed her from the Netherlands single-handed. The newspaper had run a story on him and local television crews interviewed him right after we arrived. Shortly after he left Europe, he ran into a rather severe storm. His boat had capsized in heavy seas. He feared for the worst, but managed to right it again and continue on his way. He lost all his electronics and was left with only a compass for navigation. He had a small gasoline generator on board which he rebuilt after the capsize, but even with a fresh charge in his batteries, his electronics didn't work. He had hoped to set a speed record, for the run. As it turned out, he was fortunate to have made it at all.

As soon as we registered at the marina, we learned there was a package waiting for us. It was our masthead navigation light that we had ordered months before, a prototype of one using diodes rather than regular light bulbs. It would replace our anchor light with both a bright anchor light and tricolor light. Once installed, it would make us visible for miles at sea.

First, however, we wanted to find someone to check out our steering and build a whisker pole for the boat. In case there was a following wind on any of the journey, we wanted to be able to pole out our jib to keep it full.

There was a marine repair facility, "F.K.S." across the harbor from us. They specialized in rigging and hull repair of all boats. When we called them on the radio, they sent a mechanic right over to look at the steering. After a short time he came up with a diagnosis. We had three problems. The first was that the hydraulic cylinder attached to our rudder was a bit small for the duty it would have to perform while crossing the ocean. Secondly, when fluid had been added to the system in the past, someone had used hydraulic steering fluid. Our system was designed to use A.T.F. or automatic transmission fluid. The two don't mix. Thirdly, the way our system was set up, should the system fail, the manual steering override couldn't work without our first draining the system. It would be no help in an actual emergency. His suggested repair was to replace the slave cylinder on the rudder with a new larger one, drain the fluid from the system and refill it with fresh A.T.F. and bleed the system thoroughly, and install a bypass valve which would allow the emergency tiller to be used if the system failed completely. The thought of sailing across the Atlantic with no manual override of the hydraulic steering was frightening. He was confident his repair would make the boat steer better, and be ready for our journey. We gave him the go ahead.

In the meantime we went over to the F.K.S. office and checked the place out. Their machine shop was impressive indeed. They were one of the few places where huge wire for mega-yachts could be swaged and whole rigging systems fabricated. We asked about a whisker pole for the boat. As we had spinnaker poles on previous boats, we weren't familiar with a whisker pole for a boat as large as ours. When they suggested a pole seventeen and a half feet long, we were surprised. But when we bounced the idea off a gentleman on a fifty foot Swan, docked behind us, he assured us the riggers were right.

"Just be sure to set up the pole and attach it to the mast with the jib furled," the man began. "After you clip the end of the pole on the jib sheet, pull the sail out. The pole will hold the clew of the sail away from the boat and enable the jib to fill. It will work wonderfully when running before the wind."

"What if the wind comes up too much and we want to take it down?" I asked.

"Roll your jib in first, then send someone forward to take the pole down. You don't want anyone on the foredeck with that big jib and pole flailing around. Once you have the sail rolled up, you can ease the topping lift and lower the forward end of the pole to the deck, or at least to the rail in the case of your very long pole. Then detach the sheet and the topping lift, remove the pole from the mast and fasten it in place on deck."

"You make it sound pretty easy," I said. "It seems like a huge piece of equipment to handle in a seaway."

"It is, but you'll get used to it." he replied. "Sometimes people rig a fore-guy and an after-guy to hold the pole in place and then they leave it up in all but the most severe weather. They can roll their jib in or out completely independent of the pole. They do that mostly in the trades, coming west. You won't need that till you sail back from Europe."

"Right,"

"Just be sure to set it up a time or two at the dock to be sure all your fittings work and that everything fits. You don't want to be caught short out there when the wind comes up."

He smiled and his reassurance helped us decide to go ahead and order the pole.

In the meantime, Saint Martin was a wonderful place to be. We could use our dinghy to visit the many colorful bars and restaurants in the area. The laundromat, the internet café, even a Pizza Hut was in reach. *Triplet,* our little dinghy, became like a car. We discovered a wonderful North Sail Loft and a spectacular Budget Marine Center that sold everything imaginable for cruising sailboats. We even removed *Tapestry's* main sail and took it by dinghy to North Sails where they would inspect it and further reinforce the tapes so essential for holding it in place on the furling boom. It would be finished when we returned from the States.

There was a huge lagoon in the center of the Island and it was filled with yachts of every description from all over the world. Those who lived in the lagoon, "Lagoonies" they were called, maintained a radio net every morning. They began with a weather report and then listed social events that were happening all over the island. One feature of the net was an opportunity to list things for sale.

We had both an inflatable and a hard dinghy aboard, and we felt that was more than we needed. One morning, right before we left to return to the States, we listed our inflatable dinghy on the air. Within minutes a man and his eight-year-old son showed up and wanted to see the dink. We brought it out on deck and pumped it up. The little boy's eyes lighted up and his father assured me it was just what they had been looking for. He asked if he could try it for a day before he paid for it. Unfortunately, the deal fell through, and it was too late to advertise again.

Time for our departure to the States was drawing near and the man from F.K.S. was busy working on our steering. We began to install the masthead light.

For years, whenever we needed work done aloft, Julie insisted that was her domain. On our other boats, I could winch her hundred and twenty five pounds up the mast much more easily than she could hoist my two hundred. Hence, she did all work aloft. On this boat, we had electric winches which could have just as easily hoisted me up the mast, but not if we wanted peace in the family. Julie was still the mast person. I remember watching her ascend in the boson's chair that bright morning. I was on the winch below as the halyard easily lifted her to the top of the mast. Once she was there she had to remove the old anchor light and drill new holes in the top of the mast to attach the fitting for the new masthead anchor light and tricolor. Then she would also have to wire the new fixture. It was not a small assignment.

Of course, the screws that held the old fixture in place were pretty well corroded into the masthead. Removing them was a huge job in itself. Removing them from a boson's chair while being buffeted by the wind and burned by the tropical sun involved a Herculean effort.

"Can I help" I asked.

"I don't think so," came the reply.

Naturally, there was an audience. Everyone who walked by on the dock gazed up at the woman way up there. They always had some comment, as well.

"What's she doing up there?"

"Replacing a light," I would say

"Oh," they would reply, shading their eyes and peering at Julie as she worked doggedly on. I rigged an extension cord to an electric drill and ran it up to her on another halyard.   It turned out to be a difficult job, but after several trips back down for tools or parts, she succeeded. The new light was firmly in place and wired. Before we could try it, however, we had to wire a double throw, double pole switch in the pilothouse so that we could use just two wires to control both lights. Locating the correct wires and finding an appropriate place for the switch was part of the job. Wiring it was something else. But Julie considered it her project, and she was up to the task.

When we threw the switch, it was the middle of the day. We both walked onto the dock to see whether we could see the light. What we found surprised us. Even in the bright noonday sun of the Caribbean, our new light was visible. It was even better than we had hoped it would be.

In the meantime the rudder project was nearing completion. The mechanic had drained the contaminated oil from the system, was adding new oil and bleeding the air at the upper helm. He had come to work today even though it was the birthday of Queen Beatrix of the Netherlands, a national holiday. We hoped that our steering problem was behind us.

The following day we would fly from Saint Martin to Englewood to make final preparations for our trip. We didn't want loose ends.

We were finalizing the installation of the switch for the masthead light when suddenly there was a pop and a flash of light and a little smoke. After we tested the light, we neglected to open the circuit before we finished the installation. A slip of a screwdriver caused a short. I reset the circuit breaker and we threw the switch. Outside, however, there was no light at the masthead. I checked the breaker, it was set properly. I tried the deck level running lights, they, too failed to light. What could be wrong? Was there a bad connection, had we destroyed the new light fixture, was the circuit breaker defective? It was late in the day and as it was a holiday; there was no one to call for help. A gentleman from another boat suggested there must be another "fusible link" in the system. We would just have to find it. I checked the wiring diagram and found that there was, indeed, another fuse in the system. The trouble was, it didn't say where it was. We would have to locate it in the massive electrical panel or somewhere else on the boat. The next day I searched until we had to leave for our flight, trying to trace that circuit, but with no luck. How frustrating.

Our visit home was filled with details and farewells to friends we wouldn't see until after we crossed the Atlantic. When we returned to the boat we set right to work to find that fuse. Sure enough, we located it and found a blown fuse in a small holder. It was hidden in the mass of wires near the main distribution panel. In a matter of minutes the running lights were working again. People even stopped by in the middle of the day to tell us that our lights were on; music to our ears.

We took the dinghy to North Sails and picked up the main, which had been reinforced by the sail-maker. Back on the boat we struggled to get the new, thicker tapes to squeeze into the fittings on the boom. We were determined and before the sun had set we had the heavy sail in place and ready for our journey.

That evening we made the long trek to the airport to meet Bob and Carol. A jam of people surrounded the place where everyone who had cleared customs entered the airport. Bob and Carol Markus, our crew for the next three months burst through with wide smiles. Carol was tall and slim, her red hair bounced as she walked and Bob, a large man, laden with several heavy bags, was right behind. They had five bags with them, but one especially huge duffel bag. Where would we put it all, we wondered. But it was great to see them. We all talked at once and moved toward a cab where we stuffed their luggage into the trunk and squeezed aboard for the short ride back to Simpson Bay.

But Bob and Carol were great crew from the start. They stowed their baggage in the allotted space and proved to be expert organizers. As long as we sailed together, none of their belongings ever found its way as clutter in other parts of the boat.

The next morning Julie and I headed for F.K.S. to pick up the whisker pole. It was ready for us, but it was a bit of a trick, carrying it back in our dinghy. When Bob saw us, he laughed.

"That was the funniest thing I ever saw", he said, smiling, "The two of you in that seven-foot dinghy motoring through this busy harbor with that seventeen-foot pole." We all had a good laugh. Before long we had practiced setting up and rigging the pole on the mast and attaching hold-downs so it could be fastened to the deck stanchions while it was not in use.

Later that day, Bob and I went to lunch, while Julie and Carol went shopping.

For Bob and me, it was a relaxed lunch, but for the women, it was a major investment in our future. They would be buying food for the whole trip.

When they got back to the boat they had totally loaded a taxi with food. They had cans of meat, including tuna, salmon, chicken, even Spam. Of course there were sacks of fresh food: onions, tomatoes, peppers, oranges and grapefruit, potatoes, lettuce, and eggs. There was powdered milk, Tang, lemonade, tea and coffee. We had pancake mix, popcorn, pasta, rice, cereals, flour, sugar and condiments. We had lots of prepared snack food such as peanut butter and crackers. There were jars of peanut butter as well. Finally, we had fresh foods. Five loaves of bread along with ground beef, chicken, pork chops and chunks of stew made up most of our refrigerated foods. This is just part of the list. I still marvel that the girls could stow all that food completely out of sight. Saint Martin was a wonderful place to provision. Of course this wouldn't be sufficient for the whole trip. Two weeks after we left Antigua, we should be in Bermuda. Still, this was the most economical place we would have to provision. So this is where we really stocked up.

Saint Martin is an island owned by two countries. There is the Dutch side, which we had enjoyed the entire time, and then there is the French side. It would hardly be right not to explore them both. We boarded a bus that Thursday afternoon that would circle the island and give us an opportunity to visit a bit of French Saint Martin. The scenery along the coast was spectacular. Reefs surround some of the island and the green ocean waves created vivid colors, the white of the breaking waves, the blue of the sky and the green of the sea. But it was not so much the view of the reefs that we went for. "I've been told there is a very nice beach on the French side and I think I'd like to go there," said Bob. "It's called Orient Beach."

Although we carried our passports, I was surprised that there were no customs formalities at all from one side of the island to the other. The language changed, the colors of the police cars changed, but no one stamped our papers or asked about our nationalities or birthdays. As we approached, the bus was filling up with more and more young people carrying beach gear. Perhaps because it was a Thursday, the beach wasn't very crowded. Topless young French girls and women, quite exposed, lay on the beach soaking up the rays of the sun and the glances of whomever cared to look. They plunged into the sea, strolled to the beach shower and rinsed off, and from their demeanor one had to think this to be perfectly acceptable behavior.

On Friday we went to town and watched part of the carnival. There was a parade with all the excitement and glitter of a holiday anywhere. There were semi-trucks decorated with streamers and flowers. Bands on the truck trailers played and the musicians waved to the crowd. It seemed every organization on the island had an entry of some kind. Women were dressed in exotic costumes made of all things imaginable. Some wore peacock feathers, but all of them were colorful and brilliant. Toward the end very long legged men walked by, long pants covering their stilts. The parade and party was called a *Jump Up,* and it was lots of fun. We took a bus part way back to the boat. On the way we stopped for dinner at an Indian restaurant. The international flavor of Saint Martin was everywhere.

On Saturday, we left for Antigua. If any of us had any qualms about setting off on our adventure, it didn't show. We were all quite open about our various strengths and weaknesses. Bob was great with computers and ham radio. Right away he programmed the channels we would be using into the memory of our ICOM 710 radio. He caught on to the Winlink system immediately. Ham radio and computers were his field and he was right at home. At the same time, Bob had loads of experience as an EMT and a fireman. He knew about fire control and first aid. He had driven ambulances, revived drowning persons and extinguished fires. He checked our fire fighting equipment and made sure everything was working and up to date. He organized fire drills and abandon ship drills, assigning each of us a job to do in case of emergency. We liked to not think about such things, but Bob was first to point out that if we were prepared, an emergency might have a much happier ending. He was a great asset to the crew. On the other hand, he was heavy and his knees bothered him. It was somewhat painful for him to climb the companionway ladder from the pilothouse to the cockpit. He also had high blood pressure and he became seasick easily. He had medications, and we hoped that they would alleviate any problem.

Carol, was a big asset to the crew as well. She was fit and eager. She would cook and clean and do her watch. She was meticulous about what she did and easy to get along with. Her training was also as an EMT and a nurse.

All four of us had sailed for years. We felt we were up to the challenge.

On Saturday we left. We settled our bill with Simpson Bay Marina and then cast off the lines, backed the boat from the slip and motored into the huge lagoon. The winds were gusty, and as we approached the draw-bridge the scream of sirens filled the air. They were incessant and loud and definitely coming our way. The bridge wouldn't open. Sure enough, fire trucks and ambulances raced across the bridge to an emergency somewhere on the other side.

"Might as well plan to stay here for a while," said Bob. "They won't open the bridge until they either get the injured person into the ambulance and get him back across the bridge, or at least determine that no one is injured and needs to go to the hospital."

Sure enough, it turned out to be a thirty minute wait. By then, there were dozens of boats jockeying for a space in the narrow channel. No one wanted to be caught with his or her anchor down, as the bridge operated on a limited schedule, and they might miss the opening. So we all milled about in the space in front of the bridge. When the span finally lifted, *Tapestry* surged ahead. We moved through the bridge into the outer harbor where we were going to drop anchor and do some last minute work on the boat. I knew there was a problem. When I pushed the throttle forward, there was not the smooth rush of power to which I was accustomed, but rather the engine made a hollow sound. I glanced over the side, and sure enough, rather than the usual gush of water that flowed from the exhaust, there was but a trickle. As we eased into the outer harbor, Julie ran forward and readied the anchor. I steered the boat into position, Julie released the anchor and we shut down the engine.

"I'll bet the filter's clogged," I said, as I lifted the floorboards and eased myself down into the tiny space beside the engine. I reached back and unscrewed the top of the strainer and, sure enough, barnacles and seaweed clogged the filter. We cleaned the strainer and I reached back to reassemble the unit. This place beside the engine was very confining for me, and Julie had previously maintained both the fuel and water filters which were located there. When we restarted the engine, the water gushed from the exhaust as it should. Everything was fine. I lowered the dinghy for a final visit to customs with our passports, and then back to Simpson Bay with the water key which I had forgotten to turn in when we checked out of the marina. Meanwhile, the rest of our crew slipped into the clear blue water outside the harbor and scrubbed the bottom of the boat. *Tapestry* had been in Simpson Bay for nearly a month, and a good scrubbing was in order before our departure.

Chapter 18

On to Antigua

The sail to Antigua was 114 nautical miles. The island was southeast of Saint Martin, which meant we would be sailing close to the wind to get there. Because it is never a good idea to enter a strange harbor after dark, and that is doubly true in the Caribbean, we decided it would be best to leave about noon. That way we should arrive about noon the following day. The crew would have an opportunity to practice working the boat at night, and we would christen our carefully crafted watch schedule.

Once we had hoisted the dinghy and secured it to the davits, we were excited about the forthcoming trip. The anchor came up smoothly and we set off, plunging through surprisingly large waves. The weather forecast was for wind of 20 knots from the southeast. That meant we would be heading right into wind and waves and that we were going to be in for a rough ride and a long passage. At first we shut down the engine, raised the full main, and pulled out the jib the whole way. We fell off on a port tack and *Tapestry* heeled far over. Winds were gusting well over the forecasted twenty-knots. Obviously, we were carrying too much sail. We headed into the wind and shortened both the main and jib. When the sails filled again we found that we had an easier motion, heeled less and were actually sailing faster. We took turns steering from the cockpit, but as the wind was increasing, the waves growing, and we were getting wet, we retired to the pilothouse. It wasn't long before Bob was looking pale. He grabbed his foul weather jacket, donned his harness and headed for the cockpit. I knew he was going to be sick. What a way to start a voyage across the ocean.

"Have you used your seasick patches?" I asked.

"Just put one on," He called back. Great whooshes of spray flew over the pilothouse roof and landed on him as he sat in the cockpit. "Should have put a patch on hours ago," he replied as another wave of spray washed over him.

"Hold on tight," I cautioned, "you don't have to be up there as far as we're concerned."

"I think I'll just stay here." Said Bob. "I don't like it below at all."

In the pilothouse everything was under control. We practiced steering from inside and *Tapestry* rocked and rolled through the waves as she plunged along. Carol was weathering the boat's movement well and was happy to take her turn at the helm. As the afternoon wore on to evening, Julie and Carol prepared a light supper. Bob didn't care for anything to eat, but he drank water. We all understood that it was essential not to become dehydrated.

One of the steps we had taken prior to leaving Saint Martin was to change engine oil and to change the primary filter in the water-maker. As it is important to run the water-maker regularly to flush its membrane, this seemed like a good time to do that. I stepped into the forward head and pressed the switch and immediately the hum of the electric motor accompanied the sound of wind and waves against the hull. It was reassuring to know that we were taking seawater and, by reverse osmosis, turning it into delicious, fresh drinking water. I could hardly wait for the water to start running into the fresh water container so we could offer our guests a taste. Water in the harbor at Saint Martin was too dirty to introduce into the water-maker, but out here at sea it was perfect. The device worked best in warm salt water.

I peeked into the head to see if the red light on the controller had turned to green, but not yet. Moments later the air in the pilothouse was interrupted by a loud shriek. It was the buzzing noise of the high water alarm.

"What's that?" said Carol.

I tried to be calm with my answer. "Sounds like the high water alarm," I said.

I lifted the floorboard and carried it to Bob and Carol's berth to lay it down. Then I picked up the lower board and moved it to the bed as well.

"Oh, my god," I said, "Water is running into the bilge from forward."

I lifted the floorboards in the galley and peered down into the bilge. As I feared, water was above the level of the alarm. I lifted the floorboards from the pilothouse floor and carried them to the forward cabin. There was no place else to put them with the boat surging about as it was. Water was coming from the port side. I looked in the head, but all was normal. Then I opened the *pantry* and pulled out the bottom slide, which was filled with onions and potatoes. Water was gushing from the filter canister below, which we had just serviced. I leaned into the head compartment and switched off the water-maker. Apparently the O-ring on the primary filter canister had failed and water was leaking out and running into the bilge. With the device off, the leak stopped, but just to be on the safe side I closed the thru-hull which led to the unit. The leak had been minor, and I was surprised that the bilge pump hadn't been able to keep up with it. We would make repairs in Antigua. Meanwhile, the water level in the bilge had dropped, the alarm switched itself off and everything was back to normal. We had plenty of water in the main tanks. We would just have to wait to run the water-maker.

"So, what was the problem?" said Carol.

"The O-ring." I said. "It must have broken when we replaced the filter. We have another one, but I'll replace it when we get to Antigua."

"I see. Have you had this problem before?"

"No." I said. "We really haven't had any problem with the water-maker after it was installed."

Carol seemed satisfied and the boat was obviously fine.

The wind howled, and after sunset we found ourselves surging through the darkness, our new masthead light beaming from the top of the mast. Bob was still ill, but had decided that the seat inside the pilothouse nearest the companionway might be better than the constant drenching in the cockpit. He moved inside. Perhaps his medicine was taking effect; perhaps he had nothing left to vomit. Although he was clearly miserable, at least he was safe with us inside. After a while he even ate a few peanut butter crackers.

Meanwhile, as we had been sailing for hours on the port tack, Julie and I ventured outside to tack the boat. We had done it hundreds of times and we knew the drill exactly. Julie took the helm and swung us through the wind as I released the jib sheet from the starboard side and wrapped its mate around the winch on port and hauled it in. Everything looked ship-shape on deck. Low clouds obscured most of the stars overhead. We were truly alone on a dark and windy sea as we raced along.

The night seemed endless. Although the Nauticat 35 seldom pounded as other boats often do, when she dropped off or crashed into those ten foot waves, the movement was anything but comfortable. Seas were definitely building.

A careful check of our location on the computer showed that during the previous hour we had failed to maintain course. At this rate we wouldn't get to Antigua till after dark the following day. I started the engine and Julie and I returned to the cockpit to furl the jib. We would head up a bit and continue under reefed main and engine.

Eventually Julie went to bed. Bob curled up on the pilothouse settee, and Carol and I stayed on watch.

"Is it always this hard to keep the boat on course?" Carol said. I could see that she was moving the wheel back and forth a great deal and the boat was swerving along the course line.

"You're steering too much, Carol," I said. "You only have to move the wheel an inch for the boat to respond. Remember, too, you always have to return the helm to center to keep the boat in a straight line, like driving a car. Want me to take it for a while?"

"Yes, go ahead," she said. "This is really hard."

I grabbed the wheel and held on firmly as *Tapestry* slowly moved to starboard. I corrected by turning the wheel more and more to port. The boat would correct, but then she would drift off again. I knew if I kept turning to port, eventually the rudder would reach her stops. But that didn't seem to happen. I could feel that sick feeling creep over me. Perhaps our steering hadn't been fixed after all. Maybe the man had replaced the cylinder, but that wasn't the problem in the first place. Although the wheel had worked fine in calm trials, there was something wrong now!

Then the boat was once again filled with the ringing sound of the high water alarm. I glanced at the console and saw that a red light was lit over the indicator for the bilge pump.

"Not again?" Carol said. Mild concern was written on her face.

"Oh," I said, trying to hide my alarm. I quickly switched on the autopilot and lifted the first of the floorboards that lead to the engine compartment. With both boards moved to the forward V-berth, I could see into the bilge and, sure enough, the bilge pump was covered with water which sloshed back and forth in the deep sump. I again checked the console and sure enough, the red light was on, the bilge pump was still running. Apparently, however, it wasn't pumping. I shut off the switch and grabbed the handle for the emergency manual backup. In a few minutes I had lowered the water in the bilge and finally, the irritating alarm shut itself off. By then, Julie was at my side. Whenever the boat lurched to starboard, a stream of water gushed into the bilge from the port side. Apparently, there was a leak on the port side of the boat. We quickly shut down the engine, and adjusted the helm twenty degrees to starboard so that the mainsail would fill and we would heel a bit more to starboard.

It was quiet. When we lifted the floorboards before, the engine roared loudly, but now we heard only the whistling wind and waves.

Julie, never one to hesitate, grabbed a flashlight.

"Move over," she said. "I'm going below." With that, I found the appropriate tool, twisted the safety locks under the cockpit table and lifted the table and the hinged floorboard under it as far as I could. Julie squeezed into the space beside the hot engine and probed familiar territory with her light.

"I found it," she said. "It's the water strainer on the engine. The top isn't screwed on straight." There was a minute or so of her moving around and then she re-emerged, and raised herself out of the bilge.

"I think it's all right now," she said. "Let's start her up and see."

I touched the starter and the Yanmar roared to life. We watched carefully for a minute or two and clearly no more water was pouring into the bilge. I put the engine back in gear and set us back on course. We watched for a few more minutes and all was fine. The engine gauges were where they belonged and no more water was coming in. We muscled the floorboards back in place over the bilge and were relieved to hear peaceful relative quiet return to the pilothouse.

I switched off the automatic bilge pump and worked the manual one. No resistance meant there was no water. I resolved to work the pump to check the bilge every half hour until we arrived in Antigua. Should we develop a more serious leak, the high water alarm would alert us.

Bob, who had curled up on the settee, tried to close his eyes and sleep; Julie went back to our cabin to sleep. Carol and I were too excited to rest. She took back the helm, determined to master the steering. We traded places every hour or so. Despite the heavy going, we were making good progress on our goal. I felt terrible that I had failed to properly tighten the water inlet at Saint Martin, but relieved that we had resolved the problem so well. At sea, one emergency is usually manageable, but when two things happen at once catastrophic failures sometimes occur. Our second "emergency" had involved a leak and a failing bilge pump. The good news was that the high water alarm had warned us and the manual bilge pump had been able to take care of the problem. Also we had solved the problem and brought ourselves back to normal operating procedures. Everything was okay. We handled the problem well.

The night had been filled with annoyance. What must Carol be thinking, I wondered. Each hour we would click on the light, mark our position in the log, record our latitude, longitude, speed, distance to go, barometric pressure, and then I would work the hand pump to test the bilge for water. It was our only break in the tedium of the night. On a long passage, it is the first or second night that seems so endless. After that one is able to fall into the routine.

We had a ship's bell clock on the aft bulkhead of the pilothouse. Carol seemed a little puzzled by it.

"Well, Carol," I began. "At sea, the day is divided into watches. Every watch is four hours long. You are always expected to know what time it is within four hours. So, what they used to do was use an hourglass. The sand ran out in half an hour. The man on watch would ring a bell whenever he turned the glass over. That way everyone on board knew what time it was. Watches began at 12, 4, 8 and so on. There would be eight bells on the hour. At, say eight thirty it would be 1 bell, at nine, two bells and so on until noon when it would be again eight bells. Get it?"

"Maybe some other time." she said. She was working the wheel more and more and I had an uncomfortable feeling about both the state of the steering on our boat and the tension which had developed. Carol has always happy and upbeat. Her smile was easy and pleasant. But now she seemed anxious. Perhaps that anxiety was because it was three a.m. on a rough night in the Caribbean Sea aboard a boat that had begun to leak two times and had a faulty bilge pump. Bob lay behind us on the settee and groaned from time to time. It was not pretty. I was quite certain that when we arrived in Antigua they would simply pack up their things and say good-bye. Who could blame them?

I looked at the door of our cabin and the light was on. Julie was dressed and ready to take her turn at the helm.

"Call me if you need me." I said as I slipped back toward our cabin. Light would begin to appear in the east in a few hours. I watched the spray dash onto the windshield as Carol ascended the ladder toward the cockpit to take a quick look around between waves. Even though we could see well from the pilothouse, we made regular checks outside in all weather. *Safety First*, that was our motto.

Get undressed? Not a chance. I took my dry contact lenses out in the head, brushed my teeth and reclined on the soft bed to fall into a fitful sleep. When I woke a few hours later, gray light shone through the cabin ports. Julie was at the wheel and Antigua was ahead of us. Once we were in the lee of the island, I called Jolly Harbor on the radio and received our slip assignment. Suddenly the waves were gone and though winds buffeted the boat, it seemed hard to imagine how rough it had been just a short time before. We motored into the harbor, eased through the fleet of boats at the marina and slowly moved into our slip. Bob had recovered nicely and handled lines on the bow. A young man with blonde hair and a ruddy complexion met us at the dock and helped us tie up..

"Hello," he said pleasantly with an English accent. "I'm James Hall."

Chapter 19

Parties and Last Minute Fixes

Once *Tapestry* was secured, James Hall introduced himself as the man in charge of ARC Europe. He told us there would be a cocktail party that evening where we could get to know one another. In the meantime we would have to clear customs and immigration right away. Fortunately, customs had a list of ARC participants and, as we were included, the procedure was streamlined. Right next-door was a large marine facility. Crews were busy working on yachts at the docks and in the yard. I walked into the office and approached the desk.

"I have a boat next door at the marina and we had some difficulty with the steering last night coming over from Saint Martin." I said. "It's a hydraulic system, with two wheels. I wonder if you could send someone over to look at it."

"No problem, mate," the man said. "Will you be going with the ARC?"

"Yes, we will," I said.

"Very reliable systems, usually," the man said. "We'll have John here have a look at it right away." You'll be leaving in three days time, is that right?"

"Right."

John was a big man who looked and seemed confident.

"Out last night, were you?"

"Yes, from Saint Martin," I said. "Just had the system upgraded over there. Man put a new cylinder on the rudder, and replaced the oil."

"Any leaks?"

"Not that I can find." I said.

"Probably needs to be bled. Pounding through those seas last night might have set loose some trapped air that found its way to the pumps. We'll bleed the system and add a little fluid.

That usually does the trick. You do know how to do that, don't you?"

"Oh, yes, I continued. I just wanted someone to check out the repairs. I sure don't want any problems with the steering while we are crossing the ocean." I shuddered at the thought of struggling with a manual tiller in the aft cabin while being tossed about at sea.

Aboard the boat, Bob and Carol were asleep in the forward cabin and Julie was sound asleep aft. I hated to wake her, but she got right up, we removed the bedding, lifted the plywood boards over the rudder area and revealed the new installation. John took a clean cloth from his pocket and, after looking for telltale drips, carefully wiped each joint.

"I don't see any leaks here," he said. "Looks like a tight installation to me."

At the upper helm we removed the cover to the hydraulic reservoir and slowly turned the wheel from side to side. There was room for more fluid. I added nearly half a quart before it was finally full.

"I think that'll do it," John said. "There won't be a charge for that. If you find any more problems, we'll do what we can to help. Let us know right away. We have a list of projects on ARC boats."

With that John and I shook hands and he turned and headed for the marina.

Meanwhile, Julie and Carol had made lunch and Bob was busy in the cockpit stringing our code flags together. One of the rules of the ARC is that within half an hour of arriving at each harbor, the crew of each boat will display a set of code flags along with the huge ARC pennant. They are to be left up until the start of the next leg of the race.

When we landed in Antigua, Julie and I were concerned that the Markuses might not want to keep sailing with us. But both Bob and Carol had accepted our stormy passage as 'just another night at sea' and were ready to continue the voyage.

After lunch we attacked the bilge pump. Why had it failed? We reached far down into the bilge and pulled the pump out of its fitting in the bottom of the sump. When we inspected the impeller, we found it to be clogged with dirt and oily debris. The hose from the pump to the outlet in the side of the boat was clogged as well. We attached our garden hose to the tap at the dock and used it to flush and unclog the hose from the bilge pump to where it passed through the thru-hull on the side of the boat. We had a spare pump, but once we had cleaned the old one we found that it worked fine. After we returned the pump to the bilge, we put a little liquid detergent into the bilge and flooded it with the hose. The system kicked on immediately and a solid stream of soapy water flowed from the opening in the side of the boat. We scrubbed the bilge as best we could, flushed it with more fresh water and hoped we would have no such problem again.

Now both the manual and the electric pumps worked fine. Our spare electric pump was still in its box in the tool locker. That system was in good shape.

Our cabin was still a mess from checking the steering. Before I remade the bed, I grabbed the valves on the thru-hulls. I couldn't believe it. The one Ed and I had loosened in Martinique was again stuck solid. I gave a hefty pull on it and the handle simply bent in my hand. I immediately began a check of every thru-hull on the boat. Sure enough, I found one more that was frozen. The other was on the engine sea-water intake. Right away I made another trek to the marina where I again talked with the manager.

"Go up to the marine store and see if you can find suitable replacements. If you can, we will haul your boat on Tuesday afternoon replace the valves and have you back in the water before we go home that night. You'll be good to go on Wednesday."

Luck was with me. There was a two-inch and a one-inch valve in the store. I told the yard man and he put *Tapestry* on the list to be hauled the following day.

When I returned to the boat, our colorful code flags were whipping in the Caribbean wind. Julie had replaced the broken O-ring on the water-maker intake filter and tested the system. The sun was shining and we were anticipating our first get-together of the Atlantic Rally for Cruisers.

The party that evening was in the marina complex bar room at Jolly Harbor. There were the usual introductions and then an opportunity to visit with fellow yachtsmen involved in the race/cruise to Europe. Frankly, we were relieved to see that we would be sailing with people who were pretty much like us. Most of them were retired and most had boats in the thirty to forty five foot range. Some had a crew of three and others were couples by themselves. Somehow we had expected strapping young men to be sailing these yachts, but for the most part they were regular folks. They were English, German, French, Italian and Dutch. We were the only Americans.

Later that evening we met a lady named Sylvia. She and her husband Mark would be sailing their boat back home to England. She was a petite lady, full of energy and life. Her crisp diction and wonderful inflection combined with her English accent so that she was simply a joy to talk with. She made wonderful conversation and there was something about her manner that made me think she would be as much at home at a tea party in Windsor Castle as she would be in a small boat crossing the Atlantic.

"So, Hank," she said. "Julie was telling me you have had some troubles with your boat recently, is that so?"

"Yes," I said, "We've really had our hands full. First it was the steering and then the bilge pump and now some of the thru-hulls are stuck. We are going to try to get those fixed tomorrow."

"Too bad" said Sylvia. "And what's your boat's name?"

"*Tapestry,*" I said.

"Such a pretty name. It is a Nauticat, isn't it?"

"Yes." I said. "A Nauticat 35. We bought her used a year and a half ago."

"You were fortunate to find so good a boat with such a nice name"

"Oh no, Sylvia, you see, Julie and I named her *Tapestry.*" I said.

"You changed her name?" said Sylvia. A look of mild concern spread over her face.

"Yes, of course. She was *Cloud Nine* when we bought her. Before that she had been, let's see, *Matador,* I think. Yes, *Matador.*" I said.

Sylvia's jaw dropped. She looked at me, incredulous. "Her name has been changed twice?"

"You do have her old names carefully written inside the boat, don't you, somewhere on the hull?"

"Well, no, actually we don't. Why?" I said.

"Oh my!" said Sylvia. She rolled her eyes back into her head, opened her mouth and covered it with her hand. Then she turned and moved away.

Carol, who had been standing nearby, had overheard part of the conversation. She looked at me, nodded and smiled. It was getting late. All four of us headed back to the boat. When we walked back to *Tapestry,* her flags were whipping in the wind. The dozen or so boats that would be leaving on the ARC were similarly dressed. The atmosphere was festive.

According to the official schedule, the next morning we would be assigned our handicaps and the skipper's meeting would be held. There was to be a weather briefing and clarification of any questions. In the afternoon, James Hall would visit the boat and perform an inspection. We would be asked to demonstrate our knowledge of the systems aboard and our ability to deal with various emergency situations such as fire or man overboard.

Early on Tuesday morning we noticed that the flag halyard had somehow gotten tangled at the masthead. It wouldn't come down. We pulled and tugged and tried to move the halyard around, but it was thoroughly stuck. Julie got out the boson's chair and attached herself to the spare jib halyard; I hauled her to the masthead with the winch. As soon as she got there and began sorting out the problem, a black cloud appeared over the hills. Gusty winds whipped at the boat, and large drops of rain splashed on deck. Julie was getting soaked.

Carol looked at me and I knew the words that came to her lips before she even said them.

"A pencil. Hank, get a pencil, quick."

I dashed down the pilothouse steps and returned, pencil in hand. Carol lifted the lid on the cockpit locker.

"What was the first one?"

"*Matador*, I said. *M-A-T-A-D-O-R*"

"And the second," said Carol

"*Cloud Nine*." I replied.

Carol carefully lettered the two names onto the lid of the locker. They were dark and clear.

Meanwhile the wind had let up and Julie had resolved the problem with the halyard in spite of the rain.

"OK," she said. "Bob, try the halyard now." Bob pulled on the line and it was free. It moved easily either up or down.

"I can come down then," Julie said.

On the deck below, I let the line slip over the winch and Julie came smoothly down the mast. Carol closed the cover of the cockpit locker and gave me a determined look. We wouldn't say anything about our inscription, not yet, anyway.

The skipper's meeting was routine but interesting. We learned that each of us had a handicap, but the ARC would not tell us what it was or how it was determined. The fleet of a dozen boats would be divided into two separate fleets. There would be trophies at the end of each part of the race for the winners of each fleet. There would be no overall winner. It would be permissible to use your engine during the race. If you used your engine, it was your responsibility to record the amount of time you used it and the distance traveled under power. The penalty for using the engine would be determined by the amount of time others used their engines. In other words, there was no way to know what the penalty would be before hand. We would communicate our position once daily to the fleet captain who would in turn report all positions to England. There would also be an afternoon net where we could share concerns and other interests. Bob Markus, at least some of the time, would be net control. The start for the first leg to Bermuda would be at noon the following day.

After lunch, James Hall stopped by the boat as planned. He was affable and friendly. We offered him coffee and he sat down for a chat. We were ready. We could demonstrate our man overboard drill and our fire drill. We had our first aid kit ready for inspection and our sextant and almanac on display. We had checked off every item on the list and we were ready to demonstrate our proficiency in operating or using them. But as it turned out, James wasn't terribly interested in any of what we had so carefully put together. It apparently was obvious to him that we had thought carefully about the voyage and had prepared adequately. After a half hour or so of easy conversation, he finished his coffee and headed for the next boat. That was all.

Late that afternoon I returned to the marina.

"Why haven't you called me?" I said "I have been by the radio all day just waiting for a call so we could haul the boat and install the valves."

"Ah, sir," a tall black man in overalls said.

"We are so busy today. We have no manpower to work on your boat. We are very sorry, but it cannot happen."

And so that was it. The hoses from both thru-hulls were sound and they would simply have to do. We would keep an eye on the thru-hulls, but they would not be replaced before the crossing. We backed out of our slip late that afternoon and moved to the fuel dock to fill the tanks. Back at the dock we locked the boat and headed to the restaurant for a final dinner, after which we watched a show. The star of the show was a man who swallowed swords and ate fire. He spat fire out of his mouth and extinguished flaming torches by putting them in his mouth. At the end a waitress brought him a large colorful cocktail, which he drank slowly. It must have tasted wonderful after eating all that fire! When he was finished he bit off a piece of the glass with his teeth and chewed it and chewed it, and then he swallowed it all. He continued biting off chunks of glass and chewing them up and swallowing them until the whole glass was gone.

The whole performance was disturbing. How pointless; how dangerous.

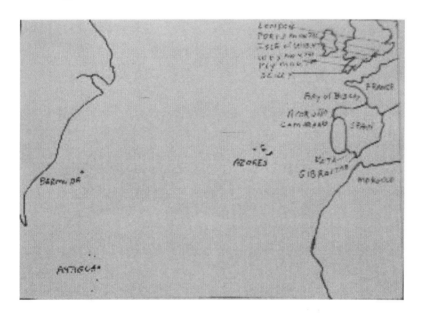

The Crossing

Chapter 20

The Start!

I had a premonition that I would be unable to sleep the night before we set off to cross the Atlantic. I was wrong. We went to bed early and slept soundly until the following morning. Carol and Julie went for a run. We had a leisurely breakfast, and the girls did some last minute laundry. Bob and I checked the boat over one more time and then lowered the dinghy from its davits and hoisted it onto the foredeck where we secured it very firmly. When Julie got back to the boat she retied the dinghy. The waiting seemed endless. We had been told a member of the ARC committee would visit us again before departure, but no one showed up. Finally, we lowered our signal flags and stowed them, cast off our lines and, with no fanfare whatever, followed the other boats out of the harbor.

The water was a blue-green when we motored out of the harbor that day. The sun was bright, and crisp white waves broke against the rocky shore. Winds were ten to fifteen knots and a bit behind the beam for our course to Bermuda. It was perfect sailing weather. The day was spectacularly beautiful. There were a dozen boats in the race. None of us had ever raced together before. Most of the boats didn't look like racing boats and once we had our sails up and began jockeying for position, it was pretty clear that line honors would not be hotly contested. After all, we would have over a thousand miles to determine a winner. No one wanted to be "over early." Still, there was one boat that hung around the line, and after racing for thirty-five years or so, I felt the need to press a bit.

The gun sounded right at noon. *Evening Star* was first over the line and *Tapestry* was close behind. We were so pleased to be second over we *high-fived* in the cockpit, eased the sails onto a close reach and charged ahead through the beautiful green water. Behind us, an Oyster 43, *Lhasa*, approached, her dark blue hull contrasted by a foaming wave at her bow. She came right behind us and tried to slide by to leeward. Nothing doing. *Tapestry* held her ground and after ten minutes or so of exciting side-by-side sailing, *Lhasa's* dark hull began to slide aft and after crossing our stern, she finally took us to weather.

Ahead there was another battle taking place. Two boats had popped their spinnakers and were sailing side by side. Further ahead was a small island, no doubt the last land we would see until we reached Bermuda. Julie checked the chart.

"Don't get too close to that island," she said.

"Shallow?" I replied.

"Looks shallow to me."

I noticed right away that the two boats carrying spinnakers were not quite able to carry them well. They were falling off more and more toward that little island. Suddenly the one to leeward, closest to the island, seemed to bump and then turn toward the wind, collapsing its spinnaker.

"I think they've gone aground," I said.

"Right," said Julie.

In a few seconds the spinnaker on the second boat collapsed as well as they hauled it in and headed a bit more to weather. The radio came to life as *Evening Star* requested assistance. They would have to return to Jolly Harbor for repairs. I could hardly believe there was so much enthusiasm in a race that was really a non-race to Bermuda. We hoped those on *Evening Star* would be able to continue as they complained only of bumps and bruises to themselves, but there was a question of structural damage to the boat. As it turned out, she was damaged severely and unable to continue the rally.

But the sailing that day was simply wonderful. With the wind aft of the beam, the motion of the boat was altogether different from the sail to Antigua from Saint Martin. We gushed along with all sails pulling. It was glorious. The boat rolled easily from side to side, a little spray might splash over the bow from time to time, but the cockpit was dry, there was excitement in the air. No one was seasick; life was good. Before long the boats began to spread out with more and more distance between them. The wind held and by nightfall the other boats were but specks ahead of or behind us.

From the very beginning we had a disciplined watch schedule. The person on watch was responsible for the safety and well being of the boat. S/he would trim sails, man the helm, or use the autopilot, and make entries into the log. S/he would be watching for ships, navigating and checking the bilge. If for any reason s/he needed help, they would wake Julie or me. Every hour the person on watch would record latitude and longitude, distance to go to the destination, and speed, all from the GPS S/he would also note barometric pressure and whether the barometer was falling, rising or steady. Finally, they would switch on the electric bilge pump (which was kept off). If the pump functioned at all, they would record the number of seconds required to empty the bilge. If the pump came on, they would notify the next person on watch and attempt to find out why. Normally the boat didn't leak at all. If that changed, we wanted to know.

Each of us had two three-hour watches each day. That would give us six hours on and eighteen hours off. There was plenty of time for rest, cooking and other activities. Of course, during the day watches were easy. Everyone was keeping an eye on things. Still, the person on watch was responsible. Ships run down more boats at sea during the day than at night. We knew we would have to be careful. The log had to be filled in each hour and the person on watch was responsible for it. We maintained a rigid rule about that.

We had our big meal around noon. That way Julie and Carol could cook and clean up in daylight. They were wonderful about doing these tasks. They had carefully stowed the provisions and the galley was a well-organized place. Through the night, the pilothouse was kept dark. Interior lights would make seeing difficult. Generally, except for the person on watch, when it was dark, everyone else was sleeping. Bob's watch was from six to nine; mine was from nine to twelve. Julie took the twelve to three watch, and Carol took three to six. It was exactly the same during the day. Day or night I was always on watch from nine to twelve.

I remember my first night watch clearly. There was a full moon and the sea was rippled with small waves. Winds were about ten knots and the boat was reaching along at about five knots. There was no land in sight, but from time to time I could see the twinkle of masthead lights far behind us. All was silent, but for the rush of water against the hull and the wind in the rigging. The moon was reflected on the water; the autopilot steered the boat. Ahead of us a tall cloud loomed. Reflected in the moonlight, its billowing white reached high into the sky and came down to the sea just a few hundred feet off the water. It looked like a thunderhead, but there was no thunder and no menacing lightning. Perhaps it will pass forward of us, I thought, and I wondered if I should adjust course to make sure. As we grew nearer, gusts of wind buffeted the boat. And the huge cloud passed just off our bow. I was in the cockpit with my safety harness attached, ready to shorten sail if need be. I was excited; I could feel adrenalin rush through me. It was almost as if I were slipping by a huge beast, a cyclops or a dragon. But the show wasn't over. A few minutes later a dark shadow slipped over the boat. I looked behind us and the light of the moon outlined the tall black cloud. Sheets of green rain slanted from the low base of the cloud and fell to the sea in a rolling torrent, illuminated by moonlight. The boat gushed along in the darkness just ahead of the storm. I was transfixed by the beauty of the moment.

Time and again while in the Caribbean, Julie and I had been buffeted by squalls such as this. We had rushed to the cockpit to shorten sail in flying spray and gusty wind. They had been an unwelcome menace in an otherwise routine night. But tonight the feeling was altogether different. What had been threatening was suddenly beautiful. It was like finding a tiger and watching it from a near distance.

"Hi."

"Oh, hi," I said to Julie who was looking through the companionway.

"I think it's my turn."

"Oh," I said, looking at my watch.

"Did you make the midnight entry?"

"No, not yet," I said, a little embarrassed. "I just saw the most beautiful cloud with rain pouring down." But the cloud was gone; it had moved out of the moonlight and blended with the dark sea. Moonlight again streamed on the sea behind us.

I climbed below, unsnapped my harness and made the required entries into the logbook. My watch had flown by. What a glorious night at sea.

Chapter 21

Dorado!

By then the breeze that had been faithful all day, had begun to wane. Our speed dropped through the night and by morning the engine was pushing us along. We had agreed that any time the boat made less than three knots we would use the engine.

A forecast cold front approached the following morning and the winds picked up; we were again under sail. The winds were predicted to be fifteen to twenty-five knots, but turned out to be only ten to fifteen, from dead ahead. Menacing clouds filled the northern sky and the wind backed more to the north. We had to fall off and change our heading to west of Bermuda. The waves were large and the going was rough. Pouring liquids became very difficult. Carol made a delicious potato salad for lunch, but eating was a two-handed experience. One hand for the bowl and the other for the fork, with one's body lodged tightly in a corner of the settee. You can imagine the difficulty associated with brushing teeth, inserting contact lenses and other daily activities.

At about two the following afternoon, Julie decided to try fishing. We were bounding along at just above five knots. She let out a long heavy monofilament line with a plug with several treble hooks attached to a leader on one end. The other end was attached to the backstay. There was a shock cord attached to the line and clipped to the backstay with a heavy clip. If a fish hit the line, it would pull on the shock cord, which would release from the backstay with a loud 'snap' as the clip was pulled free. The sudden stop when the line came taught would set the hook in the fish's mouth.

Within fifteen minutes we had our first strike. There was a loud snap and the line went taught. I grabbed the line and started pulling it in hand over hand. The fish swam back and forth from side to side through the water. When we got it close to the boat, we could see its beautiful yellow, blue and green colors. It was a Dorado. Julie grabbed it as soon as it came up the transom. It flopped on the deck and she and Bob held it down.

"Carol, the vodka," I called.

Carol appeared on deck with a bottle of Absolute. I removed the cap and poured a little on the gills of the fish. Like magic, it stopped flopping instantly.

"Powerful stuff." Bob said.

I had learned the trick from someone on Saint Martin. I had not expected it to work so well. Meanwhile, the boat was surging through huge seas, rocking and rolling. Julie got her fillet knife ready and she and Bob went to work cleaning that fish. You can imagine the two of them kneeling on that slimy deck, trying to hold on to and clean a slippery fish as the boat rolled from side to side and plunged through the seas. It took them nearly an hour, but when they were finished they had several beautiful fillets, which they carefully wrapped and put in the refrigerator.

That evening we had a second major meal of the day. Julie gently sautéed the fish and we enjoyed the sweetest, freshest Dorado imaginable. Never frozen, it was melt in your mouth delicious.

'I think I'll pass on the fish," said Carol.

"Why?" I said.

"It was so beautiful, swimming in the ocean," she said. "It had those dark eyes. I don't know, it just doesn't seem right."

The rest of us enjoyed the fish.

And so it went. We celebrated day after beautiful summer day. There was a blue sky and blue sea. *Tapestry* gushed along often with a reef in her sails, but no trouble. Bob continued to wear his scopolamine patches and was not bothered by sea-sickness. Occasionally, the wind would fall aft enough for us to raise the long whisker pole. It was always a big job and required careful balancing on the foredeck. The pole was long and heavy and awkward. I worried about putting it up and taking it down, but we always got the job done with little trouble.

One day when the jib was poled out, Bob decided it would make sense to put up a staysail. There was a small jib from one of our previous boats in our sail locker, and we rigged it to the spare jib halyard and attached it to the deck aft of the forestay. Sure enough, with that extra little sail, the boat picked up half a knot. We were in a race after all. We knew we weren't in first place boat for boat, but on corrected time, who knew?

Bob also shared "net control" on the radio net that met each afternoon. He would call each boat, take positions, and read the weather forecast which had been forwarded from England. After the formalities, there was casual conversation among the boats of the fleet. One time, Chris aboard *Lhasa*, suggested we have a contest to see who could best add a verse to the "drunker sailor" shanty. Another time we had a limerick contest. We would e-mail our entries and winners would be announced in Bermuda. What fun. We were hesitant at first, but finally made an entry. We Americans had begun to bond with our European friends as we sailed through the Southwest North Atlantic.

The following is an e-mail I sent on 12 May 2004.

Here it is the sixth day since the beginning of the race and we are plunging along on a starboard tack, much as we have been since we turned off the engine on day two. Winds are fifteen to twenty knots from the northeast and we are close on the wind with about a four-foot reef in the main. Currently our speed is about six knots, although last night there was a slight wind shift to the east and we were able to ease off a bit. Our speed jumped to as high as eight knots according to the GPS We are trying hard to keep just to weather of the rhumb line. Every few minutes we smack a wave, which sends a shower cascading onto the windshield and into the cockpit. This generally happens when Bob is checking for ships. The angle of heel is such that neither head sink will drain, and cooking has become a bit of an art.

The big excitement aboard *Tapestry,* however, is *Shoona of Mainsbury.* She has been within sight for the past four days, and the only other boat we have seen. She is a Rival 38. For most of the time she has been well ahead. At night her white stern light would twinkle on the horizon. Last night, however, as the wind shifted, she went to weather and we reached off along the rhumb line. During my watch I had the pleasure of seeing her white stern light turn to red as we inched past. At dawn, during Bob's watch, she reached down on us under spinnaker, but still was unable to pass. Bob has been busy tweaking the sails and when she was closest to us, we took down the bimini to make us more streamlined. She has gone upwind again, but we are still pretty even. It seems amazing we are so close after seven hundred miles of racing. We have been waiting for the wind to drop and shift east or even southeast, which has been forecast for the last few days, but that has not happened.

The days are sunny with scattered white puffy clouds; the temperature of the sea is much cooler, chilly in the cockpit, but shorts and short sleeves below. We had pancakes and coffee for breakfast, corned beef and cabbage for dinner this afternoon. With just 200 miles to go to Bermuda, life is good on *Tapestry.*

Hank and Julie, Bob and Carol

Our next e-mail, from May 13, follows:

> And so, as with all good things... There we were gushing along at 6 plus knots, neck and neck with *Shoona of Mainsbury* last night just as it was getting dark, when there was a call on the VHF. As it was obvious *Shoona* wouldn't make Bermuda by dark on Thursday, they were starting their engine. Sure enough, the wind was dying. Fewer waves were splashing on the windshield and the speed was dropping to the fives. We tweaked the sails and adjusted the autopilot, but there was no denying it. We carried on through the night. Finally, at about 5:30 this morning we had slowed to 3.5 knots, so we too agreed to accept the penalty and start up. At 10:30 the engine hums at 2700 rpm, we splash along at 5.9 knots with a six knot headwind. The windshield is misted, not splashed upon, both sinks work, there is hot water, and life is back to almost easy. We are 66.5 miles from the finish and expect to cross the line sometime after 11 this evening. We don't know what the penalty will be for running the engine. It will be determined by the number of boats that decide to do so. There may be radio restrictions in Bermuda, so you may not hear from us until the beginning of the Azores leg next week. All is well on *Tapestry*. Hank and Julie, Bob and Carol

As the day wore on we motored through glassy seas. Dolphins showed up to welcome us. They circled the boat and charged along at the bow. Last time we came to Bermuda we were greeted by Bermuda Long-tails, white birds with long feathery tails, but not this time. As we drew nearer to the island we began to see the gray outlines of warships on the horizon. They were silent on the radio and were obviously performing some kind of drill. We guessed they were looking for submarines, but there was no way to tell for sure. At dusk the Bermuda Islands were near and, by the time we motored across the finish line at the navigation buoy outside St. George's Harbor, it was completely dark. Julie was busy tabulating the time we had spent under power for that leg of the race, and Bob and I prepared to take the boat through the narrow entrance into the harbor.

"A little to the port," said Bob, from the nav. station in the pilothouse as I took the controls on the aft deck. He was looking at the chart on the computer.

"It doesn't look right, Bob." I said. "I see the entrance light and it's quite a way to starboard."

"It sure doesn't look that way on the plotter," he replied. "You have to go quite a ways to port."

"I really can't see very well." I responded. "It's dark right ahead, but with the lights on shore it's hard to tell quite where the entrance is. I'm keeping an eye on the depth sounder and it doesn't look like an entrance to me. Big ships go through here, Bob, and it seems to be shoaling. I'm heading more to starboard."

"Ok. But it looks as if you'll miss the entrance."

"No, I can see it clearly now. There is a green buoy just ahead and it is on our starboard. We're heading to starboard. I can see the channel now!"

And so we entered the port just as we were supposed to. It was interesting that our plotter was off by about a hundred yards. We had not noticed the problem before, but whenever Julie and I had entered harbors, we had done it from the cockpit, not the pilothouse, and so we had not used the plotter for close work. It seemed to be consistently off by about a hundred yards to port. Perhaps it was a local phenomenon. We didn't know, but it is never a good idea to rely on just one electronic device. The dock at the St. George's Boat Club was congested, but we moved through the narrow, rugged entrance with no problem. We pulled into the slip and tied up. Right away James Hall was there to meet us. A man from Customs and Immigration was with him. We quickly filled out the necessary forms and thanked everyone. We were so excited we all wanted to talk at once.

One doesn't normally think of the walk from dock to clubhouse as memorable, but that night, after being at sea for ten days and nights, the dock seemed to sway back and fourth beneath our feet. We laughed as we weaved like drunken sailors along the narrow dock. Ours was a dry ship, but I had a "dark and stormy" in my hands as soon as I could find the bar. Dark rum and ginger beer tasted good to me. We had finished leg one. Wonderful!

Tapestry in St George's, Bermuda

Chapter 22

Bermuda! Poetry and Song!

When we awoke the following morning, we were happy to find we really were in Bermuda. Julie and Carol went for a run while Bob and I explored the Dinghy Club and the surrounding area. Sport fishermen were unloading their catch at a dock near the club, and there was lots of early morning activity. We took the stainless steel helm seat, which had nearly collapsed along the way, to a welder who assured us he could "beef it up" so it would last for the rest of the trip. After breakfast we walked to town where we explored the *Deliverance*, a full-scale model of a ship built from the wreckage of the *Speedwell*.

Speedwell had set out from Portsmouth, England with the *Mayflower* in 1620. Both ships were headed for America loaded with pilgrims. Unfortunately, *Speedwell* struck the Bermuda reef and was destroyed. Her passengers and crew made it to shore, and during the following year they built *Deliverance*, a smaller ship, which continued on its way to Massachusetts, arriving just a year after the *Mayflower*.

It is interesting that virtually all of the indigenous residents of Bermuda are shipwreck survivors. The Hog Penny is the name of a popular pub on the island, but it is also the name of their one-cent coin. It was named for the wild pigs that kept shipwrecked sailors alive after they washed ashore from previously wrecked vessels.

Although they are a hazard to navigation in Mid-Atlantic, these islands are a paradise to visit. Public buildings and private homes are often colorfully painted in pastel colors and set amid magnificent flower gardens. Sailing is a major sport here and there is a view of the sea from virtually everywhere.

Shortly after our arrival we were having breakfast at a restaurant right on the water at St. George's when Bob gazed at a nearby pier.

"Look at that boat out there, Hank. It looks a lot like yours. I'll bet that's your friends, the Bishops."

I turned around and looked, but with the sun's reflection on the water I didn't see anything.

"Over there on the next pier." said Bob.

"Oh, my gosh, it is them!" I said. Sure enough Dick and Eileen Bishop, friends from the Nauticat Association and from the Seven Seas Cruising Club, were just getting off their Nauticat 43, *Triumph*. We got up from our table and dashed off to greet them, leaving our half-eaten breakfast and tab behind. There were hugs all around. We had talked to them on the ham radio during the passage, and we knew they were coming, but it was simply wonderful to see them in the flesh. We were filled with childlike excitement. We decided we would get together during the afternoon. Dick, in addition to being a fine sailor, is also an expert at all things related to ham radio and computers. Jack Webb, also a Nauticat 43 owner and an airline pilot, was their crew and anything technical that Dick didn't know, Jack probably would. We parted only when we noticed our waiter standing, hands on hips, at our table.

We took a boat ride around the island, explored restaurants and generally enjoyed the islands for the next few days.

There were half a dozen boats that came to Bermuda from St. Augustine, Florida, where the ARC had had a second start. These included two more American boats. One was *Sangaris*, an Amel 52, owned by Craig and Kathy, the other *Alcid*, a Saga 43, owned by Frank and Gail Adshead. We had met Frank and Gail years before while exploring the Bahamas, and were excited to be sailing with them again. But that was all. Of the eighteen boats in the fleet, only three were Americans. I had always believed that Americans were leaders in world cruising. But of the boats going to Europe with us, we Americans were clearly in the minority. The rest were Europeans, most of whom had crossed from Europe and come to the Caribbean the previous fall. This was their second crossing. The ARC race from the Canary Islands to St. Lucia includes as many as 250 boats, many of which sail the Caribbean for a while and then continue on around the world. Cruising is indeed a popular European pastime. Of course, the Seven Seas Cruising Club represents hundreds of American cruising sailors, but the ARC is not part of Seven Seas. It is likely that many American cruisers 'go it alone.'

On the first afternoon of our visit, I decided how nice it would be to have ice in our evening cocktail. As I am the primary drinker on our boat, and one who loves the clink of ice in my glass, I asked the ladies if there was room in the fridge for a bag of ice. They allowed that there was, so I set off in the still heat of the afternoon to find one. On my way back I met a ten-year-old English girl on the dock. Her name was Emily. She and her sister, Elizabeth were sailing on a 34 foot Westerly, *Helice,* with Jim and Ann, their parents.Theirs was one of the smallest boats in the fleet. They were smaller than us by a whole foot!

I had never talked with the young lady before, and I wasn't quite prepared for her remark.

"Got to get this bag of ice back to the boat before it all melts." I said, in passing, to the little girl.

"You Americans are all the same," she said. "You put so much ice in your drinks, you can barely taste the whiskey."

I was so surprised that I nearly dropped the whole bag. Who was she to tell me how much ice I put in my drink? But I had to laugh. She had such inflection in her voice and she seemed, somehow, so proper, I didn't quite know what to think. That was my introduction to Emily and it was far from the last time I would enjoy conversation with her.

Other issues of culture and language appeared while we were in Bermuda. For one thing, *Nona Bimba* was a beautiful

Hallberg Rassy, 43, from Italy. Her crew spoke very little English. They were delightful young men, but though they were sharing a magnificent experience with us, it was difficult to communicate with them. Of course it wasn't just the Italians we had difficulty communicating with. One night I walked into the Dinghy Club bar and was confronted by Alan from *Happy Wanderer,* an Englishman aboard an Island Packet 38.

"I'm pissed," he said to me. "I'm really pissed."

"Why?" I said, thinking that I had done or said something to offend him.

"Not you, man, me. I'm pissed," Said Alan.

Suddenly there was a loud laugh from Steve, a large man at the bar, skipper of *Shoona of Mainsbury.* He looked at me with a smile and twinkling blue eyes.

"You don't understand, do you, Henry?" said Steve. "You think he's angry, don't you?"

"Well, yes," I said. "He said he's pissed. He must be angry with someone. I thought it was me."

"Right." Steve shook his head and laughed. "To an Englishman to be 'pissed' is to be drunk. He was telling you he was drunk, man. You thought he was angry. Alan just wanted you to know he had drunk a few too many drinks." We laughed and Alan said good night.

Evenings at the Dinghy Club were something else. After dinner we sat on the porch overlooking the harbor and drank beer. Chris, from *Lhasa,* would bring his guitar and sing sea shanties. It was wonderful. Everybody joined in. Emily and Elizabeth read poems from a book and some of the men recited limericks or funny poems they had heard. Carol, Chris's wife passed out the words of songs, Chris would play and everyone would sing. We simply had a wonderful time. The nights were filled with laughter. One song, "The Quartermaster's store," helped us to get to know each other's name. We would sing along and have to make up a verse using the name of the person sitting next to us. It was easy and funny and fun and we never forgot each other's name again. Those evenings were delightful and memorable. But they were like nothing we had done as sailors in the States. I remember sitting around and singing on occasion, but these people loved to entertain us with their humor and their language and their song. I was wide-eyed. It was wonderful.

Finally, however, came the big night. The results of the race were to be announced. There was a cocktail party on the porch. The results were posted and *Tapestry* was third in her division and fifth overall for the whole fleet. We were thrilled.

We were all seated at a table on the porch when there was a loud crash. James Hall had walked through a plate glass door. Fortunately, though he bled profusely, only his hand and arm were cut. Frank, a dentist, bandaged his arm and he was taken off to the hospital. All of the rest of us had sailed part way across the ocean in small boats without a scratch and there, on the porch at the Bermuda Dinghy Club, our leader, James… Oh well.

As it turned out, trophies were awarded the following day, but only for the first two places in each division. We got no recognition for our third place whatever.

Another night there was a chicken barbecue. The ARC was masterful at getting the local Chamber of Commerce to sponsor events recognizing us sailors. It was a fine meal and we all had a good time.

In Bermuda, we ran into the issues we always faced in new ports. Imagine getting a tank of propane filled. The store where propane was sold was several miles away. One might take a bus or call a cab. However, in this post 9/11 world… We loaded the tank into a backpack and Julie and I walked to the store, sharing the load, where we left the tank to be picked up the following day.

While we were at the hardware store, we asked if they had O-rings. We needed one for the primary filter on our water-maker, and we had been unable to get one in Antigua. An elderly gentleman behind the counter smiled when I asked him.

"Yes sir." he said. "We have all sizes."

I took our only spare from my pocket and laid it on the counter.

"Want one exactly that size?" he asked.

"Yes," I said. "It has to be just right."

He turned to a spool on the wall and pulled out a bit of O-ring material of the correct diameter. He laid a length of it on the counter on top of my spare. Then he pinched the stock with his fingernail right where the proper length would be. Next he took a razor blade and cut off the stock.

"There's some super glue over there. Pick up a tube, would you?"

I went to a display and brought him a tube of glue.

He opened the package and placed a dab of glue on the ends of the O-ring material and pushed them together. The pungent odor made us wince.

"Do you think that will hold?" I said.

"Stronger than new", the man said. He smiled as he held the ends firmly in place.

We waited a moment for the glue to dry.

"There" the man said. "Pull that apart."

I picked up the O-ring and gently tugged; the joint came apart in my hands.

"I'll do this again and we'll let it dry over night. You can pick it up tomorrow, with your propane," the man said with a little less confidence than before.

The next day we walked back to the store to pick up the propane tank and the O-ring. The tank was full, but the ring was still a failure.

Finally, the day before departure, we were all assigned a time to report to a nearby pier to pick up fuel. It would be a long haul to the Azores, and we wanted to be sure that our tanks were full. The ARC had provided a tanker truck of diesel at $2.00 per gallon as opposed to the $6.00 per gallon, which was regularly charged. It was a good deal and that, along with the free dockage entertainment and delightful companionship along the way, made the ARC seem like a good deal indeed.

Chapter 23

Off to the Mid-Atlantic, Wild Weather!

We had cleaned the winches, scrubbed the bottom, and Julie and Carol had restocked the boat with food. We were ready for the second and longest leg of the trip, Bermuda to the Azores.

Shortly before eleven a.m. on the nineteenth of May, we hauled our stern anchor up and pulled *Tapestry* out of the Med Moor and away from the dock. We backed very near *Alcid,* one of the other American boats. Someone aboard said,

"Ashville, New York"

"Never heard of it, right?" I replied.

"I grew up in Jamestown. I'm John Lincoln."

I could hardly believe what I was hearing. Here was someone on *Alcid*, who was practically from our home-town. He had belonged to the same yacht club on Lake Chautauqua that I had. We had even attended the same sail school as kids. I waved, but our boats slid apart and that was it.

The plan was to start the second leg of the race from inside the harbor at St. George's. The harbor entrance is narrow, and is frequented by cruise ships. It seemed to me to be a rather exciting place to start.

As there was little wind that morning we motored through the cut to a starting line in the ocean. Winds were five to ten and with four minutes to go we eased the sheets and headed for the line. Our timing was perfect. We slid over the starting line right as the gun went off. By our calculation, we were first. Before long, most of the larger boats had caught and passed us, but we enjoyed the good start. The following morning, I sent an e-mail that ended:

"Winds have been fair, five to fifteen knots, and we had to motor for just one hour when the wind died completely last night. Currently, we are making six knots on a track of 76 degrees true. The jib is poled out, the sun is shining, and life is good. We are 94 miles from Bermuda, 1694 miles from Horta."

We got right back into the routine. Fortunately, the boat held up well as we surged along. We were truly in the middle of the ocean and the great rolling seas, which constantly surrounded us, reflected that. Bob never complained of seasickness during this portion of the voyage, though he found he couldn't sleep in the V-berth. The motion there was too extreme. Plus the sound of the bow plunging through the waves just inches from his ear tended to keep him awake. He found that the pilothouse was much more to his liking. He would lie on the settee behind the table and purr softly as the boat sailed through the night. The table held his large body firmly in place and the only way he could roll over was to sit up and switch ends, his feet ending up where his head had been. He generally did this without speaking and it occurred to me that he did it without waking as well.

Carol was a different story altogether. Whenever it was her turn to sleep she dove, often headfirst, into the V-berth and with her head right at the bow of the boat she would fall into a sound sleep. Sometimes the door to the forward cabin was left open and we could see her being tossed about as *Tapestry* plunged through the waves, but she never complained. It was quite obvious that she never woke up.

Things went well as we sailed along.

21 May 2004

Contrary winds drove us north of the rhumb line, or intended course, on Thursday. We are hoping for better winds to the north. At about 4 a.m. we ran into a squall line that surprised us somewhat. Low clouds produced heavy rain and gusty winds in the 25 to 30 knot range. We reduced both main and jib and found ourselves rolling in a lumpy sea with little wind and occasional showers. That led to a sleepless night. Finally, we reluctantly started the engine and in 35 minutes had found a beautiful fresh breeze from the north at 15, which is carrying us along at about five and a half knots, right on course for the Azores. Currently the sky is blue with scattered cumulous and stratus clouds overhead. Temperatures are warmer than expected. We are still in shorts and tee shirts.

It is 10:30 a.m., and I am on watch as I write this. Julie and Bob are resting and Carol and I are both writing on our computers in the pilothouse. *Tapestry* sails herself with a little help from Nigel, the autopilot. We have lost sight of all the other ARC boats, and have seen only one ship since yesterday at this time. It sure would be nice if this breeze would hold up through the weekend, but according to this morning's weather fax, there is calm air ahead.

Each evening at seven some of the ladies have a net on the SSB. Two pre-teen sisters aboard *Helice* are the stars. They entertain us with recipes, riddles and the occasional poem. It is delightful to listen to their crisp diction, British accents, and wonderful laughter. This has replaced the limerick contest and the "add a verse to the Drunken Sailor" contest held on Leg one.

While sailing a small boat at sea there are moments of extreme beauty. Stars in the unlighted darkness of a moonless night are deep and moving. They appear so close and so different from our world of streetlights that never turn off. Porpoises are delightful companions. Still, there are reminders that we are a small boat on a mighty large ocean. Out here when trouble strikes, there is no 911.

24 May 2004

Last evening we had a delightful porpoise show. Forty or fifty of them were jumping and diving all around us. Half a dozen played at the bow for a good twenty minutes. Even got some of it on film. As unlikely as it seems, no one has reported catching any fish yet. We tried yesterday but had no success.

Last night, on my watch, I spotted a strong target on the radar. I thought it might be another ARC boat, but as it drew closer it was obvious it was not lighted and not moving. We passed it by just two miles on our starboard side. I tried to warn other boats on both VHF and SSB, but had no success. I wondered if it was container that had broken loose from the deck of a ship in a storm. Those containers are larger than our boat. A collision with one would certainly be devastating.

That is about it from here. The weather is sunny and about seventy, and the sea temperature is just the same. Our current position is 35.00N and 56.31W. All is well on *Tapestry*. All the best,…

P.S. It is now nearly 10 p.m. 5/24, and I just realized I had not sent this e-mail as I had planned to this morning. The wind has held all day and is forecast to continue to be favorable for the next few days. It is beautiful here. The stars shine down, there is a crescent moon astern, and we are gliding due east on a broad reach. Drinking glasses don't slide off the table, as the boat hisses through the water at about six knots. We have a positive current of over one knot, so we can make nearly six knots of boat speed with 8 knots of wind. On watch I sit at the steering console, glance at the radar regularly, do a visual check outside every fifteen minutes, and record time, position, bearing, track, distance to go, distance made good, barometric pressure, and battery condition in the log each hour. I also check the bilge for water and record what I find in the log. (I turn on the pump. If there is water, I record the number of seconds the pump runs in the log.) The pump usually doesn't run at all, but it if does, we want to know why. Last night we noticed that the pump was working regularly. This morning I found that the stuffing box around the rudder shaft needed to be tightened. Tonight the bilge is dry. Things are good on *Tapestry*. We are about one quarter of the way from Bermuda to the Azores. Bearing to Horta 073; Track 090; 1296 miles to go, six miles made good in the last hour, barometer 1020. H.

We were frustrated by the lack of world news. We were able to find Voice of America on the radio, but it was always in a foreign language. But we had good weather news daily. Each morning we would receive a weather briefing from the ARC. More helpful, however was our contact with "Herb." He is a volunteer weather forecaster who offers free weather advice to yachtsmen from his home in St. Catharines in Ontario. He uses the Internet to obtain the latest information and relays it to yachtsmen on SSB. He tracks the progress of various yachts and communicates with them each afternoon. Two boats in the ARC had asked for the assistance of Herb. They were *Helice* and *Kjempekjekk* (pronounced chump a check). Whatever Herb said to either of them applied to all of us, because we were quite close together. We listened carefully and did our best to do what Herb suggested. While we were about midway between Bermuda and Horta, we got some bad news from Herb.

26 May 2004

It was just one week ago today that we left Bermuda. Tonight at 8 p.m. we got down to just 1000 miles to go to Horta. We are almost at the halfway point. That is the good news. The bad news is that there is a very impressive storm building behind us. Several low-pressure areas have joined together to make what the ARC weather people call a "possible tropical Cyclone. Herb tells us to press on to the east with all good haste to try to reach 47 degrees by some time tomorrow. So, we have started the engine and are motoring east. There is little wind, and under other circumstances we would probably sail, but not tonight. Winds may reach 30 to 40 knots by Friday if we don't get out of the path of the storm by then. It is likely that we will have some strong winds anyway, but they will be from the southwest or south so they should be quite manageable. Besides, we do have storm sails, ...not that we are anxious to use them, understand.

Tonight, we had a magnificent clear sunset with a crescent moon at about the zenith. Today has been beautiful with clear blue skies and sparkling waves. A few birds circle the boat from time to time and a huge sea turtle surfaced right beside us today. We have a radio net twice daily. Among the whole fleet, only one boat has caught a fish since Bermuda, and that is a 35 lb. tuna. The rest of us have been skunked. Frank and Gale on *Alcid*, who caught it, shared it with the boat behind them by packaging part of it in a bag of ice and tying it to a life preserver, which they set adrift. I wish we had been up with them.

On *Tapestry* all is well. We are busy reading, standing watches and enjoying the scenery: (light blue, dark blue, and lots of water). Another boat, *Helice*, is within sight now so we have some company. All the best...

For the next few days we could think of nothing but the forecast storm. Squalls generally hit hard and fast, but this system built up gradually. We knew it was coming and the waiting is often the hardest part. We checked and rechecked everything on deck and looked over things below as well. Our turnbuckles were properly fastened, shrouds were fine, there was no visible chafe on halyards or sheets, the dinghy was tightly lashed to the foredeck, and the life raft was lashed to several stanchions on the aft deck, ready to be launched in seconds if need be. All ports and hatches were tightly closed. We had a line attached to the companionway boards lest they slide overboard in a knockdown. Below, our galley was secure. Loose items were stored in cabinets. The "ditch bag" was ready to go. There was nothing to do but wait.

28 May 2004

Hello from the high seas. The promised weather has developed over night. Currently we are sailing under the main, reefed to the first spreader, and a greatly shortened jib. We are on track and sailing in a current of slightly more than one knot. Seas are in the 6 to 8 foot range. Waves and wind are from the W.S.W., so mainly are on the beam. We are making 6.2 knots across the bottom in an easterly direction. Winds are currently 25 to 30 and are forecast to increase this afternoon and tonight. We have been washed with deluges of rain as well. The boat is behaving well. Bob is asleep in the V-berth, of all places; Julie is napping in our cabin aft. Carol is reading at the settee, and I am on watch and typing at the pilothouse station. We've had gray skies and seas and no solar energy today. I will run the motor charger when I finish this. All the best. Hank and Julie, Bob and Carol.

One question that haunted us was whether we should go ahead and lower the main and put up the storm trysail. The Pro-Furl people had told us that the main was infinitely reefable and could be used in all but the most severe conditions. We knew we could shorten it to an area as small as our storm trysail and that was what we intended to do. Similarly, we decided to roll up all but a small bit of our jib rather than use the "Gale Sail" which we had purchased for a storm. There are those who say it is unwise to roll up the jib more than 10 per cent. We chose to roll up 80 per cent of it. We thought out and discussed our reasoning, especially with the jib.

First of all, to use the Gale Sail, a device intended to cover the furled jib, someone would have to go forward and install the sail on the pitching foredeck. That would be difficult and a hazard in itself. Secondly, the Gale Sail was about ten per cent of the fore triangle. What if that were too much? We would be unable to shorten it further from the cockpit or lower it without going forward onto the heaving deck in the height of the storm. Thirdly, we had heard reports of Gale Sails like ours which slid over jibs, either wearing through the storm sail where the sheets were wrapped around the jib, or causing the sheets to chafe their way through the original jib. For all of those reasons, we chose to go with our deeply reefed jib.

The rains and winds increased until we found ourselves engulfed in the storm. When it was over we wrote the following e-mail.

May 29, 2004

Our bad weather has come and gone. Winds are now in the 21 to 25 knot range, pushing along the huge waves created yesterday. We are fine. The boat proved to be up to the challenge, and the crew came through with flying colors as well. We all had three square meals yesterday in spite of waves growing to every bit of twenty feet. When I wrote yesterday, we had a deep reef in both main and jib. We reefed three more times until we had about ten square feet of main and about the same amount of jib. We had to slow the boat down and when we got down to about five knots, we knew we were okay.

During the storm, the winds rose to about 40 knots and gusted to about 47. That is a full gale. Waves came from everywhere, but mostly from astern. They would smack against the side of the boat and wash over the top, causing an impact not unlike a minor vehicular collision. Walls of spray would wash over the bow, blotting out everything until the deluge drained away. The forestay with its tiny jib vibrated back and forth and the main halyard smacked the mast in a pounding rhythm. *Tapestry* was on autopilot, following her course as well as she could. Julie and Carol were reading; I took a few videos. In the pilothouse it was relatively quiet and dry, but outside it was bedlam. Waves were long and steep and piled on top of one another. Sometimes the leeward pilothouse windows would be at water level as *Tapestry* slid sideways down the face of a great wave. Sometimes one could see a drop-off of fifteen feet immediately to leeward, and somehow the boat hung on. Similarly, walls of water would appear to windward. Generally the boat would magically rise above them, but sometimes they would smack the side and jar everyone inside. Holding on was a full time job.

Rain squalls appeared on the radar screen as a mass of tiny dots, and when they struck us it was with a roar of combined wind and rain. It was during one of these squalls, when visibility was very low, that I spotted a large solid target on the radar screen. It was a ship, and it was bearing down upon us from astern. I called the ship on the vhf radio, gave him our position, and though he responded right away, it was some time before he could see us on his radar screen. He turned his giant ship and passed us about two miles away on our port side.

Although we could easily see him on the radar, we never found him with our eyes or binoculars.

Late in the afternoon, some boats reported a lessening of wind and even patches of blue sky. By seven, Herb had reported that the first frontal line had passed, and that the second, less severe one, would pass by midnight. Fortunately, that proved to be a wind shift and otherwise a non-event. We let out some sail, but kept deep reefs in place as the night was forecast to be squally.

It is now Saturday morning and huge waves, in the ten foot range, dance about the boat, occasionally throwing us on our side. Winds are from 22 to 25 knots and we have only a short reef in the main and jib. The sun is peeking through and things are looking up.

The only damage we have found are two broken cups and a broken water bottle. The American flag on the backstay was shredded. Oh, about the vibration. The eleven on the face of the pilothouse clock is now where the twelve should be! 36 45N; 42 11W; 645 miles from Horta. All the Best, Hank and Julie.

We had a memorable net that Friday evening. The wind still shrieked through the rigging in left over gusts, and we still plunged through the confused seas. Everyone reported that all was well. Emily and Elizabeth read us poems from their book and one in particular that concerned bras made them laugh hysterically. We were fifty something adults being thrown about in small boats in the North Atlantic Ocean. At the same time pre-teen girls were reading us poems over the radio. It was a night to remember. We kept our radios on that night and I remember talking with Liz on *Kjempekjekk* as I stood watch. I had been a high school English teacher and Liz was a biology teacher in a private school in England. It was nice to know I had someone there to talk to.

Chapter 24

After the Storm: A Poetry Competition!

After the storm there was a period of very nice sailing. Currents and winds combined to move us as fast as eight knots toward our destination. We plunged though six to ten foot waves over an undulating sea. None of us was sick. It was magic. There was one development, however.

One night on the ladies net, Emily, on *Helice*, came on the radio with an announcement for the fleet.

"I have decided," she said, "to hold a poetry contest. One entry will be accepted from each boat. Poems must be two paragraphs long and about the trip from Bermuda to Horta. They will be collected as soon as we reach Horta. Prizes will be awarded."

"Wow," I said, "a poetry contest. Who has an idea?"

"Are you kidding?" said Bob. "I simply can't imagine writing a poem. It is at the very bottom of my list of things to do."

"Don't look at me." said Carol.

Julie was thoughtful, but didn't comment at the time.

I was the only enthusiastic one. Hmm, I thought to myself. Most of the poems these kids read are rhymed. I don't know much about rhymed poetry, but I suppose our entry will have to rhyme. It will have to be about the trip from Bermuda to Horta, that means the gale. I remembered teaching sonnets in high school. We used iambic pentameter and tried to write Petrarchan Sonnets, or Shakespearean Sonnets. Let's see, I thought, fourteen lines, ABBA ABBA CD CD CD But that's too complicated. We need something fun and spirited,

"Julie," I said, " Remember the poem you used to recite about Robinson Caruso."

She looked at me thoughtfully.

"Yes."

"That had an interesting rhyme scheme, didn't it? Do you remember any of it?"

Julie looked up from her book, "By a man named Carryl, I believe." She cleared her voice and began:

> "The night was thick and hazy
> When the *Piccadelly Daisy*
> Carried down the crew and captain to the sea.
> And I think the water drowned them
> For they never, ever found them,
> And I know they didn't come ashore with me.
>
> Twas very sad and lonely
> When I found myself the only
> Population on this cultivated shore.
> So I made a little tavern, in a rocky little cavern,
> And I sit and wait for people at the door."

"That's it!" I said. Now we just have to think of the words. We'll use that rhythm. It'll make a fun and lively poem. Now that we have the rhythm, we can all work on it." I said.

"I don't think so," said Bob. Carol just smiled. I wrinkled my brow and glanced at an empty sheet of paper.

Winds continued to be favorable and from the starboard quarter at about fifteen knots. We were alone on the sea, and sometimes, as I ruminated before I fell asleep at night, I would imagine the many creatures we had passed over and that might be at this very moment beneath us. Sleek sharks and huge whales must have been under our keel at times, but we went on our way oblivious to it all. Down there it was dark and cold. It was the graveyard of ships and planes and the men who had manned them. Rusted and rotten hulks must have lurked in those depths, but it was better not to think of them. For it was peaceful and beautiful on the surface and what we passed over on the bottom was better left there. Sometimes we would see a small bird and I couldn't help but wonder where it had come from and how it could survive so far from land. It was exciting to be speeding along in fine weather, and the gale of the previous day seemed distant and unimportant.

That was all it took. At about two in the morning, Julie woke me.

"Sorry," she said, "but it's steady around twenty, and we just had a gust near thirty. We better shorten sail."

I had been soundly asleep, but I stumbled out of bed and pulled on my pants and shirt. Sure enough, winds were touching 30 and rain was lashing the boat. We hooked up our harnesses and ventured into the cockpit to adjust the sails. In a few moments the boat was back under control. By morning the sky was gray and it rained hard off and on. By noon the weather cleared. It was Memorial Day. I could imagine our friends sitting on the porch of the Dunkirk Yacht Club enjoying a cup of coffee and thinking about the races to come that day. Surely the old twenty-four foot Sharks our club raced, as a one-design fleet, would be out in force. Veterans all over the country would be marching in parades; there would be speeches on the first summer holiday of the year. For us, however, it was just another day at sea.

We had heard from others that there was a positive current in the area, so we searched a bit to the north and before long our speed had gone from six to six point eight knots. The time aboard *Tapestry* was Greenwich plus two; when we arrived in Horta, because of daylight savings time, it would be Greenwich plus one. Every fifteen degrees of longitude, we would enter another time zone and add an hour to our time. Even though there may have been no one observing the change but those of us at sea, our SSB. nets were always "local time." Because we were a little careless about noting the change, we were late for the net that day. Not too cool.

But our spirits were high. It was wonderfully exhilarating, charging through the North Atlantic toward Horta on Memorial Day. We laughed about how we would celebrate the day. We were already in a sailboat race, a parade posed logistical problems, and so we decided to just go about our business. There were tens of thousands of wonderful young men and women in far more hazardous places than we found ourselves as we sailed along. We certainly owed them a debt of gratitude.

June 1, 2004
Hello from *Tapestry,*

It is just seven at night local time, and we have finally reached within 132 miles of Horta. Right now the sun is setting and casting a golden glow inside the pilothouse. The sea and sky are a light and deep blue, respectively, the air is cool, about 70 F. and life is good.

This afternoon the wind dropped a bit, causing a momentary alarm. But before long it picked up again and now we are splashing along at about six knots. Waves are small. They are about as small as we have seen since we left Bermuda, almost Chautauqua Lake size. If we maintain this speed, we should cover the 131 miles left by late tomorrow afternoon. We have run out of fresh food, but our cupboards are still packed with cans and jars. Nevertheless, I have heard more talk about restaurants than the Azores, for the past few days.

Yesterday and the day before have been our best ever on a sailboat, 163 and 151 nautical miles, respectively. The second day included an hour we lost by moving east into another time zone. Tomorrow we will most likely arrive in the late afternoon or early evening. We will have docking arrangements and customs formalities to deal with, plus a little celebrating. I am not sure what the laws are regarding ham radio and e-mail, but I think I will be able to transmit. Consequently, you may not hear from us for a couple of days. All the best, and thanks for all your notes, thoughts and prayers. Hank and Julie, Bob and Carol.

The Azores, unlike Bermuda, was a mystery to us. None of us knew anything about it. We had heard that it was often a very windy place. We knew it was Portuguese and that they spoke Portuguese there. None of us knew any Portuguese so we felt a little uneasy.

Julie and I enjoyed a little Portuguese culture while we were in the Peace Corps in Malawi, Central Africa, during the late 60's. We were teachers on Likoma Island in Lake Malawi. Just twelve miles from our island was Portuguese East Africa, better known as Mozambique. At that time the Portuguese were having a guerrilla war with the FRELIMO, a separatist group. From time to time Julie and I would board a local dhow, a small, often leaky, sailboat, and sail across to the military post at Cobue. The officers there had been drafted, many of them out of college or graduate school, and they were as eager as we to see other "Europeans." We made friends with them and whenever we arrived they would throw a party. We would have a nice meal and drink robust red wine, which came from large wicker covered bottles. They always knew enough English to get along. Sometimes they would stop and visit our island to buy fresh fish or chicken; sometimes they would visit us, too.

I remember one cool and windy afternoon there was a knock at the door of our house on Likoma Island. Several soldiers, unfamiliar to us, were there. They said the Commandant of the post would like us to join him and the men for dinner. We could come with them in their boat. I had a terrible cold, but we decided to go anyway. Their boat was an inflatable and one side was partially deflated. The four of us climbed in, and one of the men started a large Mercury outboard motor on the stern and we were off. It was choppy on the lake and the wind blew spray on Julie and me, soaking me to the bone. Armed sentries met us at the beach at Cobue, and led us to the officer's mess where the table was set for dinner. One of the officers noticed that I was soaked and shivering. He told me to go to his room and change my clothes. He found a dry pair of military issue pants and a khaki shirt for me. I noticed hand grenades and an automatic rifle in the room. No doubt they were having a serious war. The food, wine and hospitality were excellent. We laughed and tried hard to understand each other. When it was time to leave, I changed back into my damp clothes and we were escorted toward the shore but there was no boat there to take us. The soldier told us to wait on a small pier. Before long there was a rumble from the rushes nearby. A seventy-five foot, high speed, Cummins diesel powered ship, complete with machine guns, slowly emerged from the reeds. We boarded and, without running lights, we motored through the tropical African night. There was a bright moon and I remember a fat little soldier flirting with Julie while brewing her a cup of espresso. He would add sugar and milk and stir frantically so that his chubby cheeks would jiggle back and forth. I don't think any of these guys had seen a "European" woman in a year. Off the south shore of the Island, the captain shut down the engines and Julie and I said good-bye and boarded a camouflaged dinghy and were taken to the rocky shore near our house where we waded to the rugged beach. Because all of this was most likely quite illegal, we couldn't land near a village lest local officials find out. I remember stepping from the boat into the shallow water and then walking through the thick brush up to the path to the house. It was rather terrifying. Crocodiles lived along the shores of Likoma and mambas and spitting cobras slithered through the bush. The first rule of walking at night in the African bush is to carry a light. We had no light, but we stomped our feet and made it home without incident. Anyway, we liked our Portuguese hosts. They were genuine and open. Our brief friendship transcended politics and formalities. Sometimes at night during that dry season we heard what we thought was the unlikely sound of distant thunder. There were rumors of a battle at Cobue that didn't go well for the Portuguese. We never heard from or saw our friends again. They had been our one Portuguese experience, and it had been a good one.

My only other knowledge of the Azores and those who lived there, came from my childhood. They were clear and happy memories for me.

My Dad's best friend had been stationed in the Azores, to build airfields during World War II. He was still in the Islands when I was born in 1945. His name was Hank Granger and I was named after him. When he came home after the war, he talked about the Azores. I remember the look on his face when he told us about them. He said they were the most beautiful place he had ever been, and he would love to live there. He started a driveway paving business back in Lakewood in the late forties and I remember when I was a little boy, when our families would get together, he would lift me onto the seat of a huge paving roller that he kept in his garage. I used to call him "Uncle Roller." He died at eighty without ever going back to the Azores, but he and his tales of those Portuguese islands left a lasting impression on me. I knew that these islands were very special to him. I was anxious to see for myself.

Chapter 25

Horta

Through the night we raced along in unusually calm seas. On the second of June, Fial, the Island where the city of Horta is located, appeared on the horizon. Because the wind finally died completely, we had to start the engine in late afternoon, and we powered into the beautifully protected harbor just as the sun was setting. There on the dock to greet us was James Hall and right beside him was our English friend Chris with his wife, Jenny, whom we had first met in Martinique, then again in Saint Martin. How wonderful to see our friends again. Finally, the boat was secured and I was filled with childhood exuberance. Julie had prepared the 'hours motored' information and she handed it right in to James Hall. I was on a mission. I had to find Emily and turn in our poem.

We raised our ARC banner and code flags, closed the boat and stepped onto the pier. The four of us were off to dinner. At first I thought the marina was covered with graffiti, but I quickly realized that this was hardly graffiti in the usual sense. There were individual pictures covering the concrete walls, representing the thousands of yachts that had visited Horta. They often listed the boat name, names of captain and crew and then a sketch of the boat or even a sophisticated painting of it. They were colorfully and carefully done. After all, one cannot visit Horta without making a serious ocean voyage. These pictures were individual celebrations of sea journeys.

The streets of the city were busy with traffic as we walked along the harbor to a restaurant filled with fellow sailors. Wine and beer flowed freely and loud conversation greeted us as we found our way to a table. There were cheerful greetings from fellow sailors. The aroma of cooking food filled the air. This was a special place, indeed. The waiter brought us a bottle of wine and then explained we could order fish, beef or chicken.

Whatever we ordered would arrive at the table uncooked. A brick of very hot volcanic rock would then be set before each of us and we would cook our meat on the rock. It was a specialty of the house and the only way to get a cooked meal. We each ordered different fare and agreed to share. Bread and salad and a vegetable were part of the meal. Before long we were watching bits of steak and chicken sizzle before us. We shared our cooking expertise and soon determined just the right moment to flip our fish or slide it onto our plate. This was complicated, of course, by the amount of wine we drank and by the fact that the more one cooked the cooler the brick became. Then a pretty waitress would come by and pick up the cool brick and replace it with a red hot one. All bets were off. We laughed and talked and cooked and ate and by the time we were finished we had eaten more burnt beef and raw chicken than was probably healthy, but the food was fresh, all of it was delicious, and we were truly full and happy.

On the way back to the boat we walked by a little bar packed full with people who were drinking and laughing and singing. Chris Evans from *Lhasa* was there with his guitar; we had to stop in for a quick one. It was "Peter Café Sport" a bar made famous by sailors from all over the world who had visited there. What a rollicking good time. But it was not long before our eyelids grew heavy and we headed back to the boat for a well-deserved night's rest.

In the mornings, while the girls went for their run, Bob and I often frequented a small restaurant for coffee and fresh pastry. Everything was delicious. The town has beautifully paved streets with bars and restaurants reaching out onto the sidewalks on which stand tables covered with bright umbrellas. The hillsides were very green and lush. Flowers, especially hydrangeas grew everywhere. Windmills lined the tops of nearby hills. The sidewalks in Horta were a mosaic of small dark and light tiles. They were intricate and beautiful. Sometimes the designs were simple lines waving back and forth, sometimes they were pictures of ships, but there was always some design. We didn't know it at the time, but they are emblematic of Portugal. You will find the same sidewalk designs in Lisbon or Lagos.

Everything on the island was inexpensive as well. We really liked it. One day we rented a car, another day we took a ferry to Peko, a nearby towering island, while Bob and Carol, who chose not to join us, found a vacant spot and left our mark, in bright yellow paint, on a little triangle of the marina wall. Like the other yachts that had visited this famous port, we too left our names and a picture on the walls.

The day we rented the car was interesting as well. The four of us drove through the rolling green hills and saw herds of cattle on free range. Cowboys would bring portable milking machines to the herds in the summer. There would often be a horse grazing near by to help round up the cattle for milking. The men would saddle the horse and use it to herd the cattle to the milking machine. The coast was rocky and rugged, the hills steep, but the vegetation was lush and green. It seemed like a kind of paradise until one time we rounded a bend and came to a lighthouse by the sea. All that was left of it was a gutted tower. The buildings around the lighthouse had also been destroyed by fire. Nearby, a huge mound of earth obscured much of the ocean from where the lighthouse stood. We learned that a recent volcanic eruption had destroyed the lighthouse and all the buildings near it. There was a launch ramp for small boats near by, but that was about it. This was the dark side of the islands. They were, much as is the Caribbean, volcanic in origin. An eruption at any time could cause devastation and chaos. The area was carefully monitored for seismic activity.

The nearby island of Peko had a towering volcanic peak, visible from Horta, and was just an easy ferry ride from our marina. One Sunday morning Julie and I joined a number of other cruisers and visited the island. Most of the others opted to hike to the summit, but we joined Frank and Gail from *Alcid* and hailed a taxi to tour the island. It was while we were there that we learned about the fascination of these people with the

177

Holy Ghost. Catholic Churches in the Azores often have a small chapel, actually a carefully decorated and maintained building, which the islanders call the Holy Ghost Chapel.

While we were there we came upon a celebration of the Holy Ghost in which local women baked hundreds of loaves of bread that they passed out to other people in town during a special parade. We were amazed to see rooms filled with tables covered with beautiful doughnut shaped loaves. We didn't see the parade itself, but we were, thanks to our cab driver, invited to participate in a dinner that followed it. According to our driver, the men of the community get together to celebrate the Holy Ghost and raise money for the church. The tradition as well as the chapel itself, is a gift of the men of the congregation to the church, and although he may attend, the priest is not part of the organizing group. We heard others refer to this as 'some weird kind of Catholicism.' It seemed to me that these men had taken ownership of part of their church. What a good idea.

While we were in Bermuda, we had purchased a small transformer from our friends Dick and Eileen on *Triumph*. The transformer would convert 220 volt electricity to the 110 that the boat was designed to use for battery charging and hot water heating while we were in port. In the Azores, electricity is all 220. I went right to a hardware store and was easily able to purchase wire and fittings to connect the transformer to the power on shore. I was amazed at the thin and inexpensive wire used for 220. It makes our 110 lines look like hoses. As soon as we connected the system it worked flawlessly. We were very pleased with that. On the other hand, when we tried to refill our backup bottle of propane, it was not possible. No one in the Azores that we could find would fill our aluminum bottles. Fortunately, we had enough to get us to England where we would have to make a more permanent change in the gas system so it would conform to European standards.

After being at sea for two weeks and working the boat constantly during that time, there are bound to be things that go wrong. This time it was the Absorbed Glass Mat, AGM, battery, which we had installed in January. It simply would not hold a charge. Fortunately, we were always able to start the engine using the house bank of batteries, as we had designed the system that way. I called on a marine electrician to check out the system and we came to the conclusion that the battery must have been defective. The system, aside from the battery, was working fine. We replaced the expensive AGM battery with a regular lead acid model and the problem appeared to be solved. As usual, I stood by as the mechanic worked on the boat. He clearly knew what he was doing. Right after he left, I pulled the caps on the new battery. Although it was brand new, it was down half a liter of battery water. Attention to detail is so important. I topped it up and we hoped for the best. When I wrote Jack Rabbit Marine about our trouble with the battery, they gave us a full refund, even though we had discarded the old battery. What wonderful people to work with.

On Tuesday night, we got the race results. *Tapestry* was 7th of 11 boats in her division and 11th of 20 boats overall. Interestingly, among the boats we had beaten were an Oyster 63, a Wauquiez 48, a Halberg Rassy 43, and an Island Packet 38. The 23 hours of motoring we did to try to outrun the gale cost us dearly. Not only did we not succeed in outrunning the gale, the penalty was great.

After the race presentations, Emily, the young lady from *Helice,* made her way to the stage. She reminded everyone of her poetry contest and read the results, from worst to best. Of the eight entries she received, *Tapestry* was awarded first place. The prize was a silver tray "souvenir of the Azores" and a certificate. I also got to read our poem to this crowd of fifty somewhat tipsy sailors.

Horta Ho!

The wind was light and lazy,
At the start, it drove us crazy,
As we sailed our way to Horta's distant shore.
Rumbled by us, *Rumpleteaser,*
With a red sail, if you please, sir,
But *Alcid,* she was the leader more and more.
After her then, there was *Buppel,*
A strong sailor, fast and supple,
But the rest of us, we lingered,
Winds were poor.

Well we whistled up a gale then,
Winds of fifty, not for frail men,
Rattled rigging and tossed china to the floor.
While some of us thought, "Amen,"
Little girls were 'on the side' then,
Reading poems of their Ma's and bras and more.
Our laughter made us linger
To wet our pointer finger.
And find the winds were fairer than before,
As they carried us off to Horta's distant shore."

H.R.D. *Tapestry*

Actually, *Sandetti,* a beautiful Swan 40 from the Netherlands won the race, but never mind that. I was really pleased to have been selected the winner of Emily's poetry contest. After all the years I had spent "correcting" the work of high school students, it was gratifying to get high marks from these delightful English girls. We all had a good laugh; it was another memorable night.

The other big news that night was that there was a deep cold front approaching and it would not be safe for us to anchor in Jorges harbor, as planned, the following day. Winds would kick up from the south and make the anchorage unsafe. Instead, we would head for Terceira, another Azores island, and a 90-mile sail. Plans were made to leave Horta Wednesday afternoon and sail through the night to arrive at daybreak. We enjoyed our last day on this wonderful island and prepared to continue east.

We left our mark on Horta

Chapter 26

Terceira

As would be expected, winds increased as soon as we left. We shortened sail, but gusts of up to 30 knots kicked us along. Currents helped, too. The sky clouded over and rain added interest to the evening. By 2 a.m., we were just twenty miles from our destination. At our current speed of six knots we would arrive a full hour before daybreak. Finally, we rolled up the jib, halved the main, and rocked and rolled in beam seas. It was a long night, but we sloshed through the narrow opening in the rock wall at Angra do Heroismo in the gray light of dawn. We were directed to a slip near the entrance where we rocked with the surge.

The marina was new and there was an attractive restaurant and pool at the facility. The city, by contrast, was old. This was one of the very first trading cities in the Azores. Ships had been coming here for centuries. We would enjoy a tour of the island tomorrow, but after being up all night we spent our first day with a leisurely walk around town. In the evening we headed for the contemporary new marina restaurant for supper. Unfortunately, they were ready to serve drinks when we arrived at five, but the notion of dinner was out of the question. We found ourselves munching on *hors d' oeuvres* until seven when they finally agreed to bring us dinner.

Two things on Terceira were impressive. The first was a walk deep down into a volcano. The tour bus took us to the park and we descended far down into the earth through the opening at the top of an extinct volcano. The interior was lighted like a cave and it was exciting to imagine the huge "rooms" below filled with molten lava as it roared from the bowels of the earth onto the surface above.

The second thing that impressed us was the bull run. There is a tradition in Portugal that though, like the Spanish, they engage in bull fights, they never kill the bulls. Similar also to Spain, they enjoy chasing, or rather being chased, by bulls. The Portuguese pad the horns of the bulls, but bulls are large animals and the cowboys still take their knocks. We had seen videos of crowds being chased by bulls and in one instance a man being chased off a pier into the sea, only to be followed by an especially angry bull that plunged in right after him. On our bus tour we stopped at a corral where there were a number of bulls and even some cows being taunted and teased by cowboys. The animals were young and not eager to give chase, but when they did take off after the men in the pen, it was easy to see how serious injury could result, padded horns or not. It was an amusing episode and a full day. We were ready when the bus driver herded us back to the coach for the ride back to the marina.

Our departure from Terceira was at mid day in calm weather. We were headed for Ilha de San Miguel and the port of Ponta Delgada. Winds were calm when we left and we determined it would take about a day and a half to get there depending on weather. The sail was little more than a long motorboat ride. When we arrived at the port we were informed that we could not leave the fuel dock until we had visited the several offices of Customs and Immigration. That seemed redundant as we had spent several hours going through formalities in Horta. What was the problem? But we were entering the EU, or European Community; they had to get it right. We rafted to the dock and as we were all well acquainted due to our ARC activities, we were happy to be tied up together. Frank and Gail's 43 foot Saga had experienced mechanical problems during the voyage and coasted to the raft of boats. We were all there and happy to lend them a hand. The marina was new, huge, and first rate. The town was large and we found one of many nice restaurants right away.

The next day we began the customs check in. Each boat had to visit three offices where officials carefully scrutinized our papers. They slowly checked and rechecked everything. They reviewed where we had been and that we had checked into and out of each country we had visited. They tediously copied information into books and officially welcomed us to Europe. From here we would have just eighteen months to be in the EU without paying duty on our boats. That duty was serious business as it could amount to as much as 25% of the value of the vessel; no small change. Alan and Mary had purchased their Island Packet in the U.S. and had decided to pay their duty in the Azores, rather than in England, at a considerable savings to them. We Americans would have to watch the clock carefully lest we find ourselves with a big VAT, Value Added Tax, bill to pay.

The hardest part of the check-in, however, was the endless waiting on benches outside of offices. There was a young Swedish lady sitting next to me in line. I remember we had passed her and her friend who were sailing slowly in a very small home made steel sloop. Although Julie and I had thought carefully about our sail across the ocean, we had not given much thought to what we would do when we got there.

"You are from Sweden?" I asked. She looked at me with her sunburned face and shoulder length blonde hair. "My grandparents were from Stockholm and from Goteborg," I said.

"Yes, from Sweden. Have you been?" she asked. She smiled and I was pleased she was willing to pass the time.

"No." I said. "We have not decided where to go once we get to Europe. We know we will visit England, but after that we have no plans."

"You should seriously think about visiting Sweden" she said. Her blue eyes sparkled. "In summer, the islands on the Eastern side are some of the most beautiful places I have seen. You would love Stockholm. There is a canal that traverses the country. It is a wonderful place to sail in summer when the weather is nice. Of course, some years we don't have a summer." With that the door of the office opened and she smiled, stood up and disappeared into the Office of Immigration. I filed the information away and waited for my turn at customs.

Chapter 27

Volcanic Cooking, Narrow Roads and Gales

With formalities complete we learned that there was not sufficient room in the marina to accommodate us all. Some of us would have to tie to the wall and wait for a slip. The marina would notify us of openings when they became available. Julie spotted an empty slip right away and rather than tying to the wall, we took the slip and then ventured to the office to tell them. That is when we learned about Portuguese security. Not only did we need a specially programmed card to get onto the docks, we needed one to get off as well. We waited a few minutes until someone came by with a card to open the gate and then we proceeded to the office.

"We took a slip on dock B, slip 14," I said to the young lady at the desk. "Will that be all right?"

"Yes," she said. "I will mark you down." She took a blank plastic card that looked like a credit card and held it up. "You will need this to get onto and off of the docks. It will also let you into the showers and lavatories. When will you be leaving?"

"We begin the race to Plymouth on the nineteenth," I said. She typed rapidly on her computer.

"The card is good for your dock only. It will expire on the nineteenth of June."

We took the card and returned to *Tapestry*. As we approached the heavy steel gate at the entrance to our dock we found that waving the card in front of the gate caused the lock to click open, giving us easy access.

That evening was the first of several cocktail parties at the yacht club adjacent to the marina. We walked over and realized the yacht club was serious business. The first floor was an area for boat storage. It was occupied with racing boats large and small. The second floor was an Olympic-sized pool. The third floor was the bar and restaurant. The ARC people had organized a delightful evening for us at the club.

The following day we were supposed to have a bus tour of part of the island. We gathered outside the marina in the gray of a rainy morning to wait for the bus. The highlight of the tour was to be a lunch cooked in the ground by the heat caused by volcanic activity in the area. I suppose it would be safe to say that we were a bit tired of bus tours. Anyway, when the bus arrived it proved to be a fine, comfortable coach and the woman who was driving quickly displayed her ability to drive well and to narrate the history of the area. We visited a fishing village and saw small fishing boats carefully painted and beautifully cared for. We watched families baiting hundreds of hooks and at the same time keeping them and the lines they were attached to neatly organized and ready for that night's fishing. Each boat was topped with a large radar reflector many of which were decorated with colorful good luck charms of some kind. Fishing is difficult in this part of the sea, and the fishermen work hard to earn a living.

As we drove across the island, it was obvious that grapes were a large part of the harvest. There were stone walls everywhere. People had picked up the rocks strewn by the volcanoes and had piled them up as fences so grapes, planted alongside, could use them to cling to. The black rocks warmed by the sun were great for the growth of grape vines. Most of the grapes were then used in the making of wine. As on Faial, herds of cattle roamed the hillsides and hydrangeas of all colors adorned the island. They were in people's gardens, but they also lined the roads and grew wild in the fields. They loved the acid soil. The giant wipers on the bus hissed back and forth on the windshield as we sped along the paved, narrow road.

Around noon we entered the parking lot of what appeared to be some kind of a resort. The bus parked and we were directed toward some nearby mounds of steaming earth. Workmen with shovels worked up a sweat toiling in the steaming muddy earth to remove kettles of food, load them into a van and drive them toward a large building in the distance. There was the smell of sulfur in the air. It was raining and not altogether pleasant. We followed the kettles into the building and there found tables set for us with crisp white linen tablecloths and napkins. There were five bottles of red wine on each table. We took places at the tables and poured ourselves a glass of wine. Suddenly the mood changed from that of a gray rainy day to something much more pleasant. We began to talk and laugh and conversation sparkled. Steaming platefuls of beef and pork and chicken arrived along with dishes of carrots, potatoes, leeks and onions, all cooked by the heat of the earth. There was blood pudding too. The meal was a tasty delight, topped off with coffee and dessert.

Afterward, our driver, who was perhaps surprised by the animation of our group, advised us that we could have fifteen minutes to tour the botanical gardens. In spite of the rain we all headed off enthusiastically.

Right away we came to a large swimming pool filled with steaming hot water. Emily and Elizabeth had heard that there was a pool associated with the trip so they had brought their swimming suits. The ladies in our group all gathered in a tight circle to provide the girls a little privacy for changing clothes. Within minutes both Emily and Elizabeth had lowered themselves into the hot water and they were swimming in the pool as the steam nearly enveloped them. By the time they got out there was no doubt that our fifteen allotted minutes was nearly up, but we proceeded in the direction of the botanical gardens.

Here we found paths leading through trees, and plants of all types. Colorful flowers bloomed about us, huge ferns reached out over the paths and everything dripped with the never- ending rain. Lesser mortals might have retreated to the bus, but we were sailors who had nearly conquered the Atlantic Ocean. What was a little rain to us? There were ponds and streams and bright goldfish and black swans that hissed at us if we got too close. It was spectacular and it was not long before we realized we had become lost. We tried to find our way back to the bus, but our group had become turned around among the maze-like paths of the garden. Whenever we took a turn it seemed to lead us someplace new. Things looked vaguely familiar, but there was no bus and there were no roads evident. Finally, we came upon a young couple with a map. We borrowed their map and David, our leader and former officer in the Royal Navy, planned a route back to the bus. It was not long before we had found the bus and its driver. Our driver was not happy. We had spent much more than our allowed fifteen minutes touring the fragrant and colorful gardens.

In a nearby town there were hot springs and cold springs right next to each other. The cool water was clean enough to drink and tasted like soda water. The hot water was hot enough to boil an egg and roiled and bubbled as it came out of the stone wall. It was indeed a magical place.

Later we visited a tea plantation and saw iron machinery from the nineteenth century still working for processing and packaging the tea. It was a delightful tour and when it was over, we agreed we had rather enjoyed it.

But the island was large and there was a whole other half we had not explored. Bob and Carol, Julie and I again decided to rent a car. We found a museum with art and artifacts depicting the history of the islands. I studied pictures of the period around World War II, looking for "Uncle Roller," but stared only at anonymous faces of men in military uniforms. There was no English narration and even the role of American forces on the islands was not clear to me.

Later in the day we visited a volcanic peak with a narrow road around the rim. The sides were precipitous, dropping a thousand feet to two small lakes, one blue and one green in the center of the volcano. There was a small town inside, clustered around the lakes. On the outside, the mountain dropped nearly as precipitously to wide green plains stretching miles to the blue sea. The road around the rim was in places just wide enough for one car to pass. It was so steep on both sides that Bob, who had been a professional firefighter most of his life, wanted to get out and walk rather than ride in the car as we drove over the narrow part of the gravel road.

It was while we were traversing this rural mountain road that we learned something that surprised us about these people. They valued the English language and American traditions, even though they didn't always understand exactly what was being said. As we drove along we came upon several tough looking cowboys. They were searching for cattle that had been grazing on parts of the steep mountain side. One man was wearing a tee shirt with a picture of a handgun on the back. Carol asked if she could take his picture. On the front it said, "I have P.M.S. and a handgun. Any questions?" We certainly had questions about his choice of tee-shirt, but we too were lacking in necessary language skills to make ourselves understood.

Since we had the car, we decided it would be a good time to stock up the boat for the last segment of the trip. We headed for a super market in town and took a parking place in the basement parking area beneath the market. We picked up a grocery cart and a mechanical moving ramp carried us up to the level of the market. It was amazing that while we were on the ramp, the wheels of the cart locked so it could not run away, something we had never seen in the U.S. The market was large and as well stocked as many American supermarkets. We loaded several carts and filled the trunk of our small rental car with provisions that we took back to the boat.

We were supposed to leave on the nineteenth of June for the final leg to Plymouth, England, but the weather forecasts were anything but encouraging. James Hall announced that the start would be on the nineteenth, whether anyone left then or not. A number of us, especially those of us going to England had strong reservations. The weather forecast from ARC was severe. For forecasting purposes sections of the North Atlantic Ocean are broken up into areas named after women. We would be going through Uta and Sally.

> Gale Warning Update:
> It does seem likely that winds will be strong to gale force by 2359 GMT Monday in N. Meiko, N Brenda, Uta and Sally. Gales then becoming widespread and possibly severe in Uta and Sally with severe to storm force winds possible in Sally through late Tuesday and Wednesday. However, please do be aware that this is an unusually deep and active depression for mid-June. There is potential for this storm to be very serious and you should therefore monitor forecasts and warnings carefully. If you are not comfortable with strong to severe gale force winds you should not be entering areas Uta and Sally.

In spite of the warnings the race was started on time. Two boats actually started, the rest of us hung back.

"From the time I was a boy I have known never to leave in the face of a gale" said Jim MacDonald. We all understood and agreed with him. Every morning for the next few days we would hike to the library where we could go on line to check out the weather services for their forecasts. The French, the English and the Germans all have forecast offices and even though they do not always agree, they all agreed that the weather would be stormy between the Azores and England for the next few days. We waited.

In the meantime, other things were happening. In the playoffs for the European Football Championship, Portugal scored an upset victory. We watched on the television in a little bar at the marina. This generated a kind of hysteria on the island. Cars began racing up and down the waterfront and through the streets of the city, honking their horns. Young people leaned out of car windows cheering for Team Portugal. It was a mass celebration and we were surprised and touched to see such an enthusiastic response.

Also, several boats from the Nordhaven Rally entered the harbor. They were on their way across the ocean, much as we were, but with power boats rather than sailboats. We learned from them that one person had been lost in a freak accident and that they had needed to slow to below six knots in order to conserve fuel. Many of them had difficulty with their stabilizer systems and found themselves rolling uncomfortably at sea. They made us feel good about sailing.

It was then that we got word about Liz. Liz Jolleff and her husband Dave were sailing *Kjempekjekk,* a beautiful 33 footer. Liz had taken a nine month sabbatical from teaching biology to sail to the Caribbean and back with her husband. While walking downtown in Punta Delgada, she stepped awkwardly on an unmarked step and broke her ankle. It was a painful break and she had to be taken to the hospital where her ankle could be set. She and her husband would fly immediately to England where further surgery would be needed. They would have to hire crew to sail their boat home to England. What an unhappy experience.

It was the next morning when there was finally a break in the weather. A German military vessel was stopped outside the harbor. We noticed that the wind had let up and the forecast was less ominous. One by one we cast off our lines and headed through the harbor entrance to the sea. Our last leg would be 1280 miles, the second longest of the trip. Ocean waves were huge and confused and winds were light. Conditions were terrible for sailing. Bob was seasick right away and even Carol headed for a bunk to lie down. What a start. Pinball Wizard was near us and appeared on the crests and disappeared in the valleys of the waves. It was wild going. After a few days, however, things calmed down. Both Bob and Carol were again able to take solid food and keep it down. Our next challenge would be the continental shelf where the depth of the sea drops from several thousand meters to several hundred feet. Should there be strong winds, huge and dangerous waves can result. There would be nothing for us to do but gauge conditions when we drew near and make a decision whether to continue as we approached the shelf.

Our e-mails from the boat perhaps best describe the rest of the trip.

June 25th 2004

Hi,

It is raining hard here. Water drives into the reefed main, collects in the boom and sloshes onto the deck just forward of the windshield. It is cool and damp, but we wear shorts and tee shirts inside, not unlike a rainy day on Lake Erie. The barometer has been falling all night and is down to about 1011. The skies are slate gray; seas are lumpy but have been driven down by the rain. The wind is usually 20 to 25, but occasionally hangs around 30 and shocks us with a 35. We are happy as this is supposed to be as bad as it gets. The front should go through sometime between late this afternoon or after midnight, depending whether you listen to *Meteo* France or Herb. We're betting on Herb, but "the sooner the quicker" as the saying goes. The rain keeps us from opening the companionway so the windows mist over inside the pilothouse. It is a drizzly, sometimes rainy, windy morning and not likely to change much till tomorrow when the winds will become northwest and should carry us along the rhumb to Plymouth.

Not much else has happened. Jim on *Helice* came on the SSB last night to tell us that Venus Williams was knocked out of Wimbledon by an unknown. There is no news here. Several people have told us where to find the BBC, but all we got last night was soccer (pronounced football) in French. Could that be a little sun peeking through the clouds? Just a light spot.

Hank and Julie with Bob and Carol at 40.48N, 19.24W, 875 miles from Plymouth, England.

The e-mail which follows was written to my cousin, Bill Dwinelle in Seattle, who was fitting out a new fishing boat for his family.

26 June, 2004

Hi Bill,

Things are finally looking up on the good ship *Tapestry*. Yesterday we had huge waves charging by us all day and most of the night. Wind was from right behind us so we had a main with a reef and preventer and that was it. We rolled and rolled so that sometimes the decks would be awash. Still, Julie and Carol made beef stew and rice at noon and BLT's at five. It was one of those days you could never set a coffee cup down, however, last night a cold front was supposed to go through after midnight. Because it was trailing a huge low pressure area (on the weather map it was a "perfect storm") I was concerned. But we had done what Herb had suggested and the front passed without our noticing it at all. This morning the sun was out for a change and winds had shifted enough to roll out the jib and drop down to the rhumb line for Plymouth. We are making about 5.4 over the bottom and in about 17 knots of wind. Big waves are still tossing us around a bit.

Have you thought of a DSC radio for your new boat? It stands for Digital Selective Calling. We bought one before we left on this trip. One thing it does is allows you to automatically transmit your position in an emergency. It will also shift all nearby stations to the distress channel if a mayday is broadcast. If you are traveling with another boat you can talk to that boat and while you are talking to him his position appears on your radio and your position appears on his. Thus, if you found a good fishing spot, you could call your buddy with a like radio and he would know your position, but if you didn't say it, nobody else would. Also, if you program your buddy's MMSI number into the radio, you can call him on any channel and his radio will automatically switch to that channel. No need to go to 16 first.

Last night a ship was approaching us, so Julie called him on 16. No answer. She shined the spotlight on the sails, but still the ship did not respond. Bob, our radio/computer specialist called too. The ship was five miles off and steaming right toward us. Bob made an "all ships" call on the radio. That sounded an alarm on all DSC radios in the area and automatically tuned them to channel 16. Then Bob described the situation. Right away, the ship turned. It never did answer, but it turned and gave us room. It is mandatory to have them in Europe, but the U.S. Coast Guard won't require them till 2007 in the U.S. Still they are not much more expensive than a regular radio and I think they are a good idea. Ours is an ICOM.

I think I smell coffee and bacon so there is activity in the galley.

The air has cooled as we head further north. Wind is up to 19 knots and, well, there are still big waves. Bob is wearing two patches now, but we all have more or less gotten our sea legs and feel much better. All the best...

27 June 2004

Hi Everyone,

It is Sunday morning aboard *Tapestry*. Things have changed. The sun is shining. The sky and sea are blue. *Pinball Wizard* said good bye last night as she headed north for Kinsale, Ireland, and then on to Scotland. Although there are other boats within twenty miles of us or so, we cannot see them. We are alone on the sea. Currently, the wind is blowing at about force 4, or 12 knots. There are little waves on the sea, but there are also huge swells. One comes along every 30 seconds or so and raises the boat fifteen or twenty feet and then drops us back down. With these swells comes the rolling. One of the advantages of sail is that sails tend to keep the boat level. In these conditions, however, a particularly steep swell will cause the boat to heel excessively in one direction and then compensate by rolling the other. That makes life difficult, especially when one has a cup of coffee in hand, or is trying to move forward or aft. Anything the girls set down on the counter in the galley is liable to slide off onto the floor. It is especially difficult now because there is little wind. Shouldn't life be easier than this?

We are in an area of very high pressure. The barometer has risen from a low of 1009 yesterday morning to 1020 this morning. We should have rising winds tomorrow and another cold front on Tuesday with its accompanying wind shift. Good weather is forecast for the foreseeable future.

We had our own problem yesterday. We ran out of propane. There seemed to be a leak between the bottle and the hose in the bow compartment. Anyway, the new bottle we had just installed in the Azores was empty after just a week or so. It should last more than a month.

The leak was outside the boat, so it is not a safety concern, except that we may have to develop better fishing skills and hone our appetites for sushi. We have tested the system with soapy water and found no leaks. We then attached the nearly empty spare tank to the system. It should last (we hope) to Plymouth, where we will have to adapt the system to use "Camping Gas." Propane is not widely available in the UK or on the Continent. One more adventure aboard *Tapestry.* All the best...

28 June 2004

Hi from *Tapestry,*

We learned something about our DSC radio the other day that we never knew before. There was a boat traveling with us for a while named *Pinball Wizard* and we communicated frequently. We always had trouble at night, though. He blamed it on his radio because it was old. I was ready to accept that. Well, we discovered it wasn't his fault at all. We installed an LED masthead light just before we left Saint Martin. It is wonderful. The light comes from diodes rather than from a traditional light bulb, so it is pure red, green and white. There is no colored glass to fade, it uses just half an amp per hour and it is so brilliant it is visible during the day. Great, huh? Well, it also blocks all but the strongest incoming VHF radio signals when it is on. We had noticed that when we first installed it, but by rerouting the cable to it we thought we had solved the problem. Apparently the cable has slipped during the voyage and it is blocking the signals again. Perhaps that is why that ship never responded to our call. Looks like another trip up the mast when we get to England.

The seas are calm tonight. Actually, there is the rolling, still, but the winds have died and we are motoring. We have been motoring for over 30 hours straight at this point and we are a little tired of the drone. On the other hand we are moving along at 5.7 knots toward The Lizard, a peninsula in southern Cornwall, England, which is just 355 miles away. We transferred our extra fifteen gallons of fuel from tanks on deck to the main tanks today so we still have one full 45-gallon tank and another more than half full. Most likely that would be enough to motor all the way. Winds are expected to pick up from the southwest tomorrow and continue to build through the week. We hope to arrive sometime early on Thursday, July 1. Take care.

30 June 2006
Hi from *Tapestry,*

This morning we are crossing the continental shelf. That is the place where the water goes from 13,000 feet deep to about 200 feet deep in just 20 miles or so. As a result, all of that wind driven energy, in the form of waves, that has been pushing across the Atlantic from North America, suddenly has nowhere to go. So it piles up into huge swells. We've talked about big waves before, mere ripples. We were warned about it.

"Don't cross it in a storm," said Chris on *Lhasa.* " I've marked my charts with a skull and crossbones at the shelf. It can be very dangerous in high winds." How dramatic, I thought. Fortunately, there have been no high winds forecast for the last part of the trip so we didn't think much about it.

It was at about six this morning when I noticed that I was crashing around in bed. When I got up I saw that the boat was veering back and forth and that the wind was momentarily up to about thirty knots. We had been under main and engine, but with so much wind who needs the engine? I pulled back on the throttle and the main jibed. Because there was a preventer on the main, it simply backed. The preventer, a line from the end of the boom led forward to the deck, prevented the mainsail from jibing, so the sail filled backward. The boat was out of control, and trying to go backward, but the rudder kept us largely sideways to wind and wave. Bob went on deck to release the preventer, I yelled at him to be careful. I was afraid he would lose his balance as the boat rolled, or be struck by the boom when he released the preventer. This would be a terrible time to have to retrieve a man overboard. But Bob managed to release the preventer, the main jibed without incident and in a moment things were in hand. The sail was back where it belonged and we were again on course.

But the waves! We could hardly believe the mountains that surrounded us. A ship just two miles away was visible just one second in ten. Surely we were lifted thirty feet on the peaks of some of those swells. They were gentle swells, not breaking, nor in any way dangerous, but they were huge. Once we had calmed down we realized we had just crossed the shelf. Another 126 miles and we will be at The Lizard.

Another phenomenon we have discovered on this trip is Portuguese man o' war. They are jellyfish prevalent in the Atlantic on the East coast of Florida. They are often iridescent blue, but have filaments, which give a painful sting to swimmers. As we approached Bermuda we saw thousands of them on the water. The boat would plough harmlessly through them, but perish the thought of going over the side for anything.

When we left the Azores, for days we saw millions and millions of the same species, only very tiny. Each, I have been told, is actually two organisms. On top there is a bubble-like "sail" which sticks up an inch or two above the water. Half are set to one side, half to the other, so that they will disperse with the wind. Underneath the "sail" there is a jellyfish, which provides the stinging filaments. The two have a symbiotic relationship. At this stage they are little bigger than a silver dollar on the surface of the water, but their numbers are very impressive. At their most dense there were several per square meter and they were reported equally as dense by boats as far as twenty miles from us. Mixed with them were flower-like objects with a gold center and petals extending around the center, sort of like a daisy. Someone suggested that these "flowers" somehow gave birth to the jellyfish. Most of our information comes over the radio net, so it may or may not be authoritative. Anyway, there were lots of them and that is a fact! In The *Old Man and the Sea,* Hemingway describes them in the Caribbean and calls them "a*gua mala*". He calls them "whores" and tells how loggerhead turtles eat them.

We are getting "English fever" rather badly and find ourselves not tolerating much less than five knots without running the engine. Before, we would never run it unless we were going less than three knots. The winds have backed to the northwest, however, so they are favorable and, hopefully, we will be able to sail the rest of the way to England. All the best, ...

01 July, 2004
Hi Everyone,

It is now 12:30 Greenwich Daylight Savings Time and we have passed Land's End, are off Lizard Point and expect to arrive in Plymouth in about four hours. We are in the English Channel and watching six ships on the radar. A force 8 gale is forecast "soon" but that is okay. Land is comfortably in sight and there is no raining on this parade.

It did sprinkle earlier, and dark clouds formed in the northwest, but blue skies and puffy white clouds are back in the picture. We just had a little brie with apples and olives in the pilothouse, and there are rumors of more tasty things to follow. Tonight, a nice steak and a pint or two of English ale sounds good.

We are all smiles. Ahead of us is the Eddystone Light, Drake Island, and the Mayflower Marina, where we will stay in Plymouth. All the best.

Chapter 28

England! Success!

And so we made it to England. We sailed into the busy harbor at Plymouth, which was crowded with warships and pleasure craft moving rapidly through the channel. For the first time we had to unlearn our American tradition of "red right returning" and accept the fact that on this side of the ocean green is on the right as one approaches a harbor. We passed through the break wall and then over the "bridge" which is not a bridge at all, but a cut through a rock shoal that gives access to the marina. As when we left Antigua, there was no fanfare at all. We were just another boat looking for a slip at an English marina. We raised the "Q" flag, an orange flag that notifies customs that we are an arriving vessel waiting to be inspected. We walked to the marina office, anxious to touch English soil and to check in.

"Hello, we're *Tapestry,*" I said to the man in charge. "Just arriving from the Azores. Do you have a number we can call for customs?"

"Yes, *Tapestry.* With the ARC, aren't you? About customs, you don't need to call customs, I'm quite sure. You came by the Azores, didn't you? You checked in there. I'll call them to be sure, but I know they won't want to speak with you. And take that damn yellow rag down, will you? Just draws unnecessary attention, you know."

"Yes, all right." I said.

"The ARC has paid for you tonight; after that it will be the regular rate. You will want private heads, won't you? That will be a ten pound deposit, returned when you check out. There might be mail for you. You can check that desk over there."

"All right." I said, "But our crew will be leaving right away. Does customs have to know that?" I asked.

"I don't think so. I'll call them. Don't you worry about it unless I get hold of you."

I paid the deposit for the private heads and that was it. We had made it. We were in cold, rainy England.

Bob and Carol were getting their things together. We wheeled their duffel bags onto shore where they called a cab and we said our good-byes. They had had enough of cold and wet and were headed for a heated hotel room where they could reorganize and begin a tour of England and France before returning to Florida. They had no interest in waiting for the last of the fleet to arrive. Celebrations were low on their list.

We hauled down the yellow "Q" flag, replaced it with the British Flag, and found ourselves alone again. We had made it. We had been warned of pirates, and terrorists, and storms and sharks and whales and domestic hostility, but we had made it in spite of all the rest. The boat was intact, we were still friends with our crew, and we had entered the Old World. Crossing the Atlantic had not always been easy. Like most life experiences, it was filled with moments of beauty and terror with the beauty outweighing the terror a hundred to one. Still, life continues even when one is crossing the ocean. A good friend back home had suddenly become ill and died. Another friend had lost his father. We would be able to attend neither memorial. Now that we were here, we had another adventure before us. There were things to learn, to taste and to weigh. This was the land of our grandparents. They too had crossed the ocean, but in the opposite direction. They had said good-bye to their parents and brothers and sisters and towns and churches with the firm belief that they would never see any of them again. They had made the trip in wooden vessels with sails of canvas and lines of hemp. Now we were back.

We enjoyed the hospitality of our ARC friends that night in the marina. Dave from *Kjemperjekk* was there to greet us, but only briefly as Liz's leg was uncomfortable in her cast and she had stayed home. It was great to see him. After he left we sang and laughed and enjoyed a fish and chips dinner. We learned that although things are cheap in the Azores, by American standards, they are not cheap in England. A large cup of coffee cost several pounds or almost five dollars. Right away we were told that our English friends, with whom we had sailed the Atlantic, seldom visited restaurants. They would more often visit pubs and eat bar food. That is, they would order their food over the bar and take their food to a table, eliminating service charges. That night, rain and wind washed over *Tapestry.* We snuggled in bed to keep warm, but we slept well.

The following day the ARC had a luncheon to celebrate the end of the event. Jim and Ann and the girls arrived just before the festivities. There were no prizes as there had been no race at least officially. There was some dissatisfaction with the fact that the Azores/Plymouth leg had started in such foul weather, but there were no speeches. James Hall slipped away quietly. The ARC was over and that was that.

Chapter 29

A Warm Pub, An English View, Poole

3 July 2004

Greetings from England,

Today we will embark on getting cooking gas to work on the boat. We are still running on the part bottle of propane we installed on the way from the Azores. *Helice* has offered us two empty English bottles for camping gas. How generous of them. That will be a good start; we will get them filled with the butane/propane mix they use here and buy a different gas regulator. *South Saxon* gave us a cell phone. We will just need to purchase a sim card to make it work. These people are very generous. We cannot walk into a bar without someone buying us a drink. They have been more than generous; they are true friends.

Our flags whip in the wind and rain. The temperature has barely touched 60F since we got here. Unsettled weather or "Wimbledon weather" is upon us, but it is expected to improve in a week or so, maybe. No shorts, I am wearing a wool shirt and think about sweaters and jackets when I go out. Quilts? Heaters? We have neither, but they are on the list!

Plymouth is an inspirational place. It was fire bombed to all but complete destruction in WW II, but has been rebuilt. In the center of town is a bombed out church with only the walls standing amid a green lawn. It is a touching memorial, and a grim reminder of the horrors of war. On the shore there is a huge park called The Hoe. A large stone citadel overlooks the harbor, but the rest, a grassy park, contains memorials to the boys from Plymouth lost in two world wars. It is awe inspiring to see so many names in bronze. There are thousands from this one city alone. How can one comprehend such sacrifice?

Our boat is moored overlooking the outer wall of the marina. It is spitting rain, blowing 20 knots, less than 60F degrees out and families with sailboats are loading picnic lunches and heading into the harbor. Ferries, military vessels, cargo boats all chug past just a few hundred feet from us. Waves lap over the floating docks. It is cold, but no one seems to notice. There are flowers everywhere. It is very green.

One thing I have found interesting here are the bathrooms. There are immaculate public heads at this marina. They are clean, well maintained, heated and fine. But, if you have a slip here, you can pay ten pounds deposit for a key, and then use the private heads. There you can get a whole bathroom to yourself. These are also heated, with heated towel racks, clean and fine. This morning there was a line waiting in the cold rain at the private heads, but the public ones were empty. You can guess where I took my shower.

This afternoon we will head for town to do more shopping. Who knows, by evening we may even have a phone number. All the best...

We did get a phone number, from Virgin Mobile, but we found out right away that the old phone we had been given wasn't up to it. We would need a new one.

On the night of the Fourth of July, we found ourselves back at the bar at the marina. Chris walked in toting an American Flag and an envelope filled with tea, in honor of American Independence Day. We had a laugh about that, but I was impressed with how much he knew of our history and how little I knew of theirs.

In conversations around the marina, we began to get another worldview, something akin to what we had learned from our friends on the ARC.

I noticed that a number of people who sailed to the Caribbean had avoided stopping in the U.S. I wondered why. One night I was at the bar and some of the conversation turned toward the States.

"My wife and I have sailed the Intracoastal waterway several times," I said. "We've cruised in the U.S for years."

"Never had any desire to visit the States, myself," a man across from me said. "Too many guns for me."

"Well, I suppose there are guns, but I've never seen a problem with it." I said.

"More guns in the States than there are people," he said. "And that's a fact." A man across the bar jumped into the conversation.

"We stopped in Miami and Marathon and Key West," he said. "Never felt comfortable on the streets at night, really."

"I remember a number of years ago, young people were shooting Europeans who rented cars in Florida." The other man said. There was a nod of agreement and the conversation died.

Suddenly I felt rather defenseless. I thought about Tortola and our friend, Hastings. We were talking about taking our boat to Crown Bay to do the installation of the generator back in January. "I hate to go to the U.S. Islands," Hastings had said. "Everyone carries. Get in an argument in a bar over there and like as not you'll get shot."

Even Jim, our English friend from *Helice,* had told me that while he was in Miami he never ventured onto the streets without three adults.

The previous evening, before I had fallen asleep, I remembered feeling a bit superior because I didn't insist on using the private heads at the marina in the morning. But after this evening's conversation, I had a different feeling altogether. These people thought of us Americans as cowboys, our world a kind of quick draw contest for survival of the fastest. Guns and bombs had devastated England through two world wars. Policemen had prided themselves on being unarmed in England in the past. Were we somehow less civilized because of our dependence on firearms in everyday life? It was something to think about.

In the privacy of our cabin on *Tapestry,* our new 220-volt space heater hummed quietly and warmed our bedroom as wind driven rain once again pattered on the cabin top.

Our plan to sail north to Sweden and Norway and then to store the boat in Finland fell through. Most everyone we talked to said it was far too late in the season to begin such a journey. Martin and Erika on *Buppel* had suggested we still had plenty of time for the trip, but others, who had never tried it, insisted that we would need an earlier start. Besides, when we began our search for charts, we failed to find the ones we needed.

A second suggestion was to sail around England and Scotland with several visits to Ireland. Again, we could find no one who had done the trip, but the prevailing opinion was that we would end up in a number of places that were shallow and stormy with dangerous and challenging tides. They thought, that too, was a voyage best begun in early June, rather than mid July. Besides, as before, many of the crucial charts were not immediately available. We would need another plan.

Consequently, we decided on a trip across the southern coast of Britain to Portsmouth and back, after which we would head south to the warmer climes of southern Portugal and Spain. Everyone we talked to thought that would be a splendid way to spend our summer. We bought the charts and the following day we were off.

Dartmouth was just up the coast, our first destination. Like Plymouth, which was at the mouth of the river Ply, Dartmouth was at the mouth of the river Dart. We entered the harbor and were enchanted by the two medieval castles that guarded it, one on either side of its mouth. We sailed up the river to the town where Chris Harrison was waiting on a small pier. We had cruised across the Atlantic never far from Chris and Jenny, last seeing them in Horta. They had insisted we visit them in Dartmouth and so we gave them a call. The tide was in flood as we approached the dock, and what a current! The dock was a "T" shaped affair and as we approached the inside of the "T," we found we were being sucked powerfully into the walkway that led from shore to the "T." I slipped the shifter into reverse and speeded up the engine as Julie handed a line to a man who owned a trawler tied to the dock. I revved the engine for all it was worth to stop us before we slammed into the wooden pier. Thank goodness the boat behaved properly.

We visited Chris and Jenny in their home. There were colorful formal flower gardens in a park by the river just a short walk from where they lived. It was a flat in three levels and very comfortable indeed. I noticed that the refrigerator in their kitchen just reached up to the counter top. In England they shop every day for fresh food. There is no need for a huge fridge. That evening we dined with them in a stone walled hotel by a comfortable fire. The building dated from the 1700's, very old by American standards. Dartmouth, unlike Plymouth, had little industry at the time of World War II, and hence it was spared much of the bombing. Many very old and beautiful buildings remained.

After dinner that evening a deep and powerful cold front passed through. We ran frantically from Chris and Jenny's home back to *Tapestry* as the rain poured down. The wind was screaming through the trees and a helicopter roared over head, no doubt to rescue someone at sea. It was a wild night outside, but the boat, secured to the pier, was safe and warm.

The next morning was gray and blustery. Jim and Ann from *Helice* picked us up for a tour of the moor. Julie and I climbed into the back seat of their Volvo station wagon and we headed into the countryside. Their Volvo was a big car and there was room for the four of us plus their two daughters, Emily and Elizabeth. We saw Dartmoor Prison and felt the gloom of the place so often mentioned in English fiction. We had lunch in a pub with a huge fireplace where a small fire flickered.

"That fire once burned for a hundred years straight," said Jim. " And then some bloke let it go out one nice day. That was a hundred years ago, and they still haven't forgiven him."

In spite of the fire, it was cool in the room and we sat on benches. I walked to the bar and got two pints of dark English ale for Jim and me and other drinks for the ladies. The barmaid pulled hard on a long wooden lever, which pumped the brew from kegs in the basement. How different from the pressurized taps back home. Returning to the table, I stepped over the bench and sat down. I looked at the old fireplace and thought of the others who must have sat here before me and probably talked of the victories of Admiral Nelson, trouble in the Americas, and then, centuries later, the bombing of London. But I was quickly jarred from my reverie. Next to us a party of four adults talked and laughed as they drank dark beer. I felt something warm against my leg. It was dark in the pub, but snuggled beneath the next table was a collie and two English springer spaniels, comfortably nestled around their owner's feet.

"Are these your dogs?" I asked the man sitting near me.

"Yes, of course. Are they all right?" He looked at me as if something was wrong.

"Oh, yes, I said. Julie and I had several springer's ourselves. I was just surprised. They are so good, so quiet and content."

"Yes. Old family pets. Lovely dogs really."

I looked down and the nearest Springer was looking up at me, his stub of a tail wiggling, but making no move toward me. I wanted to give him a hug, but I petted him on his brown head for a second and scratched under his chin when he raised his head. He relaxed and closed his eyes. By then our lunch had come.

Later that day we visited a museum where we saw how peat, tin and granite had been mined on the moor. It was interesting that the first reforestation project took place on Dart Moor in 1790.

The following day we walked, again in the rain, to one of the castles at the mouth of the harbor. Although they were never used in battle and were built in the Fourteenth Century, they were designed to be defenses against cannon; the turrets had walls four feet thick and built of rock.

I remember a comment from the owner of a small gift shop adjacent to the castle. He asked me what I thought of our invasion of Iraq. When I told him I thought it was a bad idea, he disagreed.

"No," he said. "You Americans are doing the right thing. We English tried to ignore a tyrant like Saddam Hussein two generations ago; look what that did for us." He shook his head and then he gave me a coaster as a souvenir of our visit to the castle.

It reminded me of what another Englishman had said when we first got to St. Lucia, back in the Caribbean, because it was so different.

"*Noocular* George." he had said when he realized we were Americans. "I have always been impressed by the fact than in America anyone can become president. But I always thought you had to go to school first!"

After Dartmouth, we sailed for Weymouth. To get there we would have to pass "Portland Bill" a point of land around which powerful tidal currents often created dangerous conditions.

"There are two ways you can do it," Jim MacDonald had told us. "You can either pass four or five miles off shore or else go right within a stone's throw of the point. Personally, I prefer the off shore method. It may take a bit longer, but I think it is the safest." He went on to tell us that, especially with a contrary wind, the tidal rips off Portland Bill could be very dangerous, even to an ocean going yacht or a small ship.

Chris Harrison had warned us about transiting southern England.

"When one transits the south coast of England, it is important to consider the state of the tide at your destination when you plan to arrive," Chris had said. "Then, considering currents with or against you, you can determine the appropriate time of departure." Obviously there was more to cruising this part of the world than getting an early start on the day.

On the 11th of July, after our stormy, but delightful stay in Dartmouth, Julie and I set sail for Weymouth. It was a forty-mile sail, but tides were critical for getting out of Dartmouth and getting into Weymouth. We poled out the Genoa (a first for just Julie and me with our 17.5 foot pole) and sailed down wind, first slowly into the tide and then faster and faster as the tide turned. GPS put us at 7.8 knots at the max. We had to round Portland Bill, which is a steep sided point with a shoal called "The Shambles" just outside. The question was outside, or inside? Jim had suggested, "Outside is always safe." Chris had said, "Save an hour and go inside in good weather with the tide." The tide was with us; the weather was fair, winds 18 to 23. We went inside. Waves peaked and broke and *Tapestry* just plowed through. We rolled up the jib, dropped the pole, and sailed under just a full main. The current was in control; the marks for The Shambles came upon us quickly, but we missed the shoal easily and just as it began to rain and the wind touched 27 knots, we slid into the harbor. What a relief. It was cold, more like an October or April day in Western N.Y.

Once inside, we found ourselves in a city with boats moored five deep from pontoons. We called ahead and got permission to tie up to a pontoon in third position. Neighboring boats were wonderful. They helped us tie up and directed us toward the harbormaster's office where we would pay our fee.

The next morning we discovered something more about English character. The man inside us in an H.R. 34 was having a little trouble with his mainsail "single line reefing." He was an older white haired gentleman. I saw that he was frustrated. He was wrapping his reefing line around a winch and grinding on the line for all he was worth. Still the line did not move.

"Excuse me," I said. "We had a similar problem with single line reefing on our previous boat." He looked at me and paused. His face was quite red.

"Really?" he said.

"Yes", I said. "My wife figured out that there was a tangle inside the boom and she understood how to fix it. She's out for a run right now but I'm sure she'll be happy to help when she comes back."

"I see." the man said. Just at that moment, Julie appeared behind him in her running outfit.

"Jul," I said. "This man has a tangle in his single line reefing. Could you give him a hand?"

"Hi," said my wife. "I'm Julie."

"How do you do? My name is Wellington. Your husband tells me you know about these things."

"Yes," said Julie. "There are two 'cars' that float inside the boom there. Sometimes they get twisted around and it is possible to pull them out the end of the boom and straighten them. It's easy, really," Julie said. With that she unscrewed and removed the end cap, eased the line from the winch, pulled out lots of slack and pulled the 'cars' out from inside the boom. In a few minutes the lines were untangled and the problem was resolved.

Once Wellington realized Julie had solved the problem, he looked at us and asked, "Where are you two headed?"

"We're going east." I said. "And we are looking for a place to meet our friend Michael who we haven't seen for over twenty years. "He and his wife worked with us in Africa in the 60's, and since then she has died and he has remarried. It will be a grand, though a rather sad, reunion."

"I wish you would meet them in Poole," said Wellington. "I have a slip at the Royal Motor Yacht Club there, and I'm going to give them a call and tell them that you are coming. It will be a fine place for you to meet your friends. My crew and I will simply stay out a few more days. It will be no problem. In fact it will be a pleasure."

"Thank you," I said, "but that won't be necessary."

"But I insist," said Wellington.

Weymouth is a beach town with arcades and beach rides and amusements. It turned me off at first, as we walked around in the rain. But Sunday was nicer, and we learned there was a National Model Boat meet in town. Model ships and boats of every description were on display in the conference center. Battleships, carriers, sailboats, and wonderful steamboats were there for all to see. Later, at a nearby lake, they all performed. It is easy to imagine power boat races of every description from high speed racing boats to foot long plastic boats in a demolition derby.

Of course, there were sailboat races, too. But the real drama awaited us. At about four in the afternoon, several battleships, destroyers, and cruisers, each over a meter long, accompanied a freighter and appeared in a reenactment of a WWII convoy. Suddenly there was a "bang" as an explosion and fire blossomed aboard the freighter. It was a submarine attack. Real smoke and fire belched from the freighter. The warships circled and dropped depth charges as water and noise splashed astern. The fire was contained aboard the freighter and we were told: "The German U. Boat has been sunk." (The English haven't forgotten.) Later, several "square riggers" sailed out and engaged in battle. They fired loud smoking broadsides into each other until one ship lost two masts and listed seriously to one side. (The French one of course.) Fire erupted aboard, and the English had clearly won the day.

Finally, two huge WW I battleships, each four meters long entered the scene. We were told a diplomat's daughter had been kidnapped and was being held in a fort, a replica of which was anchored in the bay. The fort fired on the battleships and the ships fired back. It was very loud and grown women, as well as the kids, had their ears covered. Fireworks erupted from the fort and black smoke filled the sky. No doubt, the girl had been rescued and the battleships were victorious. When the battleships got to the windward side of the fort, the whole deck lifted up to reveal a man inside these huge models. It was a kind of bow and also a chance for the "driver" to get a breath of fresh air. The audience had enjoyed this wonderful display and it brought generous applause from the crowd.

On the way back to the boat we stopped to buy fresh tomatoes and beets from a roadside stand, then went to a movie, *Around the World in 80 Days*, a humorous twist on Jules Verne's classic and a wonderful end to a delightful day.

The following day, we set out in early afternoon for Poole, as it was a relatively short sail and the tides dictated our after lunch departure. We called ahead when we approached the Royal Motor Yacht Squadron, but got no reply except from the English Coast Guard who told us to use channel 37 to call yacht clubs and marinas. Well, American VHF radios don't have a channel 37, so that was that. We made our way into the club and found Wellington's slip. We pulled in and Julie gracefully dropped to the dock and tied us in place. Our ARC flag and the Stars and Stripes were flying.

People seemed cool as we walked down the docks. One pleasant lady who helped us with our lines spoke to us. "I believe that's Wellington Carr's slip," she said.

"Yes," I said. "We saw him yesterday in Weymouth."

"You'll have to check in at the office, you know. We don't generally reciprocate with other clubs." she said. Her tone told me she was quite certain she was right.

Julie and I headed for the office. The club was nice, but nothing really special by American standards. The office was closed for the day. If our reception was cool, it was a good match for the weather. That night, as we walked along the dock, we stopped to visit with a man in a small outboard cruiser.

"You're the American's are you?" He said, looking up from his boat. "Do you know that this club is located on the fourth most valuable residential land in the world?"

"I had no idea," I said.

"Yes, we're quite proud of our club." He smiled and went about working with his boat.

Next morning at eight a.m., we headed back to the office. It was open this time and an impeccably dressed woman greeted us. "You must be the Danielson's. Is that right?"

"Yes, ma'am," I said. "We spoke with Wellington Carr in Weymouth and he told us we could use his slip here for a night or two.

"You'll have to speak with the manager." she said.

"Yes, of course," I replied.

The manager was a smiling man, dressed in a brown suit.

"Ah yes, the Danielson's," he said when he saw us.

"Wellington called and said that he had told you that you could use his slip. It is a bit out of the ordinary, you know, but of course you are welcome, foreign flag and all. There will be no charge."

"Why, thank you," I said.

"If you would like to use the dining facilities, you are welcome to them. Shirt and tie are required for the dining room; casual attire will do for the grill or outside on the porch. We hope you enjoy your stay."

"Well, thank you so much." I said. We're really grateful. We will be meeting old friends here we haven't seen in over 20 years."

"Of course. I'm sure you'll be leaving Wellington a fine bottle of whiskey before you leave," said the manager as he turned to walk away.

"Yes. I'm sure I will," I managed to reply.

Later that morning, Michael Ryan appeared at the Yacht Club with his new wife Margret. Michael and his first wife Ann had lived in Nkotakota, Malawi, while Julie and I were on Likoma Island in the Peace Corps during the '60's. We were fast friends and we visited them in England in 1981. Ann had suffered a sudden onset of dementia and died several years before our current visit.

Michael and Margret came with a bottle of champagne to celebrate our reunion and to introduce us to Michael's new wife. We had a fine time aboard the boat and then ventured to the club for lunch. As we approached the entrance, a mature gentleman dressed in black slacks with a white coat and a towel draped over his arm looked at us in our casual clothes.

"Mr. and Mrs. Danielson," he said. "Will you and your guests be dining in the grill or on the porch this afternoon?"

I was at a loss for words. This man we had never seen before spoke to us as if we were royalty. His good-natured formality made me feel I had been a member of this club for years. I almost couldn't think of what to say. It was sunny and 60's. We decided to dine on the porch.

Before we departed, I left a very nice bottle of whiskey at the office for Wellington. Our experience at Poole Royal Motor Yacht Club was one we shall certainly never forget.

Chapter 30

The South Coast of England

From Poole, we headed for the Beaulieu (pronounced Bulie) River, where we wended our way through the English countryside to Buckler's Hard, a place where much of Admiral Nelson's fleet had been built. When we looked at the chart, we were a bit put off. Depths at the mouth of the Beaulieu were very shallow. But when we remembered that depths are recorded at low water and that there is a considerable tidal range in the area, we knew that at high tide we would be all right. Of course when one explores in a sailboat, one does so on a rising tide whenever possible. That way, should the boat run aground, the rising water helps re-float her. Julie carefully checked the tide tables and we figured backwards to determine our departure time from Poole. We knew we could do this.

We slogged through the Solent with winds behind us at about 20 knots under a reefed main. We entered the river cautiously, but found good water between the buoys and moved up river easily. By 7 that evening we had tied *Tapestry* to posts in the river off Buckler's Hard. The next morning we lowered the dinghy, attached our trusty Honda outboard and started it on the third pull. It was the first time the motor had been started since we left Saint Martin. Ashore, with the dinghy tied to the dock, we walked to the nearby shipyard museum. Part of the old town had been restored and the buildings were of some interest, but the museum held plans and models and paintings. It was fascinating to see how so many great British ships, including most of Nelson's fleet, had been lofted and constructed there. Buckler's Hard is also the home of Sir Francis Chichester, a noted solo pilot and record setting solo sailing circumnavigator during the 1960's.

Around noon we walked the two and a half miles to the town of Beauleau. Here we enjoyed our first ploughman's lunch in a comfortable old inn. Down the street you could purchase a beautifully restored MG, Triumph, Jaguar or Bentley for a truly exorbitant price. A ways further down the road was the National Motor Museum. Inside we ogled spectacular automobiles from sedans and trucks to Grand Prix winners. There was a Lotus, and huge land speed record holders, driven by a man named Breedlove. There were other sports cars and motorcycles, too. I remember the many Mini's and the movie about those tiny cars. I was moved by the pride the British take in their automotive history. After that we visited the Montague Estate where we were allowed to visit a few rooms of the house as the Lord was away. Nearby was what was left of a very old abbey. It had been built in the 13th century, then dismantled at the command of King Henry VIII. The Catholic Church didn't go along with the King's idea of changing wives from time to time, so Henry had this Abbey and many others torn down and used the stone for the construction of several castles. What a beautiful place it was. Many of the arches are still standing, surrounded with contemporary sculpture amid carefully groomed lawns. We visited with a priest who told us a bit of the history of the place. It was fascinating, indeed.

As we returned to Buckler's Hard, we walked along a footpath. Beautiful estates could occasionally be seen in the distance and sometimes hand woven wooden fences separated the path from the homes. There is a freedom of access to the countryside in England that was new to us. At the same time there was a kind of aristocracy with which the English seemed more comfortable than we were.

Next morning, with the ebb, we sailed down the Beaulieu to the mouth and then back into the Solent. Just to the east was Cowes on the Isle of Wight. We had been paying about twenty pounds per night for dockage, but we had been warned that at Cowes, the center of sailing in England, things would be much more expensive. We sailed up the river Medina and found a pontoon with an available space. We tied up and before long a man in a boat came by to collect our fees. As it turned out it cost only nine pounds per night. It was the cheapest dock we had found in England. We were a bit dismayed to find that there was no walkway to shore. We would have to take the dinghy. We walked through town that day, exploring myriads of marine stores and chandleries. We found a museum where the gaff of the yacht Britannia was suspended from the ceiling. The curator, a lady, told us of her grandfather's days sailing on the great yacht. Off the shore, Beneteau Yachts were having their World Championships. It was a sailor's dream.

The following day we bought a rail pass and toured the island by bus and train. Part of the way we rode a double-decker bus giving us view of the countryside from a second story window. We stopped at Newport, Ryde and then Sandown where there is an impressive display of dinosaur bones. Finally we went to Yarmouth, where we found The Bugle. Outside, the harbor was busy with yachts coming and going and sailing in the sparkling Saturday afternoon sun. Someone was getting married in an old church down the road, and he and his lovely bride were about to run away in an ancient white limousine. Flowers were in bloom everywhere. That is when we stepped into this lovely old inn, The Bugle, and had a quiet drink. It was glorious England in summer. It was a moment to be saved in poetry, a bit of what we had come for.

Across from the Isle of Wight, just to the east, is Portsmouth. We met Chris and Carol Evans from *Lhasa* there and enjoyed the area with them. Navigating the busy harbor is a story in itself. First, one must call harbor control and announce his or her intentions. Then he may only cross shipping channels at right angles to the direction of shipping and only when the coast is clear. It is a very busy place. Three attractions dominate the port: the *Victory*, the *Warrior* and the *Mary Rose*.

The *Victory*, carrying 104 guns in three tiers, is an impressive three masted wooden vessel. The place where Lord Nelson was standing when he was shot and the place where he died are carefully memorialized aboard the ship. Nelson was a hero of enormous stature in England in his day. *Victory* was the flagship of the British fleet when they won the Battle of Trafalgar. The officer's mess was a beautiful cabin aboard the ship. Among other interesting facts about the ship was that the ration of beer was eight pints per man per day. At the same time it was a rule that men not "appear" intoxicated. The vessel is no longer afloat, but a permanent exhibit on shore.

The *Warrior* was a complete surprise to me. I had always thought that the Americans had built the first ironclad ships for use during our Civil War. Not so. In 1860, *Warrior* was launched. She was a combination sail and steam vessel built with an iron hull four inches thick. The hull was backed with eighteen inches of teak and lined with a three quarter inch thick iron liner. Her cannon fired rifled, breach loading shot, which made every existing fort and warship in the world obsolete. She was so feared that not even England's traditional enemies ever fired a shot at her in anger. Both her smoke stack and her propeller were retractable. It took the strength of 600 men pulling together to hoist her 24-ton propeller and shaft into an aperture in her hull. She could make 11 knots under sail, 14 under steam and 17 using both sail and steam. It took six men to handle her helm under full power, a serious design weakness. Although her cannon were "state of the art" they tended to overheat and explode. The British sold her original cannon to the American Confederacy, which used them in the defense of Richmond, Virginia. All the cannon on the *Warrior* today are plastic reproductions.

The story of her restoration is amazing. She had been abandoned after her useful life ended. She deteriorated into nothing more than a coal bunker. After she was rediscovered, a successful brewer bought her and spent a fortune on her restoration. The restorers removed two and a half feet of concrete from her decks and replaced it with teak. They spent eight years on the restoration whereas the original construction of the ship was completed, from drawings to launch, in 17 months. We had never seen such a magnificent job. From her teak decks, iron masts and "working" replica steam engine, she was simply magnificent. I admired the rifles lining the walls below and the carousels of Colt pistols ready to arm the marines at a moment's notice. Her wardroom was elegant and the dented copper pots in her galley shone like mirrors. What a proud lady she was. She was afloat, too, looking ready to back from her slip and sail out to sea.

The third ship on display in the harbor was the *Mary Rose*. She was built in 1511, and was the first English ship built purely as a warship. Thirty-four years later, in 1545, she was in the Solent, heading from Portsmouth toward the coast where some French ships had come to invade England. Henry VIII had dinner with the captain the night before she left, and he sent her off to do battle with the French. She was fully loaded and had her normal crew of 415 along with 300 others. To show her resolve, all her guns were run out as the sails were raised. King Henry watched from his seaside castle (Built from Beauleiu Abbey stone) and the shores were lined with onlookers. As the sails were raised, a gust of wind caused her to heel, water rushed into the lower gun ports, she heeled farther and she tipped over and sank.

About half the ship was recovered in the 1980's and she has been undergoing restoration ever since. She was being sprayed with a plastic "wax" that, by 2011, would stabilize her hull. We watched the process through glass windows in the shed where she was being stored and treated. Meanwhile artifacts of wool, pewter, leather, wood and silk have been recovered, remarkably in tact. Her bronze and iron cannon are in fine condition. There are needles and wool hats that look as though they might have come from any museum. Hundreds of artifacts are on display in the museum dedicated to the *Mary Rose*. Again, this was a worthwhile and memorable exhibit.

The next day we followed Chris and Carol up the Hamble River to the yard where Moody yachts are built. We stayed at the Moody Marina there where we filled in paperwork as though we were entering the country. It was pointed out to us that there are few American boats in England. It is true. We hadn't seen another Stars and Stripes since our arrival in Plymouth.

That night we enjoyed steak and kidney pie with a few pints of Old 66 Ale at "The Jolly Sailor," another delightful pub with walk-in fireplaces and wonderful ambiance. The next morning we sailed down the foggy river, passing the thousands of yachts moored there, and headed west, through the Needles and past the Shingles toward Weymouth, where we would spend another night tied fourth from the wall, without water or electricity. In other words, the harbor was so crowded we were rafted to another boat which was rafted to two others. When we left our boat, we would have to climb over three other boats to get to shore. It was, to say the least, inconvenient, but the price was still 20 pounds.

The next day we again found ourselves motoring west. There was little wind, but it was westerly and we motored against it. Rather than go straight to Plymouth, we decided to call the Brixham Yacht Club on the cell phone and see whether they had room for us at their pontoon. Sure enough, there was a spot, so we sailed into the harbor and tied to the float. Like Cowes, we had to use our own dinghy to get to shore, but that was no problem. The yacht club was busy. They were having a dinner that night and we were invited to join the festivities. We visited with local sailors and enjoyed a few pints of ale while we waited for the dinner to be served. A friendly man named Roger insisted that Americans didn't know how to enjoy good whiskey because they always mixed it with water and drank it over ice. After dinner he brought me a glass of "good English whiskey" and asked me to drink it slowly, enjoy the aroma, warm it with my hands and savor the moment. That was not a problem for me. What a delight it was to spend 20 pounds for dockage, dinner and drinks, rather than just for dockage.

Early the next morning we walked along a footpath to Berry (means fortress) Head, a defensive headland used since prehistoric times for the defense of England. The first defenders there were in 660 B.C. The sky was pure blue for a change and the sea was calm. Birds migrate to Berry Head from the Arctic, Africa, and Northern Europe. It is a stunning place to visit and we enjoyed a cup of coffee at a small restaurant nearby. By 1:30 in the afternoon, the tide finally shifted and we sailed round the head, viewing the spectacular headland from shore. We continued on to Plymouth, where we found an anchorage for the evening. For some reason on the 24th of July they had an amazing fireworks display. We never talked with anyone ashore to find out why, but it was truly impressive from our anchorage in the bay.

From Plymouth we continued on to Fowey (rhymes with boy) and Pulruin, the town on the other side of the bay. Liz and Dave Jolleff lived in Fowey in a home overlooking the entrance to the harbor. Liz was recovering, in some discomfort, from her ankle fracture suffered in the Azores. It was great to see them. It was they who suggested that we visit the Eden Project, a short distance away.

So the next day we bussed and walked to the part of Cornwall called The Eden Project. (If you arrive on foot the entry fee is cheaper.) Here huge white, semi-transparent domes, resembling giant golf balls, and suspended by pumped-in air, enclose flora and fauna representing various climates of the world. In separate enclosures, there were plants from the jungles of Africa to the desert-like climate of Southern California. They were impressive to walk through and inspiring in that they showed how good environmental practices could reclaim land decimated by mining and the resulting erosion. The park was built on the site of an abandoned mine where clay had been taken and turned into fine English china. Recycling is a major theme here as is energy conservation. It was a kind of Disneyland atmosphere celebrating nature. Outside the domes, flowers and shrubs were blooming along paths and walkways. It was a fragrant and colorful treat. Obviously, it is a large and expensive undertaking and a very worthwhile one.

Falmouth is a rather large city at the mouth of the river Fal. We bypassed the city and sailed upriver to Smuggler's Cottage, a small inn where General Eisenhower met with English officers to plan the D-Day invasion of France. We picked up a mooring outside the inn and went inside for lunch where we visited with the proprietor who told us he was a very young man at the time of the invasion, but that he had a dim memory of it. Outside there were photos and articles posted around the property as reminders of the significance of the place in the outcome of the Second World War. The cottage itself was a beautiful one with a thatched roof, nestled comfortably into the countryside. *Tapestry* swung on her mooring in the river, her stars and stripes proudly flying from her backstay. Although the guidebook said there was a ten-pound mooring fee, perhaps because we flew the Stars and Stripes, there was no fee for us.

01 August 2004

Hi from *Tapestry,*

After Falmouth, we again waited for tide and headed for the Helford River. Everyone has spoken of it as a "must do." The entrance is broad and easy, so we motored in and took a mooring. Ashore, we found a little town with a pub and a few stores. There was a footpath toward the headland, so we took it. It is part of a trail that goes all the way around Cornwall. There are gates where the trail crosses people's land, but the land is deeded as a trail and it will be here forever. There are bridges, walls, and elevated parts, but it is definitely a trail and these trails are open to everyone. We walked two or three miles to the mouth of the river and back, and we passed perhaps a dozen other hikers along the way. Walking is a popular pastime in England.

When we returned, we went to the pub for lunch. I had a "pasty," meat and potatoes in a thick crust, with salad and a pint of local beer. Tin miners used to take pasties into the mines with them to eat at noon.

A large part of the World War II D-Day invasion came from this river as well as from Falmouth. Before the invasion, thousands of landing craft had to be hidden under tarps along the river. Many of the troops who took part waited here as well. When the man came by to collect mooring fees, he saw the American Flag, and passed us by.

From there we sailed (motored) to Penzance. You remember The Pirates of Penzance? This is the one. It is a town very near Land's End. This harbor "dries out." That means if you anchor there your boat will be on its side half the time. Not good. However, they have a small harbor controlled by a lock door. They open the door one hour before high tide, and close it two hours after high tide. We arrived a bit early and had to wait at a buoy outside. Inside we rafted to a French boat with three young men aboard. The town is just a town, but several miles away, a short bus ride, there is a castle called St. Michael's Mount, built on a tall pointy island. There is a path to shore that is only available at low tide. Lifeboats carry hundreds of tourists out to see the place each day. It was begun in 1070, has been owned by the same family for 400 years, and has been recently deeded to The National Trust, an organization in Britain that takes over things old and beautiful, and prohibitively expensive to maintain. It is in remarkably good shape and the tour included some magnificent gothic furniture in room settings that were comfortably small in such a huge building. Fireplaces were everywhere, from beautiful tiny ones to huge ones, but virtually none of them work. Today it is not possible to get small boys, chimney sweeps, to clean the flues in the convoluted chimneys popular when "sweeps" were available.

That night we had dinner in a pub built in 1430. We both had fish and chips and I had a beer. When we sat down there was one couple with their kids quietly enjoying appetizers across the room. When dinner came for us, behind the waitress came 20 men and three women, all intoxicated, shouting and laughing and taking pictures of each other. There was nothing pleasant to remember about that meal.

Next morning we walked to Newlyn, the next town, and back. We left the harbor, and passed through the doors with the tide around one that afternoon, and waited on a buoy outside the harbor till morning. We motored from there to the Isles of Scilly.

These islands are past Land's End and according to the Pilot are hazardous to the newcomer. As it turns out, the entrance is well marked and we easily picked up a mooring in St. Mary's Harbor. The islands are owned by Prince Charles, but inhabited by fishermen and others. There are 365 islands at low tide and 52 at high tide. Everyone who lives here pays rent to the Prince. The Islands are serviced by helicopter and plane and one ferry. They are expensive and very exclusive tourist destinations. We launched the dinghy and walked around a bit. We found a number of restaurants, but ended up standing in line fifty minutes for fish and chips, take away. The man next to us had been part of a classic automobile 'round the world' race and entertained us with stories of his adventure the whole time. Besides, anything with a line that long has to be good. It was one of the tastiest meals we had while we were in England.

Next morning we again took the dinghy to shore. What to do with the dinghy is always a problem. The tides here are 6 meters. That is about 20 feet. The answer is to use a long painter and tie the boat to a ladder. We did that. We had planned to take *Tapestry* to another island that day, but with the low tide at about noon, we decided to spend the day at St. Mary's. We rented a tandem bike and covered every road we could find. We probably went about ten miles, but we did enjoy the rocky coastline and the beautiful scenery. We even stopped to purchase a pastel from a local artist, Jo Probert, as a souvenir. When we got back to the dinghy, we found our little *Triplet* on the ground twenty feet down from where we had tied it, a dozen yards or so from the water's edge. These are high tides, indeed! Scilly gets its name from the Romans; it means "sunny."

This morning, August first, the sun shone bright as we readied the boat for our sail across Biscay to Spain. A tame, banded pigeon came aboard, sometimes a portent of a storm, but left after gentle coaxing.

We had enjoyed a fine time in England, but we never saw another American boat while we were there. Perhaps it was the cost of things, maybe the weather.

Finally, back at sea, there was some wind. Ten knots were forecast along with thundery rain. We got the rain and thunder all right, along with a good bit of lightning, but now, at 5:30 the skies have cleared and the wind is just over 20, fortunately, from the port quarter. Next stop, La Coruna, Spain, 348 miles away. All the best, Hank and Julie

Chapter 31

Biscay and La Coruna

We sailed across the Bay of Biscay and then visited the city of La Coruna on the mainland of Europe, the northwest corner of the Iberian Peninsula. We had been warned by Chris Harrison: "Get across Biscay as quickly as possible and if at all possible, do it before the first of August. It is no place to linger." Hundreds of ships have been lost here after being driven into the bay by westerly gales and finding themselves unable to escape. Of course, in the old days ships didn't have reliable diesel engines as we do, but a word to the wise…

Perhaps the best way to tell the story of our crossing and of our time in La Coruna is to quote from an original E-mail source.

10 August, 2004

Hello from Spain,

When I last wrote, the clouds were clearing as we sailed across The Bay of Biscay. With the clearing skies, the wind dropped and we motored nearly 50 hours till we approached the continental shelf. Here the water drops from 4000 meters to 200 meters in about 20 miles. If it is windy from the west, it can be horribly dangerous. But winds were calm as we approached. As we drew nearer, the breezes switched from south to west and grew to about fifteen knots. It was very dark under cloudy skies, around midnight. I shut down the engine and raised sails; within fifteen minutes I had added a deep reef to the main. Waves were building and *Tapestry* surged ahead. Things were manageable, but sleeping impossible and, well, one's imagination tends to soar. At

25 knots the winds steadied and then dropped as we approached La Coruna.

The marina here is delightful. It is right in town and modern with laundry and other facilities close by. Nice.

Betsy, Julie's sister, had contacted her former exchange student, Miguel, who lived here. Julie had taught Chemistry to three of the five siblings in Miguel's family. We wanted to contact them. On Wednesday, the day we arrived, we slept much of the day, but Thursday we found Miguel. We had lunch with him in a fine restaurant, at around three.

Dinner? We met Rosa, his girlfriend, and enjoyed dinner at the new restaurant of a friend. Delightful. We finished at about midnight. On Friday we explored the city, from the Roman built lighthouse to the internet café, to the Millennium Obelisk. Spectacular. Isabel, Miguel's sister picked us up at 8. We visited his mother's apartment overlooking the city where we enjoyed cool white wine. Then it was on to Miguel's apartment and more wine with dinner. We were back at the boat around 2 a.m. Most of our meals consisted of mussels, which are harvested in great quantity here, octopus, squid, tiny minnow-like fish, small green peppers, and bread. Soft cheese is also often part of the meal. Of course, there is wine. Foods are cooked in different sauces and beautifully presented. Meals often take hours. Truly, to these people, a meal is a ceremony. Oh, and the ceremony begins late, generally after nine. Dinner is always a late affair by American standards, and one generally returns home, in our case back to the boat, well after midnight. Still, even at 2 a.m., we found affable people in the streets. Sidewalks were peopled with friendly smiling folks. Of course, there are few people with guns in Spain and we felt no fear in the streets of La Coruna, even in the early morning hours.

On Friday we drove with Miguel and Rosa, about two hundred miles exploring the rocky Spanish coastline. We drove south past several estuaries, exploring ancient dwellings at Castro de Baiona. We met Rosa's parents at Portosin, where they fish, grow fresh vegetables and raise poultry, to sell at the local market. We enjoyed a large lunch at Isla de Arosa, and then a Spanish omelet at Rosa's home. Saturday night we ate canned lasagna on board. So much food!.

Sunday we went to Miguel's mother's to meet the rest of the family, all of whom had returned to La Coruna for the weekend. There were Mrs. Paya and the children who are no longer students. Miguel, is a civil engineer, Javier, a lawyer, Carmen, an international wine merchant, Beatrix, a physician/psychiatrist, and Isabel, a research pharmacist. All of the children had spent time in the U.S. and were fluent in English. We had a delightful dinner, and afterward, "a little whiskey is good for the digestion." Then the whole family, including Beatrix's two infant children and Mrs. Paya, came to see the boat. It was a wonderful day.

It was Isabel and Beatrix who wanted to show us Santiago de Compostela, the nearby city where pilgrims from all over the world go to visit the cathedral where Saint James is buried. That would be Monday. They would meet us at noon at the marina.

Hurricane Alex, or what was left of it, had chased us to La Coruna, and the low pressure area and cold front that followed it had stirred the sea into a frenzy. We were stormed in.

The drive to Santiago was long and at lunch, Julie mentioned to Beatrix that she had been suffering from a rash on her back and under her arm. One look and the physician/friend took us right to a hospital. An intern, a second physician and the head of the neurology department examined Julie, gave her an injection for the pain, several prescriptions, and released her. She was diagnosed as having "shingles." Beatrix had interpreted and talked with the other physicians, and had facilitated her treatment. We were hours in the hospital, and when we left there was no charge. We could hardly believe the generous, helpful attitude of these wonderful people. Truly, we were humbled. By then it was seven in the evening.

"Do you still want to see the Cathedral?" asked Isabel.

Well, huge doesn't say it; magnificent, you pick the adjective. There must have been close to a thousand people inside while we were there, and it seemed empty. Begun in the 12th century, it is built on the site of the burial place of St. James. In one of the alcoves he is depicted on a great white steed, slaughtering Muslims with his sword. Perhaps that explains the rather large police presence on site. Anyway, there is also a hotel where the Catholic King and Queen, Ferdinand and Isabella stayed. Columbus talked with Queen Isabella, remember? This place is old. Souvenir shops sell silver. A nice silver chalice will cost about $1500.

We found a little restaurant along one of the narrow streets in the old city and had tapas. It was a meal of mussels and cheese and octopus and bread and, of course, a bottle of wine. We were home by midnight.

Seas are still reported to be "rough to very rough" and winds force 7 and 8. It looks as if we will be here for the next few days. There could be worse places to be stormed in! All the best! Hank and Julie

We stayed a few more days in La Corona. Julie was healing nicely, her rash was responding to the treatment and medication she had received in the hospital was working.

One of the reasons we stayed, in addition to Julie's health, was because we were waiting for mail. We had called our mail service in Florida and asked them to forward our mail by courier to the marina in Spain where we were staying. When it didn't come after the third day, we called the courier company. They located the shipment in Madrid. We waited a few more days and still, it did not show up. Finally, I asked the man at the marina, who spoke beautiful English as well as Spanish, to call for me and explain where the package should be shipped. Still, it did not come. There was only one city marina in La Coruna, how could this be so difficult? Finally, Isabel said she knew someone in the courier office. She called and had our package, which had been delivered to the oil shipping terminal rather than the marina, forwarded to her mother's address where we were able to pick it up. It all seemed terribly casual to us.

On Friday, the 13th we ordered a case of good wine as a thank you to the Paya's. They had been so wonderful to us. At the same time, we called our Englewood, Florida, bank. We received a recorded message. "We will be closed until further notice due to the approaching hurricane." We made several more calls to friends on the Key where we lived, but got no answers. Finally, we reached Janet in Martha's Vineyard.

"Doesn't look good, Henry," she said. "Category IV and heading right toward Manasota Key."

We headed for an internet café where we found the National Weather Service site which listed both Venice and Fort Myers as 99% likely to be struck. As our home in Englewood was right between, what chance did we have?

That night there was a concert at a plaza near the marina where *Tapestry* was moored. It was a spectacular show featuring some of Spain's leading singers. It was nationally televised and featured giant TV screens, flashing lights, smoke, the works.

Plus, there were well over a thousand people there. It was wonderful and all free.

Saturday morning we learned that Hurricane Charley had made an unexpected right turn at the last minute and had gone into Charlotte harbor and missed Englewood altogether. Whew! To celebrate our good fortune, we decided to cast off the lines and head south to Camarinas. Strong headwinds soon turned us back, however. We re-entered the marina just at dark.

On Sunday we again strolled the streets of beautiful La Coruna. We had a wonderful seafood dinner at a sidewalk café, and then returned to the marina where there was another surprise in store for us. A small decorative "fort" had been set up on the point near the marina. There were huge stereo speakers set up there as well.

We found what we thought was a good spot to watch. We saw men load and fire off huge old cannons until our ears rang. But that was just the beginning. When the festivities started in earnest, dramatic music roared from the speakers and we learned that Sir Frances Drake had landed in the harbor and was about to take the town. There was a wild battle right in front of us with men and women dressed in costume, fighting with the British soldiers. Swords, knives, and pitch forks armed the Spaniards. It was, all done to martial music with the volume way up. Of course, the cannon continued to boom in the background. By now thousands of people had gathered, most of them far behind us, to see the festivities. Those around us, like us, had fingers stuffed into their ears, as the noise was overwhelming. At this point, when the British seemed to be winning, and the fort was burning, a woman, Maria Pita, wife of a captain killed in the battle, came to the front and said, "Never stop fighting thc British." With that the music resumed and we were treated to an hour of fireworks. Colorful explosions of color came from everywhere, ahead of us, behind us and across the bay. They were truly spectacular. What a night! There is a statue of Maria Pita in the large plaza in front of City Hall, with an "eternal flame" burning at her feet. To honor her bravery and patriotism, she was awarded a military pension after the battle.

On the seventeenth of August we finally headed out of La Coruna. We had been so wonderfully welcomed by our friends and this generous city, it was truly difficult for us to leave. Rain drops were falling as we left the harbor, but winds were reasonable, although they were forecast to again increase later in the week.

Chapter 32

Camarinas

We arrived in Camarinas that evening and found a slip in the marina. We walked through the little town and were impressed with the women and girls working at making lace. Groups of teenage kids might be gathered around a few girls who were busy weaving thread between pins on a board, which would later become expensive lace. The stores sold the finished products and they were beautiful in an age-old tradition.

Unfortunately, *Tapestry's* steering still wasn't right. Again, we noticed that the boat tended to weave back and forth under autopilot much as it had in the Caribbean. I took the bed apart and stared at the quadrant and the rudder post, but couldn't really see a problem. But when Julie appeared with our "million candlepower" searchlight and a mirror, I knew something was about to happen. We shined that light into the abyss surrounding the shaft and reflected the light up under the quadrant, and there it was. There was a stainless steel plate which was badly corroded and which connected the hydraulic cylinder to the shaft. Apparently it had been overlooked at both Saint Martin and at Antigua. As there were no pleasure boat facilities in the area, we hiked to a building with a marine railway, which we thought must be a boat building facility. Inside the door we were met by the strong smell of fish and were told we had found our way to a fish packing plant. The secretary there, however, spoke English and was able to direct us to a machine shop.

When I opened the door of that shop, there was a large drill press, a band saw, and a lathe. There was stainless steel stock near by. I knew we had come to the right place. The man there, however, spoke very little English. I managed to get across to him that I had a boat in the harbor and that I needed some work done. He understood and right away he turned to a younger assistant, Pepe. They spoke rapidly in Spanish and then the young man's face lit up. I understood that he would be at the boat in a short time. He went outside and started his car as Julie and I headed back to the boat.

A few minutes later Pepe was standing on the finger pier next to *Tapestry*. He had a young boy, Juan, probably nine or ten years old, with him. He was his son, he explained, and he asked if it would be all right if they came aboard. Actually, we communicated mostly with my Spanish, and though I was quite sure it was pretty good, he didn't verbally respond to any of it. The little boy, though, was wonderful. He didn't say anything, but his eyes missed nothing. He gazed at the galley and the forward stateroom. He was too shy to think about opening a door, so I took him around. I remember when I was young, I too was fascinated with boats and trucks and airplanes. It was wonderful to see and share his enthusiasm. His father was sure the boy knew some English from school, but no word passed his lips.

Meanwhile, we showed the mechanic the problem and he understood right away. He immediately took tools from his case and went to work disassembling our steering system. In a few minutes he had come to the piece in question. Sure enough, it was almost rusted through and was corroded and loose where the key on the rudder shaft came in contact with it. In fact, it looked as though it could fail at any moment. He carefully lifted the corroded stainless steel piece from the shaft and looked at me.

"*Manana*," he said.

I must have looked concerned as he bit his lip and then pointed to his tools. "*Manana, Manana*." He insisted. He got up to leave and left a large tool box on the floor of the pilothouse. I took that to mean that he would be back in the morning with the replacement part. He and his son climbed through the companionway and headed back to their car leaving our steering system in pieces, one crucial part missing. But, I was reassured by the large tool box on the floor, that he would be back, and soon. Sure enough, first thing the next morning, there was Pepe, a shining replacement part in his hand. It was beautifully made and, hopefully, of good grade stainless. As he had spent his career working on fishing boats, I had high hopes. He slipped the fitting over the end of the shaft and within a few minutes the system was back in working order, but this time there was no question. There was absolutely no play in the system; success at last.

While we waited, another gale had come up. Winds were about 35 knots and huge waves crashed over the wall of the port. We were not about to leave. We were enjoying our stop and so another day or so was not a problem. In the meantime, Julie had run out of her pain prescription. We weren't sure just what it was, but it had worked really well and the prescription was good for a refill. We found a pharmacy in town and when Julie laid the script on the counter, the pharmacist disappeared in the back room, I checked my wallet to be sure I had enough cash. In a moment, the lady returned, laid the package on the counter and in English she said,

"That will be two Euros one cent." I could not believe that I had heard her correctly. We both stared at this lady who misunderstood our incredulity for hostility.

"You must pay me two Euros, one pence or you may not have your prescription!" She was standing tall and her voice was firm. I quickly reached into my pocket and produced the coins and then reached for the package. She frowned, pushed the penny back toward me and said.

"Now you must leave."

She didn't get high marks for courtesy, but one thing is for certain, the price was right.

Before long the weather had cleared and we again headed south. Ahead of us was Cape Finisterre, which in Latin means "the end of the earth." Fortunately when we rounded, the winds were calm. It is one of the Great Capes and sailors are warned to use caution. We stopped in Cascais, in Portugal, where we visited Lisbon and even the Royal Palace in Sintra. From there it was on to Lagos, rhymes with 'by gosh'. Portugal did not disappoint us. Their enthusiasm for sailing and sailors was evident from the start. In Lagos we saw a yacht club with 80 Optimist dinghies, some of them in aluminum. They had large fleets of stars and snipes and dragons to name a few. Local sailboat races made the television news every night.

But our American friends, Dick and Eileen Bishop and Frank and Gail Adshead had found a place in southern Spain they thought would be perfect to leave the boat over the winter. It was Rota, located in Cadiz Bay, and they were there already. We decided on a marathon two-day sail and headed for Rota. We continued down the West Coast of Portugal and then swung east along the Algarve until just before sunset one evening, the outer wall of Rota pulled into view. We could see the warships at the military installation across the bay, but we were headed for the marina at the fishing harbor. The lights of the town were twinkling on. What a beautiful summer night.

Chapter 33

Rota, Spain

There were our friends waving to us from the wall as we pulled in to the harbor. They directed us to a slip. What a sight! The night was warm and soft and gentle and *Tapestry* behaved beautifully as I guided her into her slip. I idled the engine for just a minute or two until she had a chance to cool off, and then we shut her down. The evening was filled with the quiet sounds of water lapping on shore, the hushed talk of fishermen, quiet engines and other sounds of evening. We opened a bottle of wine and the six of us shared our wonder at the past year's adventure. Somehow it was time for closure, for an end to the magnificent year we had all shared.

There were nights of watching community performances of flamenco dancing and dinners in little restaurants along the streets, a day trip to Cadiz. We were excited that our nephew, Toby, Julie's sister, Betsy's son, a U.S. Army Captain, stationed in Germany and headed for Afghanistan, would be able to visit us over the Labor Day weekend. We shopped and planned a wonderful party for Toby. We rented a car and were all set to pick him up at the airport when we got an e-mail. His C.O. had changed his mind. He wouldn't be getting the time off after all.

Of course, we had the party anyway, but there would be no Toby.

It was about that time that we got a very disturbing e-mail from our friends Ed and Joan, back in the States. Hastings had died. He was the young man who had been so lively and helpful to us in Tortola. He was the genius mechanic with the wonderful laugh. Hastings and his wife had been visiting Ed and Joan in the States and before he left, he had been uncharacteristically quiet. When they got back to Tortola, he was quite ill. He developed a fever, and took some aspirin. When he got more and more ill, his doctor thought it might be some rare disease associated with the filth found in the bilges of boats. His condition suddenly worsened and he died. The autopsy showed he had suffered a ruptured appendix.

I remember a surgeon friend of mine who said a cardinal rule of medicine is "Don't look for zebras." If it gallops like a horse, looks like a horse and smells like a horse... Apparently whoever diagnosed Hastings hadn't heard of that rule. Suddenly things weren't going quite so well. It was time to go home.

We made flight reservations and contacted the local police about placing the boat in bond. It would then be sealed and the clock would be stopped on our eighteen month time limit in the European Community. In spite of our loss, the memory of the last days in Rota and the trip back to Florida were happy ones.

We made arrangements to haul the boat the day before we left, as they would not allow us to stay aboard, even one night, once she was on land. It was explained to us that we would have just one hour for the mechanical lift to haul the boat and set it in place in the yard.

When it came time to haul the boat we were right on time. We had filled the tanks with fuel, there was no wind, a lull in the tide, a perfect time for hauling a boat. But the boys at the hoist were unimpressed.

"You have to go to the office first." they had said.

"What?" I said as the boat danced between the rough concrete walls of the slip.

"To the office. You must pay your bill and show us a receipt before we can haul you." said the man seated on the travel lift.

I got off the boat and headed at a run for the office that was way out on the end of the pier. Then I realized I had forgotten the checkbook and returned to the boat for it. Several people in the yard watched as I dashed into the cabin and then set off again in the hot morning sun.

Of course, I was third in line at the office, and those ahead of me were not as anxious as I. They visited and flirted with the girls behind the desk as I sweated and did my best to look cool. When it was my turn, they told me that the computer was down and they would have to figure our bill all out by hand.

"Now, how many days water, electric?" said the blonde girl who kept blowing wisps of hair out of her eyes. "And a ten per cent discount for paying in advance. You will have hauling and hard storage...."

It was endless. Finally the girl gave me the total in Euros.

"I want to pay in dollars." I said. I knew that was a mistake as soon as the words escaped my lips, but as it turned out, I was wrong.

"Just write the check in dollars for the same amount,"she said.

I did what she asked and she stamped "paid" on the bill. What a nice surprise. I knew the hour we had been allowed for hauling was almost up, so I hurried and tried to run back to the boat, only to find *Tapestry* cozily resting in her cradle, braced for winter. Julie had coaxed the men into getting the job done on time and tended to the many details of properly bracing the hull.

We had visited the Guardia Civil the day before to arrange the bonding. The Commandant had signed our forms and had promised to bond the boat on Saturday night at 2000, or eight o'clock. We worked like slaves all day Saturday till just before eight. Sure enough, right on time, two young men showed up with forms for me to sign and a paper to tape over the companionway. In ten minutes the deed was done. We went from the water to bonded for the winter in just 8 hours. Whew! We grabbed clean clothes and headed for the shower. Our 'wheeled duffels' groaned and rattled behind us as we walked along the cobble stone street, loaded with an extra bag and the computer. The showers were busy that Saturday night. Then it hit us. We left our towels on the boat.

As the boat was bonded, there was no going back. It was locked and sealed. Sweaty and grimy, we turned toward our hostel. We rattled along past restaurants and dressed up Spaniards dining at sidewalk tables who, at least in my imagination, cast disparaging glances our way. I fumed. But the hostel had a fine room with a clean bath and shower, and snowy white towels. Before long we were clean and appropriately dressed and off to a night on the town.

Next morning we hiked toward the bus terminal. The hostel keeper explained that the coffee machine was too noisy to use at 7:30 in the morning, and of course, no restaurants were open at that hour. We boarded the 8:30 bus, hungry. A little KAS soda held us over until we finally found breakfast at the terminal at Sevilla. Our hotel, the Alcazar, was very near the bus station. We were stopped on the way by a man who offered us a room for 12 euros each. We turned him down and found the Alcazar delightful. It was air conditioned, a good idea in Sevilla, clean, and the price included a full breakfast. We spent the day at the real Alcazar, touring the garden and the beautiful palace. We even rented a four wheeled pedal yourself buggy for a garden tour. That night we had, perhaps our best meal ever in Spain. Our table was outside a cheap hotel and next to a parked motorcycle, but the host was delightful, the salad fresh, crisp and tasty, and the fish stew, complete with clams, mussels, and periwinkles in their shells, delicious. It was just around the corner from the fancy places, but the price was right and it turned out to be the beginning of a fine evening.

On Monday we toured the cathedral. It is the largest Gothic cathedral in Europe and the third largest in the world. Some of the massive columns that support the roof/ceiling were crumbling at the base and the reconstruction effort was truly impressive. One cannot help being awed by any edifice so large, so beautifully proportioned and so simply massive. The work involved is unfathomable. Anyway, Mass was being chanted while we were there and a few hundred worshippers were seated in the nave. Tourists milled about, taking photographs, and it was business as usual on a Monday morning. I looked down one time and at my feet was a rectangular plaque with 'Cristobal Colon' written on it. The grave of Christopher Columbus was right below me. Wow! It is a long way across that ocean. I know!

Before lunch we got our bags and waited for bus 21 which would take us to the high speed train to Madrid. The bus was crowded, standing room only. Because we were traveling to catch a plane, we got a 25 per cent discount on the train. The train was a real surprise. Seats were comfortable, the ride was very fast and smooth. Most amazing was the sound. It was quiet, much quieter than a plane or car. We could use some trains like that in the U.S.

Our hotel in Madrid was the Orly. The room was on the seventh floor of an old building. The hotel was truly grim from the street, but there was an elevator and the room was clean with its own bath and a balcony, which overlooked the noisy street. We walked to the Plaza Mayor for another outdoor dinner. Clams from certifiably bad beds and wilted, soggy salad went poorly with weak sangria.

On Tuesday, we made three subway connections, clicking luggage in tow, up and down stairs and escalators, to finally arrive at the airport. The attendant at the door told us that we would have to find Terminal 1. It was a long walk. When we got there, another 'guide' assured us he had never heard of Delta Airlines. But he was wrong. It was right there and we were in plenty of time for our flight. Madrid is a very large airport that gets even bigger if one wheel on your baggage goes sideways as one of mine did. The flight was fine. We had two meals and lots of cool drinks. It was the best flight we had experienced in years.

Bob Markus met us at the airport back in Tampa, and we were home in Englewood by 9:30 that night. Of course there was no water at the condo, the car wouldn't start, and the phones didn't work. But then Charley had missed us and Hurricane Ivan wasn't heading our way either. Our plan was to weather the winter in Florida and return to *Tapestry* in the spring.

Little did we know that a second bout with breast cancer faced Julie, along with the agony of chemotherapy and discomfort and uncertainty that goes with it. Would we be back in Rota in 2005? We wondered, was this the end of a dream or a bump in the road? Only time would tell.

Part II

Exploring

The

Med.

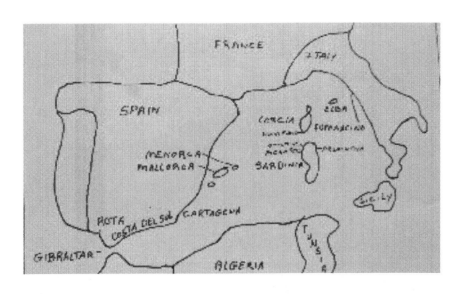

Chapter 34

EASTWARD

After the crossing, and back in Englewood, we packed the car and headed for Ashville, NY. It was late summer. The boat was safely stored in Rota, Spain. Back home, Julie had an appointment with a doctor. There was a problem.

After sixteen years, her breast cancer had returned. It was the same breast as the previous condition. This time there would be a mastectomy; there would again be chemo and radiation. My poor wife, after defeating polio and breast cancer the first time, was again afflicted. Here we were with the largest investment we had ever made, our girl, *Tapestry*, in Spain, and Julie suffering from this life-threatening disease.

The surgery went well and we made arrangements with a treatment laboratory in Venice, Florida, to take over the chemotherapy when we got there. A port was surgically implanted in Julie's chest where the chemo would be inserted. It had a direct line to her heart. We bought a new car, a VW Passat, diesel. We were going to get through this. Julie lost her hair this time, but she never missed an appointment. We walked, we exercised, we did what we could. She even rode her bike on 30 mile club rides in Florida with a chemo pack at her waist. There was no sign of spread. By early spring, it looked as if she would be okay. She wanted the port removed, but those administering the treatments thought I should learn to flush it instead of their removing it. That way, if she should need further treatment…

But Julie wanted nothing to do with that. She found a physician who was willing to remove the port, scheduled it, and in a few days the job was done. We made reservations and before long we were on our way back to Spain and *Tapestry*. Hooray! We were healing and we were traveling and, to help get through this, Julie brought her paints, sketched and painted as we went. Me? I wrote a few poems.

Rota

A small town
On the Southern Coast of Spain
The Algarve.
Home to Ponce de Leon,
One of Columbus' pilots,
And the U.S. Navy;
Thousands of scooters,
Narrow streets,
Small cars,
Friendly Spaniards,
Wide beaches,
Narrow glasses of hot coffee,
Flamenco dancers,
Late night dinners,
In Tasteful restaurants.

Rota, a place to
Come home to.

Swaying palms,
Friends,
A little bit of home,
In Southern Spain.

H.R.D.

Of course, the first thing we had done when we got our airline reservations, was to schedule *Tapestry's* launch. They would have painted the bottom and have the boat ready when we arrived. There was an issue. "The Festival of the Horse" was a big deal in Spain, and it would be happening and we would need to have the boat launched within four hours of our arrival, or wait two weeks when the festival was over. Obviously, not wanting to wait two weeks, we opted for the immediate option. After the flight to Madrid, the train ride and bus to Rota, we found ourselves dragging our bags over the rough streets on the way to the marina. Quite intentionally, we stopped at the local police station. The police agreed that they would send a man right away to remove the official bonding from our boat. We thanked them, and headed out the door. As we walked along, our bags bumping behind us, a police car zoomed by. We broke into a run. Did we have to be there when the bonding was removed?

We made it to the marina just as the policemen were searching for a ladder. They climbed into the boat, removed the seal and that was it. The E.U. clock had started again. We walked to the marina office where we were informed the boat would be launched right away. There was another hitch, however. Remember the frozen thru-hull valve we wanted replaced in Antigua? The one the folks in Antigua just didn't have time to tend to before the ARC began? They were supposed to have replaced it in Rota over the winter, but... something about the language.

I asked the man in charge and he looked at me with wide eyes. Did it really need it to be replaced? Yes, I was sure we really needed it. With that he looked at the thru-hull on the bottom of the boat, dashed for his car and sped off out of the marina. Now what? I wondered. Meantime another man who was not an English speaker climbed with me into the boat. I took him to the aft cabin where we removed the mattress from the bed and the plywood boards underneath. I got him a wrench and a screw driver and he removed the hose and struggled to remove the valve from the thru-hull connection. I heard a car pull up outside and then there was the yard foreman in the cockpit, the valve in hand. He had a tube of sealer as well and he began applying it to the threads. Meanwhile, there was a deep rumble in the air. I looked out and the huge travel lift was coming our way. I could hardly believe my eyes. The vehicle straddled our boat, straps were attached fore and aft and with the men still working in the aft cabin to attach the valve, we began to be lifted from our winter cradle and moved toward the water. Over the haul out slip, the boat was gently lowered into the clear water as the men finished up their installation. No leaks!

I pushed the stop button and turned over the engine for ten seconds or so to move oil to the cylinders of the engine after its long winter rest, and then, when I released the button, the engine burst to life. A smooth stream of water flowed from the exhaust. Everything was fine. We were back in the water. It had been a harrowing 24 hours.

We had driven our rental car to Tampa airport, where we turned it in, and boarded our plane for Madrid. In Madrid we had taken a train and a bus to Rota where we frantically launched the boat all in a period of 24 hours. It was time for food and sleep. We were exhausted.

We took a slip for several days at the marina and we enjoyed the area. There were outdoor presentations at night, music and dance. With our friends on *Triumph* and *Sugilite*, we attended the "Festival of the Horse" where men in formal dress with black suits, ties and hats demonstrated their skill and horsemanship. Women and little girls in high heels ran alongside. It was an amazing community event. There were parades and demonstrations; it was wonderful.

Chapter 35

GIBRALTAR

The Rock

Under the Rock at Gibraltar
We swing back and forth.
Should we go ashore?
Low clouds shroud its massive strength
Jutting above the strait
Defying wind and weather,
Guardian of the West,
Symbol of endurance.
We, in our plastic boat,
Waver.
We plunge ahead, slowly,
As the plates beneath us grind,
And even "The Rock"
Moves.

H.R.D.

Back on the boat, we pushed off from the marina at Rota and headed for Gibraltar. I remember a former football coach at Jamestown High School telling me a story about Gibraltar. He had been in the Navy in WW II. He was on a destroyer and worked in the engine room. He specialized in diesel engines and because he was good at what he did, he was transferred from his ship to another ship in the fleet that, after crossing the Atlantic, desperately needed his services. He was angry at having to leave his friends. When Gibraltar came in sight, the fleet came under a U-boat attack. The ship he had been on was lost, with few survivors.

I could hardly get that picture from my mind as we entered the channel to the Mediterranean Sea. Powerful currents determine passage for small boats and shipping always has the right of way. Thirty thousand ships each year make the passage. The ancients believed the cliffs on either side of the straits were the Pillars of Hercules. They separated the Mediterranean from the Atlantic, heaven from hell, the real world from the mythical one.

We entered the harbor at the great rock and dropped anchor near the airport. At first, we anchored in Spanish waters, but then we moved to the English side where we would check in. We could take the dinghy to shore and shop in the city there. It is a small city, but when cruise ships drop thousands, it becomes very crowded. We did a tour of the Rock by taxi rather than by tram and were assailed by delightful monkeys. Unlike the shy ones we had encountered on Likoma Island in Malawi, these were eager to please. They mounted passing cars. We fed them bits of macaroni and they climbed over us. At one point Julie had two sitting on her shoulders, one parting her short hair, as it searched for lice or ticks or something. We saw gun emplacements overlooking the strait. It was an English enclave in a Spanish world. Delightful.

Gibraltar

The Pillars of Hercules,
The Gate to Hell,
At the entrance to the ancient world,
An opera house,
A still lake.
Towering caves and a
Neanderthal skull,

Island People: Deep Water Dreams

Gunpowder
And wetted wooden wedges,
Helped carve these dark tunnels;
Man-made caves that still house
Steel cannon,
As
Playful apes
Pounce on tourists,
Eat macaroni,
And fight amongst
Themselves.

H.R.D.

One night there was a "dry squall" that struck the small harbor late into the night. We woke with wind screaming through the rigging. I remember being awakened and climbing from my bunk to check our bearings. We were fine; though we had straightened our anchor chain, the anchor was holding. Ahead of us, however, a French boat had arrived after we had retired. It was dragging its anchor and moving right toward us. The boat was completely dark, the occupants apparently unaware of the impending collision. I moved to the helm in the pilothouse and in the darkness, pressed frantically on the horn button on the console, but in the screaming wind I could hear no response. On and on the boat came, narrowly missing our port side as it jerked its anchor and plowed stern first toward the airport runway just behind us. My finger was numb, but it was only after Julie turned on the pilothouse lights that I realized I had been pushing the "stop engine" button rather than the "horn" button right next to it. Fortunately, the bounding anchor on the other boat did not snag our anchor chain and dislodge our anchor. Otherwise, there would have been two boats aground rather than just one. It wasn't until the next morning that we learned the couple on the other boat had been sailing for several days and were so sound asleep they were never awakened by the storm. Winds had been 40 knots that night, serious wind, but our anchor had held; good news for us. A few days later, we were ready to head out and decided we should take advantage of the cheap fuel available there. Ahead of us the Mega-Yacht, *Clementine* was filling her cavernous tanks. A tanker truck arrived with additional fuel. It took three hours and by the time we got to the fueling station, the price difference was hardly worth the wait.

Gibraltar

Chapter 36

MOROCCO

Rather than return to Spain right away, we headed for Morocco. We transited the strait, through the Pillars of Hercules, and in spite of two freighters that made things interesting in the gusty winds and current, we had no issues. We arrived at Smir around 5:30 in the afternoon, without a scratch in spite of the strong winds and the concrete piers where we landed the boat. Smir is a very safe harbor; it is where the king of Morocco keeps his yacht! We checked in to customs and officially left the EU, so the clock would stop on our 180 day limit.

Tetouan

Rashid in a silver Mercedes,
Driven by profit,
"I will make you happy.
Police have two eyes,
They see and they don't see."
Arab women with covered faces
Sell their goods from tiny spaces.
Berber women in conical hats
Laden with goods
Turn from the camera.
Beans and lentils, dates and nuts,
Skinny chickens
Hung by the legs,
And huddling in cages;
Cigarettes one by one,
Weavers of rugs,
Sellers of gold,
Ancient narrow streets,
Very, very old,

Henry R. Danielson

"Have a sardine, grilled or cold."
Averted eyes of bearded sages,
Strawberries and fresh fruit.
"Let me show you a rug,
People die, rugs last forever.
Make me an offer,
Two-hundred years,
Silk from the mountains,
Alpaca and wool,
We take plastic,
You know what I mean?"
Speed limits on rear bumpers?
Depends what you pay.
Morocco, land of dust and sand
And
"You paid too much,
Sucker!"

HRD

The next day we did the town. Rashid picked us up in his Mercedes cab and took us to Tetouan. Morocco used to be owned by Spain and France. Casablanca was the French Capitol, and Tetouan was the Spanish capitol. It became independent in 1956. People there are Sunni, so they don't like to cause trouble. Nevertheless, there is always a policeman along whenever Americans tour the "Medina" or old city. It was fascinating. Vendors were selling everything from live chickens and parakeets to fresh meat and fish to handmade clothing and rugs. Of course, this is the land of the magic carpet and here, "You may grow old, but rugs never wear out! Guaranteed for 200 years." They started out trying to sell living room sized ones, but when they got to 3 by 5 feet, we bit and bought one that would fit the pilothouse floor on *Tapestry*. Lunch promised to be "very cheap," but it proved to be huge and expensive.

Still, the streets of the city were narrow and crooked and winding, simply wonderful. Carts loaded with a huge variety of goods from fresh vegetables to even mattresses wended their way among the vendors of oranges and strawberries and fish. Sometimes the carts were powered by smoky engines. Bedouin women carried loads of produce on their backs wearing colorful outfits and straw hats. Men, too, wore headgear and full length gowns. A man with a pack of Marlboro's sells them one at a time to passers by. Colorful doorways line the narrow walkways. Inside, some men embroider with silk thread. A clothes vendor dressed Julie and Eileen in traditional garb. In other shops jewelers work with 18 karat Moroccan gold. A man calls us to prayers from the top of the mosque. It is sensory overload. Another man grills sardines over a charcoal fire. A tannery belches foul odors into the street. Our guide seems to know everyone and receives calls on his cell phone as we walk. Always, the plain clothes man is behind us, smiling and watching.

It was six in the evening when we got back to *Tapestry*. Security guards were standing around the boat. An alarm was wailing on the radio. The new radio, in the locked pilothouse, automatically sounded an alarm if it heard a distress call. I had accidentally left the radio on while we were gone. How embarrassing. I unlocked and opened the companionway and turned the radio off. I never was able to discover what triggered the alarm. From there it was back to Spain and the Costa del Sol.

Smir, Morocco

Chapter 37

The Costa Del Sol

The Costa del Sol, the Mediterranean coast of Spain, was lovely. We stopped at several ports and had wonderful experiences at them all. Velez and the Almerimar were two places we enjoyed. There were old stores and lovely condominiums in town. Restaurants were inexpensive and the food was superb. We bought *gazpacho*, a tomato drink, in cardboard cartons. One thing that sticks in my mind was a lunch where Julie and I were simply enjoying our lunch at an inside table. There were old women at a table near by enjoying their lunch, when a group of teenage girls walked by. " *Mi abuela*!," cried one of the girls and she ran to the table occupied by the old women, and gave one of them a warm, loving hug. They visited intimately for a few moments before the young woman gave the old one a parting kiss and rejoined her friends who waited for her on the street. I was touched by the intimacy of this young lady for her grandmother. How wonderful that she would show such public affection, even breaking from her friends, for this old woman. I was moved. As an English teacher in the U.S., I knew most American children would be much more reserved when encountering a grandparent in public. They might wave, but the hugs and kisses; I would be very surprised.

A week or so later Julie and I were having dinner in a seaside restaurant with tables inside and outside along the shore. There was a family at the table with several generations present. Grandparents and parents and children, teens and younger were all there having dinner together. They were celebrating a birthday or an anniversary, something special. It was obvious that some of the teenage children had dates. Everyone was dressed up and everyone shared wine when it was served. They were supervised by their parents, of course, but they were treated as young adults and they were given a glass or two of wine. They were truly a part of the celebration. Everyone was laughing and telling stories. I was transfixed. In New York, I had to be 18 to share a glass of wine or a cocktail. Most Americans have to be 21 to do so. Do American parents ever really teach their children the wonders and dangers of alcohol, or not? Do American adolescents enjoy being treated as children at family events? Perhaps this introduction to wine has something to do with the way Spanish adolescents treat their grandparents in Spain. It was a telling moment.

As we sailed the coast, we saw thousands of greenhouses covered with huge plastic tarps. The Costa del Sol is where virtually all the vegetables consumed in the rest of Europe are grown. Some of the mountains along the North Coast of the Med are 2500 meters high. There was still snow on the top in May, though the temperature on the coast was generally in the 70's F. It was wonderful sailing.

Almerimar

What a lovely marina with stores and
Condominiums and parking and all for just
Six euros a night.
We rent a Fiat with three
Cylinders for the four of us
And tackle the roundabouts and
The motorway to go see
Granada where the Alhambra
Lies in splendor, bulging with
Tourists who appreciate
Fine architecture and wear stickers
On their shirts and follow the man with the
Flag. (Please don't lag behind!) but we're
Told the Alhambra is sold out for the day, so
We see the gardens, instead. Roses and
Flowering shrubs with mystical views over

Henry R. Danielson

Soaring planes are restful. We are not pushed
Or hurried by the man with the plastic flower
Who herds his flock while speaking several languages,
But move quietly through magic
Architecture older and more delicate
Than brick and tile.
On the way home, three cylinders takes
Us through the mountains, up
Steep hills and then down through
Switchbacks; near dizzying drop offs,
With dandelion guardrails and
Unsettling skid marks to
A mall where Julie buys
Running shoes and we
Eat Spanish dinner.
Another stitch in the tapestry
Of Europe. Triumph in
The face of rejection.
We try to squeeze into
The culture of Spain
And
 Hopefully
  A little of it
   Has rubbed off.

H.R.D.

In Almerimar we rented a car to drive to the Alhambra in
Granada. It was my first experience driving through traffic
circles. We were able to go the whole way without having to
stop but once or twice. One has to slow or stop for traffic in a
circle, and traffic all comes from the left. It was harrowing at
first, but as I got used to it; I found it worked well. Unlike traffic
lights where drivers speed up for yellow, caution, slowing was
essential for entering the circle. The roads in town were very

narrow.   Navigating our little car was challenging with motorcycles and bicycles sharing the road. I can't imagine how bus drivers do it, but they drive their huge vehicles through the city with seemingly no room to spare on either side. When we got there, we found the Alhambra had been booked solid for the day.   We toured the gardens instead.   On the way home we drove through the Sierra Nevada mountains where nothing but driver vigilance protected us from plunging off sheer roadside cliffs.

Alhambra Gate, Granada, Spain

Chapter 38

CARTAGENA

Cartagena Afternoon

The May sun beams down over Julian's Castle,
And Isaac Pearl's first submarine rests on a fountain.
Africans built this city to thwart the Roman invasion,
And Hannibal brought his elephants here to ascend the Alps,
And slow Roman advances.
City of marble and granite,
Of Roman statue
And outdoor theater.
Strategically placed;
A perfect harbor,
Conquered and conquered,
To rise again, better than
Before.
Cross shaped cranes pick at the dead
City and from the ashes,
The ancient is revisited.
The modern and the very old,
Protected by heavy steel and locked doors,
In a city in coastal Spain,
Sit side by side,
And slender women,
In fine clothing, shop and watch their men toil
Until mid afternoon,
When everyone
 Goes
   To sleep…

H.R.D.

Our last stop on the Costa del Sol was Cartagena. We planned an overnight, but fickle winds, a specialty of the Med, allowed us to stay all week. Remember Hannibal, the man who used elephants to cross the Alps and slow the Roman conquest of Europe? Cartagena was founded by Hannibal's brother. The family came from Carthage on the North African Coast, a city completely destroyed by the Romans. Cartagena is very old. In the museum there we saw pieces of human bone 1.4 million years old. Founded in 425 BC, it was a significant port even then. The Romans took it soon after and added a theater large enough to seat 5000. It had a traditional Roman stage, complete with columns, carved marble figures and beautiful walls and floors. The theater was being excavated as we watched. Every shovel full of soil revealed more items to be identified, tagged and numbered. The archeological museum is built around an early graveyard and preserves items found there. Amphorae from well before the time of Christ are on display. They were used to transport wine, olive oil, and salt fish.

The place is unique as there is no one there to clap his hands and yell should you reach out and touch something. Though these things are fragile, one is encouraged to experience them. A sculptured marble foot looked so real it seemed ready to move its toes. Some priceless vases and sculpture were behind glass. Amazingly, a driver's license or passport paid the price of admission.

Siesta

It is afternoon in Cartagena, the pure golden
Mediterranean sun pours from blue sky.
Winds northeast at twelve, a cooling breeze
In the heat of the day.
The streets of town are empty.
Tables and chairs stacked neatly,
Doors closed and only a beggar,

Henry R. Danielson

Playing his flute, gazes hopefully
Our way. His sad tune echoes
Along the narrow street.
This busy city is quiet,
Resting up for Friday night revelry,
Cocktails and late dinner.
A gentle tradition made old by
Euro values, industrial demands.
A Romantic ideal, closely held,
But slipping away.
Soft music on the radio.
Tapestry rolls gently in her slip,
Tugging at her lines. Oil checked,
Fuel and water good. We're off at
First light, bucking wind and waves
Balearics bound, plunging through
Mediterranean blue toward even greener
Grasses.

H.R.D.

Chapter 39

The Balearics

Ibiza

The islands off the coast of Spain called the Balearics was our destination. Our goal was Ibiza. At one time, during Franco's reign, it had a reputation for being a place where people who were wanted by authorities could live with impunity. During the '60's it was a place where American draft dodgers went to escape conscription to fight in the Viet Nam war. We wondered what we would find.

Of course we had to sail through the night to get there, and we arrived at about 8:30 in the morning. We found a little cove on the protected west side, and anchored in ten feet of clear water over sand. There was a lovely beach ashore and, well, it was wonderful. People were arriving at the beach and sunning themselves. There was some kind of show going on and women appeared to be modeling swimwear and cover ups on the beach in front of a film crew.

Naturally, some of the men and women sunning themselves farther down the beach had nothing on at all. Somehow, I thought we might grow to like this place. We spent the rest of the day at anchor, and the next day we headed for the city of Ibiza.

What we found there was impressive, indeed. The marina was huge, with hundreds of beautiful yachts, and wi-fi was available everywhere. Boats ranged from the most modest day sailor to the most luxurious 100 foot yacht. The marina held 350 boats. We rented a car with our friends, Dick and Eileen, from *Triumph,* and enjoyed the island. Prices were reasonable, and we found an amazing walled city. Sheer drop-offs demanded the full attention of the driver, but this was no longer the home of vagabonds or draft evaders. There was an aura of wealth about the place. Rolls Royces, Bentley's, a customized Corvette, and a twin engine, four-wheel-drive Citron 2CV, along with a beautifully restored P-1800 Volvo, like the one Julie and I had owned, fascinated old car buffs like Dick and me. The island had obviously become the home of the rich. When we got back from our drive, the marina staff was setting up a stage in the parking lot for a free concert to be held that evening. Wealthy English and German tourists enjoyed the place. Our English language was never a problem for us.

Ibiza

Chapter 40

Mallorca

From Ibiza, we headed for the Island of Mallorca. After a 30 mile sail to weather, we arrived in the harbor at Andratx, (rhymes with crotch). The harbor is protected by high rocks at the entrance, with lovely homes built on top. In the '60's it was a fishing harbor, but by the turn of the 21st century, the streets were lined with lovely tapas bars and restaurants. In June the temperatures were in the eighties and there were no bugs. Tables were available right on the water, across the street from the restaurants. The place was magical. In the evening Dick and Eileen, and Julie and I would stop for *tapas* at one of the tables on the water. We would be served by a waiter who brought food and drink across the street to our table. Later we would stroll along the sidewalk by the water where some kids were still swimming and nicely dressed adults, men in slacks and sports shirts, women in dresses, began filling the linen covered tables. Windows above were open without screens, people lounged in balconies as the sun set and lights came on.

We made two trips while we were there. The first was to Palma where a marina held many very large mega yachts. These monsters, much like those we had seen in Crown Bay in the U.S. Virgin Islands, years before, were huge and impressive, indeed. It was the trip to Soller, however, that was truly memorable.

It was a Sunday morning in June when we traveled first to Palma, then we caught the train to Soller, a port on the other side of the island. We knew the train was a "retro" affair, electric and all, but really we had no idea. The train was mahogany. The running gear was iron and very old, but the coaches were varnished mahogany, polished and smooth. That was true inside and out. In our car, the seats were leather, the ceiling was white with bright brass fixtures, but the sides were

267

varnished mahogany wood with windows that fit perfectly and slid up with a pinch of stainless steel releases to let the air in. It was beautiful! We traveled through the mountains for about an hour to Soller. We passed houses with closed shutters and hundreds of roses and flowering plants in their yards; past horses and corrals, past olive and fig and almond orchards, past mountain scenes to take your breath away. We wove across trestles and through tunnels, one of which left us for seven minutes in the dark. This was not your modern railroad. The tracks were not welded, but just bolted in place and the cars bounced and wove, and groaned back and forth. An open window made the sound loud, like a radio left on too high. In the tunnels the smell was dank and musty. The ride reflected an earlier time.

At the Soller station we got off the train and picked up a street car to the port city of Soller. If I had been thrown back to my father's era in the train, imagine the street car. It was what my parents had talked about as a "summer car" in their youth. It was what used to take them to Celeron or Midway Park along the lake in Chautauqua County, New York. It was a streetcar with no sides, just wooden benches of varnished wooden slats. It was neat and clean and magnificent. We rumbled through city streets, past the Cathedral and on down to the old port city. When we got there we had breakfast. Then, after exploring the town, we had lunch and headed back toward the City of Soller. There we entered the cathedral and watched old folks walk home. We imagined them never wanting to be more than a mile from where they were born. We saw their grandchildren play near the fountain in front of the church, saw them have lunch with their children. The train took us back to the twenty-first century, where we found *Tapestry* hanging tight to her anchor chain just as we had left her. After a brief rest, we took the dinghy back to town where Julie drew an image of an old olive tree, I finished reading a novel, and we enjoyed cocktails and tapas. (tripe and sausage with sauce, olives and tomatoes and peanuts) as the sun set over beautiful Andratx Bay.

Chapter 41

Cabrera

We sailed from Port Andratx, south along the coast of Mallorca, to a little beach area about ten miles from Cabrera. The wind was contrary, but we were able to sail for, perhaps half the way. There were charter boats near us so it became a race. We pulled out all of *Tapestry's* sails in about fifteen knots of wind and heeled our girl over like a racing boat. Of course, we had to close the sink drains in both heads or we would have taken on water, but she leaned to the wind and most of our Beneteau rivals found they could not pass. One exception was a 35 racer, flying just a jib, but she later revealed her true colors by sailing way to windward. (She was using her engine!)

The beach where we anchored was "Rapida", a large public bathing beach along the coast. It was well protected and we anchored in about ten feet of crystal clear water over white sand, reminiscent of the Caribbean. Our friends on *Triumph* had caught a tuna and invited us for dinner aboard. Next morning we motor/sailed to Cabrera in light winds. The harbor there is completely protected by high hills and a medieval castle overlooking the entrance. There were fifty moorings in the harbor, which is a national park, and it is necessary to get written permission beforehand to stay there. We got a (free) two day pass. After picking up our mooring we walked to shore and climbed the rugged hill to the castle. It was a difficult climb, more suited to Land Rovers than humans, but we eventually followed a rocky path to a spiral staircase, especially designed for the non-claustrophobic and strong of leg, which led to a terrace with a magnificent view in all directions. The descent was equally exciting. (Pamphlets, available in the information office, remind tourists, "We are concerned for your safety, but not responsible for it.") There would be a guided tour at six.

Island People: Deep Water Dreams

After a nap and a light dinner, we found ourselves in a sprinkle of rain as we headed for shore at six. Friends from an H.R. 50 were there with two young park rangers. We set off despite the precipitation. The trail was steep and gravelly and long. Our friends were celebrating their 52nd wedding anniversary. He was a pancreatic cancer survivor. Strong people. Our male guide had long dark hair and a thick beard. He and his cohort, in her 20's with blonde , streaked hair would explain what we were seeing. It was the young woman, however, who stole the show. Although some might question her credulity, what with a jewel implanted on a front tooth, a pierced tongue and tattoos creeping from cuffs and waist, she struggled to translate and make us understand his narrative.

She told the story of how, during the Napoleonic Wars, French prisoners, many of whom were ill, were left on the island of Cabrera by the Spanish. They lived off the sheep and goats on the island. Unfortunately, as there were 9000 prisoners, the food supply soon gave out. They resorted to cannibalism. By the time the French had negotiated peace, there were only 3000 left. The male guide showed us a toxic onion that the last survivors boiled with leather and ate to stay alive. How ironic that so many should suffer on such a beautiful island. Imagine being left on a beautiful island to be starved to death by your enemy. Imagine resorting to killing and eating others to survive. It says something else about being human.

In modern times the islands are very protected. There is only one harbor of the dozen available, where sailors can moor. Most of the islands are restricted and protected.

Chapter 42

Porto Cristo

We motored from the Islas de Cabrera on to Porto Cristo. This a tourist town on the east coast of Mallorca. One of the main attractions here is the cave. How could we be here and not see the cave? We purchased tickets. Our tickets said that we would leave at two.

We, literally hundreds of us, were herded, via a cement walkway probably eight feet wide, into the underground caverns. They were huge! We walked on a regular road through the place, but around us were steep inclines, sheer drop offs and all the other more common features of caves. The bottom was filled with clear sea water, and formations were illuminated with spectacular lighting.

It was beautiful.

Among the list of "no's" was photographs. They wanted us to buy photos in the gift shop, not delay the line by trying to take pictures. Of course, people were popping flashes as we walked, frustrating the guards who diligently tried to make us not shoot pictures. Finally we came to a huge auditorium-like room with hundreds of seats. In front of us was a lake, illuminated by floating lights. It was spectacularly beautiful. Once all of us were seated, a narrator came on and explained to us, in five languages, that we should be quiet and then we would see a performance of classical music played by musicians riding in rowboats. Everybody finally got quiet and the lights went down and it got really dark.

Soon three rowboats, illuminated by small lights around the edges, came into the scene as a keyboard, a violin and a cello played. It was an eerie and beautiful sight, but obviously, to the very young, it was terrifying. Every small child in the place began to scream and cry. More flashbulbs began to pop, frustrating the guards further and drawing a rumble of complaint from the audience. Finally things settled down and when the concert was over, we could choose whether to ride out of the cave in a boat or walk. We chose the former.

We boarded 16 man lifeboats and were rowed to (where else but) the gift shop where we disembarked and had a chance to buy souvenirs.

Porto Cristo

Chapter 43

Menorca

We sailed from Porto Cristo to Menorca where we enjoyed the first full day of summer. It was hot, Caribbean hot. At night the mosquitos found us and they buzzed in my ear most of the night.

We rented a car, an Opal, Corsa. It was the least satisfying of the three cars we had rented thus far. It was slow and cramped for the four of us, but it had air conditioning and that was important. The driving on Menorca was less challenging than on Ibiza or the mainland. There were fewer sheer drop offs or treacherous roads, more country lanes and lovely scenery.

The place is old. We visited a ruin of a Talayotic Culture that was here about 1300 B.C. There was a huge rock balanced on top of another, Stonehenge style. Some dwellings, a cistern, and underground storage places were carved out of solid limestone. Huge rocks were lifted into place to make a stone ceiling. Small rocks were wedged into place to make a kind of vaulted ceiling. As we stood beneath them, our friend Eileen, from *Triumph*, thanked me for reminding her that these cisterns would be a terrible place to be in an earthquake. Rock fences surround the place. There were underground burial chambers, a defensive tower and other buildings. It was all very impressive.

Rock formations dominate the arid and barren Menorcan landscape. There are miles and miles of stone fences which cross fields and descend to the sea. The roads, though plenty wide for two cars to pass, are often bounded on both sides by high stone walls which appear to have been built long before cars were ever invented. Tall cliffs surround the island and supplemented by walls, were a major part of the island's defenses. The south coast is lined with narrow bays which terminate in sandy beaches, very much appreciated by the local population who love to swim and sun bathe.

The city of Mahon is built in front of and atop a huge cliff. Some of the seaside shops use the rugged rock cliff wall as the back wall of their businesses, where they show fine china and clothing. Subtly lighted, it makes for an elegant contrast.

We anchored in the town of Puerto Mao, or Mahon, a long and wonderfully protected harbor filled with yachts and fishing boats and recreational craft of all kinds. Freighters and ferries plied the waters. The wind was very still, the harbor just rippled by a zephyr as the full moon rose in the east. The cooling breeze was most welcome.

In case you think Menorca is "almost heaven," it is well to remember that in 2003, an earthquake in Algeria caused a tsunami, which devastated many of the boats in Menorca's harbor.

Chapter 44

Ciutadella

This is a beautiful town on the north end of Minorca. Marinas and anchorages are full there for weeks because of the Festival of Saint Joan. For that reason, we left the boat in Mahon, and took the hour long bus ride to Ciutadella. Saint Joan is actually Saint John in Catalan, the local language.

While walking into town, we stopped into a marine store. Dick was busy talking with a clerk when suddenly there was a huge crash as a shelf filled with cans of paint came crashing to the floor. A customer was struck as he struggled to get out of the way of the tumbling shelves and flying cans of paint. To our horror, the man was covered in red when he struggled to his feet. Fortunately, it was all red paint, not blood. Was this some kind of foreshadowing?

We wandered around town, had coffee, then lunch, and admired the views and enjoyed the thousands of people, young and old, gathered in the streets for the festival. At around two, a man on a mule rode to the church and asked the priest of it would be all right for the festival to begin. The man was dressed in a black suit with a white shirt and a black hat. When he came from the church, he rode to the town square. People rushed to greet him waiting for his message. He announced, "Let the Festival begin," or something similar in Catalan. He had a drum and a fife, which he played, and everyone cheered and jumped up and down. Then, pretty much everybody headed for the bars.

In the bars loud music was playing and people were dancing and when a favorite traditional song came on they would sing and bounce up and down. In contrast to the horse festival we attended in Rota, people were not dressed up. Jeans and tank tops were the dress of the day. The beer taps were flowing, of course, but the drink that day was a mixture of lemonade and gin which is sold frozen in liter bottles by the bars. It is cheap and very plentiful. Walk into a bar and someone would hand you a plastic cup full of the stuff; there was no need to buy it. With temperatures near 90F, it was refreshing, too. Although the party had officially started at two that afternoon, one had the feeling many of the revelers had most likely begun a little early.

While walking around town, we noticed that heavy wooden boards had been bolted over plate glass store fronts. The next phase began at 4:30. Ominously, seven ambulances had gathered in the police parking lot. EMT's were busy counting bandages. Huge crowds of people were gathering in the square. Music was playing and young people would leap high in unison as they sang and danced. At this point, down one of the streets came a line of men on horseback. The horses were covered with beautiful tack, and their riders, dressed in black formal wear with boots and hats, urged them through the crowd.

Young men began to charge the horses and the horses reared up, prancing on their hind legs. It was magic. This was not a sober crowd, but it was a happy one. Riders, who ranged in age from 20's to 80's, smiled and waved as their mounts reared and flailed their hooves again and again. We never saw a rider fall. Young men charge, horses rear, and the rest of us keep out of the way. Of course, in the narrow streets, that is often difficult. There were perhaps 80 riders and horses and they kept charging through the crowd from 4:30 to 6:30 in the afternoon.

One horse reared in front of us and dashed perhaps fifty yards on his hind legs toward the square. The crowd went wild! Finally, there was a pause and then two horses raced at full speed past us down the street into the square. With that the mob followed the horses and there, in the square, a brass band had assembled. Each horse rode past the band and reared and received tumultuous cheers from the crowd. Finally, the horses disappeared and the crowd went back to the serious matter of partying. It was seven in the evening when we headed back for the bus. On the way, we saw three EMT's with backboard and defibrillator, looking for a patient who had somehow disappeared.

We had never seen such well trained horses. Taunted and pushed by this drunken crowd, they reared and pranced and no one, that we saw, got hurt. It seemed that the potential for a blood bath was huge, but the only red we saw that day was the man in the hardware, covered with paint.

The Spanish people have a love for animals and for interacting with them that seems to me to be unique. Whether it is running the bulls at Pamplona, bull fights, or showing horses, they are in a class by themselves. I might add, they have a delightful sense of fun as well. They love to drink, but we saw no one who was sick, fighting, or obnoxiously drunk. There were police around, but few by American standards. It was a thrilling and exciting afternoon. What a wonderful way to end our almost three months in Spain!

Chapter 45

SARDINIA

We motored and sailed to Sardinia, nearly 200 miles, through calm seas. For a time there would be winds of perhaps ten knots, but nothing exciting and barely enough to allow us to sail. Still, we sailed anyway, as much as we could. The highlight of the trip was when *Triumph* called us on the VHF and told us they had caught another large tuna. After they had filleted it, they wrapped a generous portion in plastic bags, attached them to an old fender and dropped fish and fender over the side. We came by and "caught" it with our boat hook. It was probably one of the few fish ever caught and eaten by two different boats on the same day!

The entrance to Sardinia, near Porto Conte, was dramatic. Tall rock cliffs with a lighthouse on top and round forts near the water greeted us as we approached. We anchored in ten feet of crystal clear water, very near shore. The weather was calm, the anchorage okay, but only for one night.

Stintino

Thick buildings of white and
Tan, pink and brick rest on a brown land with green
Bushes, thick and untended.
Red and beige tile roofs
Against a perfect blue sky.
Stone streets and sidewalks
With surprise steps;
I glance at a pretty face,
And stumble!
Curvaceous sloops,
Lateen rigged, ply
These waters adding

Henry R. Danielson

Bright colors to
Pastels.
Church bells play
Ave Maria at seven.
"Buon giorno,"
"Giorno"
"Grazie"
"Prego"
"Ciao."

H.R.D.

That evening we went ashore and for the first time I greeted a stranger with the Italian, "Buon giorno." She looked at me with bright blue eyes and said, "You must be English."

She was a fellow American. Julie and I went to their boat for coffee. Not an auspicious beginning for my Italian!

Still in Stintino, we again experienced strong wind. We secured the boat to a pier and waited it out.

Pressure

Tied to the dock in Stintino
There is no need for lines;
The wind presses us onto the
Pier, crushing our fenders,
Heeling the boat over the quay.
There are no wispy clouds
Or angry thunderheads in
The sky, no threat of rain.
Wavelets smash against
The side of the boat; wind
Sings in the rigging.
There is no escape from this

Island People: Deep Water Dreams

Place, pinned down as
We are, forced to listen to
An unfriendly song.
We find no threatening
Clouds, but clear blue sky,
Italian sunshine and a
Ripping Mediterranean
Wind.

H.R.D.

Next day we headed for the old city of Alghero. It is a beautiful walled city with walls easily 30 feet thick, surrounding the old part. For three days we enjoyed the city.

Alghero

To Italy we sail, motor really,
Pounding diesel over mirror sea.
Mediterranean blue; hot days
A cool night,
From Spain's reserve to Italian intensity.

Henry R. Danielson

Greeted by towering cliffs and
Ancient turrets, we anchor in
Porto Conte, move on to Alghero,
A walled city with pill boxes,
German built to keep out Americans,
Vandals, Goths, Visigoths, and other visitors,
But they are here anyhow,
Buying the Colors of Benetton,
McDonalds and pizza as they
Wander through the city gates,
Snap photos and leave euros.
Old men sit in the shade of the wall,
Watch us, smoke and
Pass the day.
Only Ferraris go fast on this
Island where, officially, things happen,
But nothing happens right away.

H.R.D.

We were in Sardinia, in Italy, but the important part was
Julie. Her hair, ever so slowly, was growing back in. She was
well, gaining weight, as much a part of the journey as before her
terrible bout with disease. She had clawed her way back with
smiles and pleasantries. She had brought her paints and during
quiet times in this beautiful place, she painted.

Artista

She sits in the cockpit,
Knees together, looking forward,
Then down,
At the pad in her lap.
Her hands move carefully.
On the paper, she draws

Island People: Deep Water Dreams

The wall, the tower,
From the American perspective;
A visitor to Italy
With American baggage.
She looks and tries to understand,
To feel the texture,
The curve, the line,
The thickness of the wall.
She finds the gate
By drawing the wall;
She penetrates a little
Of this Italian world,
A pink house with
Green shutters, open
Just a crack.

H.R.D.

A pink house with green shutters, open just a crack.

Many of the shops and restaurants in Alghero are literally built into the wall. One place where we had dinner had vaulted ceilings, stone walls and a glass floor which covered an ancient well. Neat, but a bit difficult to navigate after a glass of wine. Although very picturesque, the city was also very tourist oriented with hundreds of jewelry shops, clothing stores and restaurants. It was also hot!

We purchased white material which Julie, after borrowing Eileen's sewing machine, sewed into a cover for the pilothouse. We got the temperature down from 93 to 88 degrees F. during the day. We also got a *constituto* here which would, hopefully, prove that we had reentered the E.U. after our visit to Morocco. It was free, and the Coast Guard officers who issued it could not have been more polite, in spite of working in an upstairs office with no a.c., not even a fan, and temperatures near 100F. The Chief of Police, on the other hand, whom we asked to stamp our passports, told us to come back two times and finally demanded four photos of each of us, two copies of each page of our passports, and 14 euros each, before he would make the stamp, which he said couldn't be done until the following Saturday. We said, "No thank you." That evening we spent in an abandoned marina with several dozen other boats, listening to an accordion serenading diners in outdoor restaurants across the bay. The next morning our friend Kathleen on *Vivache* would begin Italian lessons aboard at 9:00 a.m. We would be there.

PORTO POZZO

Fourth of July at Porto Pozzo

On Sardinia, Porto Pozzo, we gathered,
Eight of us, American yachts,
To celebrate a non-event in Italy.
"Happy 4 July" we write in code flags.
Italians smile and wave.
It is hot and our dish
To pass is a large watermelon.
Dinner on *Vivache*,
Sixteen Americans (and two Brits)

Sixty-five feet of sailboat,
With 7 dinghies in gusty winds
And a muddy bottom
And *Vivache* 's anchor slides and slides
Across the bay.
But the reset held, dinner was
Fine and we had our
Fourth of July,
After all, in Porto Pozzo.
A little American celebration
Afloat,
In
Sardinia,
Italy.

Fireworks?
They came on the fifth.
In howling winds
Smoky brushfires
Raced across the shore,
Checked by brave Italian
Pilots in red and yellow
Seaplanes that scooped salt water
Roared low over our masts,
And doused the blaze.

H.R.D.

It was the Fourth of July and there were six boats from the U.S. in the harbor at Porto Pozzo. We had a party aboard a McGregor 65, and to show we weren't prejudiced, we invited the people from a British boat, too. No sooner had we arrived aboard *Vivache* than the wind came up, and up. With seven dinghies and 14 extra people aboard *Vivache,* of course she dragged her anchor. A reset took care of things, but through the evening, anxious glances back at our respective boats reassured us a little. Back aboard, the wind died during the night, but the next morning it rose to new highs. White caps filled the bay and *Tapestry* swayed and tugged at her anchor as though she were struggling to drop back to the jagged rocks that lined the shore astern of us.

Still, we had wonderful entertainment. The sail school at Porto Pozzo is serious. In spite of the 25 plus knot winds, there was no "chalk talk" for these kids; they were out sailing! Their instructors were intrepid, cheering them on and picking them up when they flipped.

There was a young lady in an inflatable, responsible for several boats, and she was truly amazing. There was a fifteen foot boat with four 12 or 13 year olds aboard. They had tipped over several times and no one was doing much of anything but holding on. At one point they headed right for *Triumph* which was anchored just ahead of us. The young lady instructor saw what was happening and got her rubber boat between the kids and *Triumph,* just in time to prevent a crash. She pushed the kids away and again they flipped. She tried her best to get them to right the boat and sail on, but, in desperation, they headed downwind, right for us! Someone tossed out an anchor, but it was too late. The boat was trapped on our anchor chain and leaning against the bow pulpit. I went forward and pushed them off, but the anchor caught on our chain and slid up, right to the deck. Fortunately, I was able to free it. The boat capsized again and headed for the rocks. The young lady did all she could with kids in the water and an overturned boat to make things right. Finally she got one boy in the dinghy with her, one in the boat, got the other two to right the boat and swim to shore. Then she towed the boat back to the club.

Finally she came back and picked up the abandoned sailors and anchor, and stopped by *Tapestry* to apologize in her best English. What a neat young lady. But that wasn't the end. Wind surfers rocketed by in the gusty winds and fleet after fleet of kids and adults in small day sailors came by to try their hand at dealing with heavy air. They tipped over, shredded sails and generally got beat up, but they all wore pfd's and were fine. It was really a great example of the enthusiasm that exists in Sardinia for sailing. They truly love the sport.

After our big day in the wind, we woke to calmer seas. Right away we raised our anchor, with some difficulty, (I had fantasized we might finally break it free and all the lights in the village would go out!) pulled out our jib and sailed from Porto Pozzo along this simply lovely coast of brown rock and green scrub reflected in bright green and blue water, to Arzachena, a well protected town with much better holding. Along the way we passed ferries, other sailboats and powerboats of all kinds. It was a spectacular sail under bright blue sky and moderate winds. After little more than a two hour sail, we anchored in ten feet over clear white sand.

Julie and I went to shore and found lovely stucco villas and restaurants. Frangipani and Hibiscus were brilliant, lawns were watered and neatly kept. We went into a restaurant for a drink and *creme brulee*. Wonderful!

Later in the afternoon, we were startled by a plane flying low overhead. It was really low and caused us to jump to the cockpit. To our amazement, white smoke was rising from behind the hill right ahead of the boat. Sirens were wailing in the "he haw" tone prevalent in Europe. The plane circled above the blaze (which was out of our sight) and then headed back for the bay where it did a touch and go, filling its tanks with water. It then flew over the fire and spectacularly, dumped its load. This was a twin turbo "flying boat" built in Canada. Each run, from water to fire to water, took about three minutes. Each time the plane took off it cleared our masts by only several hundred feet. Very exciting! The wind had risen into the 20 knot range again and the fire was clearly gaining ground.

Before long a second plane appeared and joined the fight. With the two of them dumping hundreds of gallons of water per drop, the smoke began to subside. Before long a chopper joined the two seaplanes. It was an hour and a half before the flames were brought under control. We had cocktails on *Alcid* as the planes continued their bombardment. The pilots were fearless, handling these large planes with wonderful dexterity as they dived through thick smoke to drop their payload and swooped onto the bay to pick up water. While we were on *Alcid*, the winds again picked up. Out of the 20's and into the 30 knot range they raged, swinging the boats back and forth, whipping canvas and challenging chain and anchor. The ride back to *Tapestry* was a wet one.

Fortunately, the winds again subsided for the night. Next morning we went to the little village for coffee and grocery shopping. A wonderful butcher shop, a vegetable store and a bakery greeted us, along with a small market. By noon the winds again screamed, reaching 40 knots, but the anchor held.

Sardinia Morning Coffee

Before the wind is up,
We take the dinghy to shore
And find a *ristorante*.
Outside, in the shade,
Plastic chairs
A cotton cloth on a plastic table.
Coffee with milk.
A little expresso coffee
In a glass of hot milk.
"Europeans wouldn't
Drink pot coffee."
A little tablet, a twist
Of a lever, a hiss of
Hot water in a tiny
Cup, poured into milk.

Island People: Deep Water Dreams

A paper packet of sugar.
"Chocolate Croissant?"

H.R.D.

Sardinia

Chapter 46

Cala di Volpe

So, we left Sardinia. After passing up a number of small harbors crowded with yachts and no space for us, we finally found ourselves in *Cala di Volpe*. At *Cala di Volpe* on *Isola de Maddelana,* there was a giant anchorage with hundreds of yachts. There was an immaculate pre-WWII four masted schooner and numerous giant and elegant sloops and ketches. There were many power yachts in the 150 foot plus size range, some with as many as four decks. We anchored in front of most of the fleet near the area reserved for water skiing. It seemed as though the dinghy of choice for these vessels was a hard bottom inflatable with one or two huge outboard motors. These boats were about twenty-five feet in length and could carry eight or ten adults, no problem. They would dash between the yachts and the hotel on shore, which was the only attraction at the place. To do this, of course, they had to weave through the fleet of moored yachts. Slowing down did not occur to any of them that we saw. Add to the "dinghies" plenty of jet skies. Of course, there were water ski boats too, but most of the time they stayed in the area reserved for them. Wakes crossed and criss-crossed, making getting home from *Alcid* in our seven foot dinghy a bit of a challenge, although we made it safely. We did not even go to the hotel for a drink. The cost of which we learned was truly excessive.

After dark, the air was filled with the hum of generators as all of the yachts run generators 24/7. Deck lights and spreader lights were lit as well as lighting inside the opulent cabins. Some of the larger yachts had underwater lights which illuminated the water around them a brilliant green. It was a stunning sight. It was as though we were in the middle of a city in the sea. Most of the larger yachts were British. The six of us were the only U.S. boats we saw in the harbor.

The following morning we six American boats, broke up and went our separate ways. *Tapestry* headed North toward a small NATO island with a submarine base and a submarine tender. As we drew near, there was a great deal of squabble on the radio in Italian. We thought they might be yelling at us, but we continued and anchored in a cove too shallow for shipping. There was an eleven boat sail school sailboat race nearby. The winners were doused with buckets of water by the "instructors" at the end. Good fun. We went to town for lunch and shopping and returned to the boat in time for a swim before dinner. Everything was fine until at dark a boat approached and told us we couldn't anchor where we were. I asked him if he was a policeman or if he represented the Italian Navy. He assured me he was "just a citizen." Did he own a marina? We decided to stay 'til morning when we would head for Bonifacio, on the French island of Corsica. We would have to learn to replace *buon giorno* with *bon jour.*

Chapter 47

CORSICA

City of the Strait

Napolean and Charles V
Lived there in the old city,
High up the hill in Bonofacio.
Built on chalk cliffs
That overhang the sea,
Grottos beneath echo
With thumping waves
As restaurants above teeter
On perilous ground.
Tourists climb from
The ancient harbor
To the walled city,
Walk narrow streets,
Buy souvenirs, and
Eat French food
In rough dark rooms.
It takes your breath away,
This ancient city,
Of Corse.

H.R.D.

But then, there are places like Corsica. We headed across the straits of Bonifaicio to the French island of Corsica. The wind was on the nose at first, and the diesel droned as we plunged through small waves. On the port side we spotted "The Bear," an overhanging rock formation that looked for all the world like a bear sitting on its haunches. Homer mentioned the formation in *The Odyssey.*

Finally, we entered the Straits of Bonifacio. This area is renowned for strong winds, but today they were moderate, about fifteen knots. It was a beautiful day. Gradually the winds fell off to port and we raised sail and shut down the engine. As we sailed along, the white chalk cliffs of Bonifacio rose above us. Yachts of all sizes, along with a huge container ship, showed us what a busy port this was. *Tapestry* heeled far to starboard, we gushed ahead under full sail. It was wonderful. By ten thirty we had arrived at the cliffs and spotted the harbor entrance. It was narrow, but very busy. Yachts, large and small were motoring in and out in a constant stream. We fell into line and suddenly found ourselves being passed by a sightseeing boat to starboard as a huge sailboat approached to port. I tried to take video, steer, and control the speed all at once. Not possible. We squeezed through the entrance which opened to a beautiful harbor, but a very busy one.

Suddenly there was an inflatable dinghy pressing against the side of the boat. A red faced French boy was yelling something at me in French. I assumed he wanted to know if I needed a slip. We spotted our friends on *Sugalite,* and pointed. He raced ahead and found us a spot just one boat away. We squeezed into the slip and finally tied up. What a beautiful and spectacular place! Tall cliffs with beautiful buildings surrounded the water. There was a huge fort at the harbor entrance.

Homer describers Bonifacio in *The Odyssey*. His fleet sails into the harbor, hidden from the sea by chalk cliffs, and most of the ships head for the interior (where we were) to anchor for the night. Odysseus is suspicious and anchors in a little cove near the harbor mouth. The locals attack during the night and rain rocks down on the fleet. Only Odysseus and his men escape. We should have followed his example!

After just a few minutes we were greeted by James and Karen from *Blue Heron*, an H.R. 43. They are American friends from San Francisco, and invite us for drinks and suggest we all walk up to the old city for dinner before the fireworks. The next day, the fourteenth of July, is Bastille Day, a big deal in France.

We walk up the long ramp to the fort and the walled city. It is a magnificent edifice with breathtaking views. Later we enjoy cocktails aboard *Blue Heron* and then climb again the stone ramp over the drawbridge to the old city. Dinner is in a hole in the wall restaurant with rough stone walls, lovely French speaking waitresses and wonderful food and wine. Later we return to the boats as fireworks rain down on us from the fort. The fireworks turn to music. We were stunned.

After getting off to a fine start in Bonifacio our first day, things seemed to be even better the second. We took the dinghy and explored the harbor entrance. There are cannon mounted in the chalk cliffs as are the old winches used to hoist submarine nets and cables in World War II. Best of all, however, are the grottos. These caves at the water's edge are nearly 100 feet deep. We motored into one in the dinghy. It was a large room with a perpetually dripping ceiling that had been carved right out of the chalk cliffs. It is fascinating to see these cliffs. They are hundreds of feet high and very undermined by the action of the waves on the soft chalk walls. One can see where they have been eroded and have fallen in over the centuries. Yet, the French have built large buildings with restaurants and apartments on the outer edges of these cliffs, overhanging the water. That takes a kind of faith not present in this American.

When we got back to the boat later in the afternoon, we saw that a hit-and-run boater had struck *Tapestry* on the quarter inch thick head, or bathroom, port protruding from the side, which had been left open and was now broken off and sunk. We questioned people around us, but no one said they had seen anything. Dick, from *Triumph,* and I closed the hole where the port had been, with a heavy piece of plywood from his ship's stores. It would be safe, but the head would be without sunlight for the rest of the summer, or until we could get a replacement from Nauticat. Julie and I really appreciated Dick's help.

Bonifacio was truly a special place. Like Odysseus, we probably should have anchored near the entrance rather than sailing way into the harbor.

Bonifacio

Odysseus had it right
About Bonificio, I mean.
He never sailed way into the harbor,
But dropped his hook
At the entrance to
Avoid treachery and
Large rocks thrown
By the locals.
We went way in
The deep harbor
And squeezed in
A narrow space.
The locals
Haven't changed.
It was Bastile Day,
And fireworks
Rained down on us,
Prices skyrocketed,
And someone smashed
Our window!

H.R.D.

After Bonifacio, we visited the crowded Sanguinaires Islands and then Cape Rossu, a mass of brown and red rock covered with green moss and scrub. There are grottos along the water's edge that are often deep enough to motor into with the

Henry R. Danielson

dinghy. One such "cave" made sucking and thundering sounds as the waves rolled into it. We explored each grotto and tiny harbor in our little seven foot dinghy. The wind was about ten knots and the waves less than one half meter; still the spray splashed over our heads. Had the waves been higher, the ride would not have been possible. It was delightful.

We did have a bit of an adventure on the way to Cape Rossu. As we motored along, a large gray ship with an orange stripe from deck to waterline approached *Sugalite*, our friends from Seattle. Four men boarded their boat and did a thorough inspection including lockers, tool boxes, bilges, anchor wells, etc. They checked all their paperwork and made sure everything was in order. They were very thorough, and spent more than one half hour examining their boat. When we arrived at Cape Rossu, the same ship was anchored there. After an hour or so they boarded *Triumph*, our friends from Michigan. They inspected their paperwork as well as doing a brief boat check. We had the Stars and Stripes up on *Tapestry*, and were ready for a visit as well. They paid no attention to us at all. Must have been our deodorant! From there we headed to Calvi.

Calvi

We roll and we rock
In following seas and

Island People: Deep Water Dreams

Contrary winds from
Calvi, motoring east on the
Mediterranean Sea.
Calvi, which might be the birthplace of
Columbus and is
Certainly where English
Lord Nelson lost an eye
In a vain attempt
To conquer this walled City.
Calvi, a French town
On Corsica, home to
Tourists, fragrant shops,
Fine restaurants, loud music,
And the French Foreign Legion.
Calvi, a jewel on Corsica,
Steeped in history, ice cream,
Souvenirs, and pizza;
Spanish, English, French,
Italian and German.
We struggle to understand,
To try to survive without
The walls.

H.R.D.

The mountains on the north of the island of Corsica are some three thousand meters high and snow covered. The view is spectacular, right down to the water. Sometimes range after range of mountains disappear into the haze as we look shoreward. Haze is the key word here. The weather in July is hot and humid. We noticed the barometer was falling and there were 7's and 8's on the Beaufort scale in the forecast. That means big wind. Calvi offered moorings, a safe place to be in a gale. Calvi is interesting in that it is at just 42 degrees of latitude, the same as Dunkirk, New York, where The Dunkirk Yacht Club, our home club was.

The old city is surrounded by a wall and perched on top of a hill. It is picturesque to view from the sea. Lord Nelson lost his eye trying to take Calvi, and they say Christopher Columbus was born there.(They say Christopher Columbus was born and buried in many places!) Calvi is also the home of the French Foreign Legion. Their recruiting office is at Calvi. It is interesting that the Foreign Legion takes only non-French nationals. It asks no questions about the past of its recruits, and for five years of service issues them a French passport with any name they choose. Thus, past indiscretions are forgiven for five years of very rigorous military service. The only requirement to join is that one pass a very demanding physical.

The city is largely tourist oriented with lovely shops set into the ancient city. There are many restaurants and ice cream shops. One thing we reaffirmed here is that there is an absolute tourist staple in Europe. It is pizza. Everywhere we have visited, there is at least one restaurant calling itself a pizzeria or *pizzateria*, often with a wood fired oven, and pizza is almost always on the menu of all but the most expensive restaurants. It is okay, too, with thin crust and familiar toppings. Fresh fruits and vegetables are delicious here, as is meat, chicken and fish. The French love good food. The wine is something else. It is cheap by American standards, and even to my inexperienced palate, superior to that of Spain or Italy.

When we returned to the boat after our first visit to town, the wind was rising, as forecast. It was cloudy and during dinner it began to rain. The rain would come in short bursts, as though it really wanted to rain, but just couldn't. There was lightning in the distance, even a roll of thunder. I stuck my head out at one point and was amazed to find that the wind was hot. The storm was coming from the southeast, right out of the Sahara Desert. Wind barely exceeded 20 knots so sleeping was easy. The next morning, the boat was covered with red mud.

Island People: Deep Water Dreams

Although rain is infrequent in summer, when it rains even here, as in Spain, it rains red mud.

The next day we went to town early and caught a diesel tram to L'ile Rousse, a little town down the coast. The tram was noisy and hot. Diesel smoke blew in the windows and it went just a little faster than I thought might be safe. As unlikely as it seems, I was sure the driver was shifting gears. The ride took about a half hour and carried us along the coast. The wind was really whipping and the sea was bright with white caps. After we arrived, we walked through town and sat in a shady square for coffee. It was a dirt floor with tables set up under huge old shade trees. People were visiting and reading and laughing and the atmosphere was wonderful for conversation. Later, we bought cheese, wine, bread and sausage, and enjoyed a picnic in the same park. Real wine glasses were cheaper than paper cups, so we went first class. By then there was a group playing music nearby. The six of us had a delightful lunch. We walked the beach and enjoyed the scenery, and by three had ridden the tram back to Calvi and were back aboard our boats. Winds gusted to 35 knots as we snaked back and forth on our moorings. Suddenly we noticed smoke in the air and before long those familiar twin engine sea planes were scooping up sea water and dumping it on several fires that had sprung up suddenly. There were three planes this time; serious business.

Our last night in Calvi, Julie and I dined in a little French restaurant next to a church still pock marked by shells from Lord Nelson's attack on the city toward the end of the 18th Century. Our table was on the street and next to a couple from Switzerland who spoke only French, Italian and German. We could converse with them fluently in English, but they didn't think they spoke that well enough to count. Julie had lamb and I had veal. The food was rich and good, but the star of the show was a Brittany spaniel who was snoozing on the street. He would roll over and over down the hill, catching the attention of everyone at the outdoor tables of the restaurant. If you made eye contact, he would walk over to your table and beg, but just with his golden brown eyes. He never barked, or pawed, or drooled; he just looked at you. I scratched him and petted him, but though he looked at the bones on my plate, I never fed him. That was fine, he just moved back to his spot on the street. Another couple near us fed him a piece of bread, which he took to the street and dropped. He made it plain that bread was not what he had in mind. Neat dog! It was 10:30 by the time we left the restaurant and the streets of Calvi were packed with people. There were lines at restaurants and shops filled with talking and laughing people. Wandering minstrels were singing their songs, and bands were tuning up for the evening. Wow!

After our night in Calvi, the weather truly settled and we headed for St. Florent. All along the coast of Corsica and Sardinia are watch towers which were used as lookouts during the 18th century and before. It is said that if an invader approached the shores of Corsica, a message could be sent all around the island in less than an hour using cannons. At St. Florent, Lord Nelson attacked and conquered the city quite easily, except for the tower located at the mouth of the bay. Fire at it as he would, he could not destroy this round stone structure. He finally had to send a detachment of marines to take it. He was so impressed, he took the dimensions of this structure. He built similar towers and they were used, ironically, to keep the Corsican, Napoleon, from the shores of Scotland in later years.

Tapestry, Sugilite, and *Triumph* had a delightful *bon voyage* dinner at St. Florent; I had roquefort spaghetti and salad. The company was the best, the food delicious. There was only one trouble. There was no friendly dog.

Chapter 48

ELBA

Elba was a surprise! Elba was made famous because Napoleon was exiled there after his unhappy defeat at Waterloo. Our first harbor there was Portoferraio. We went to the large harbor and anchored. The harbor is a ferry stop, as its name implies, and it was a bit of a tourist destination. Still, it was a place where people could work and live other than in the tourist business. There was a large grocery, a bus terminal, and other things that gave it a "real" feeling.

Soon after we got there, Dick and Eileen on *Triumph,* said that they had met another American boat called *Odyssey* while they were in their dinghy. Dick said that their names were Joe and Marie, and they were sailing a Nonsuch 36. It hit me like a brick. There had been a boat by that name in Englewood harbor in 2002. We met the couple, Joe and Marie, and we had them for dinner in our condo. They had sailed their Nonsuch 36 catboat (boat with a single large sail) from the California West Coast, through the Panama Canal and as far as Englewood. They were preparing to head for Europe.

The next morning we took the dinghy and motored over to their boat. It was indeed the same couple. They had headed for Bermuda the previous year, but faced with eighteen foot waves in a storm, they had aborted and headed for New York City. They then returned to Fort Lauderdale where they raised the money needed to ship the boat to Europe. At that time they were able to live aboard the boat while it was in transit. They would stay aboard at night and climb down a ladder at meal times to move to the ship's dining room and eat with the ship's crew. They endured constant movement and spray as the ship crossed the ocean, but the ship's engine propelled them.

They had relaunched in Mallorca, Spain, and continued along the Riviera. They found what they called exorbitant prices and tacky harbors. Marinas were "full." They might find room for you if you were willing to pay for a very large slip, come late and agreed to leave early the next morning. Obviously the marinas were geared for much larger vessels. Joe and Marie called it the worst sailing experience of their lives.

Elba, on the other hand was the very best place they had found, and, even though they had been there six weeks, they were not planning to leave any time soon. "The people here," Joe said, "were real. They worked for a living, they fished, made leather goods, farmed, but they didn't just cater to tourists." He said there is everything on Elba that there is in Italy. Joe spoke Italian and that made him somewhat of an expert. He said we had to go to Marciana, a small mountaintop town on Elba. We were so excited to see Joe and Maria there, we could hardly believe it. Small world.

MARCIANA

So, that morning, in spite of the fact that we had invited four friends for dinner and had not shopped yet, we took the dinghy to shore and the bus to Marciana. The "half hour" ride turned into almost an hour of sharp switchbacks and narrow winding roads that often caused an oncoming car to stop if the bus was attempting the hairpin curve. When we arrived at the town, we were amazed. It was a city built high on the very top of a hill. Streets were stairways sometimes carved into the granite rock. Narrow and twisting, they wound their way to the top. Crossroads were level, but just two or three pedestrians wide; no motor vehicles had graced these "streets." (We did see one motorized wheelbarrow with tracks like a dozer, that could negotiate steps, but only one!)

The view from the town was spectacular, gorgeous, wonderful. People were genuine. They didn't speak any English, but they wanted to talk with us. We had lunch there and waited an hour at the bus stop for fear of missing the next bus. We were learning to love Elba. In spite of our trip, dinner on the boat was a success.

Back at Portoferraio, the streets also often ended in stairways. We had lunch at a restaurant with tables built on the stairs. So different!

NAPOLEON

Finally, we climbed the hill to Napoleon's house. He was exiled there after he was defeated at Waterloo. His house was elegant, with lovely furniture, immaculate gardens and a spectacular view of the sea and the harbor. Why would anyone have wanted to leave? He had hundreds of his followers there with him. He could have entertained them all at one time in his house had he wanted to, but instead he "escaped." He had been there ten months and after all, if one calls you an emperor, you should be off fighting wars, right? He took off and fought again and lost again and within a hundred days of his "escape" he was dead. Am I missing something?

Exile

You could exile me
On Elba, I suppose,
And I wouldn't mind
Very much.
Especially if you gave
Me a two-story house
With lovely gardens
Overlooking the bay;
I'd stay.
I wouldn't run away
As Napoleon did.
To fight another day.
If I met my Waterloo
And they gave me

Henry R. Danielson

A pad on Elba,
I wouldn't
Flee,
Not me.

H.R.D.

MARINA di CAMPO

Still on Elba, we sailed to Marina di Campo. This was definitely
not a tourist place. There were no ferries nor tour boats here at
all. It was real. There were hardware stores and drug stores and
dress shops as well as cafes, bars and restaurants. Of course,
there was a huge beach there, too, but mostly for local
consumption. Europeans, be they Spanish, French, or Italian
love their beaches.

One night, after dinner, we decided to head in for a
drink. It was nine thirty when we arrived. It was dark, and the
town was warming up. The bars, restaurants and ice cream
(*gelato*) shops were busy and the whole town was doing a brisk
business. What caught my attention, however, was a woman
who was telling a story to perhaps fifty children of elementary
school age. She would sing and play her guitar and at one point
she got all the kids (and many of their parents) to follow her as
she walked, then ran through the streets. Drummers accelerated
the pace until, pied piper style, she led them back to their
"theater" which was just plastic chairs in a roped off corner of
the street. Then she sang and read and taught the kids a chorus
which they would sing out in unison from time to time at her
command. It was a wonderful way for these kids to learn
language and literature and music.

It was there that night that I realized how much I wanted
to talk to some of these people. I wanted to tell them that in
America, I had spent a career teaching English to people named
Palimino, and Gulotti, and Cali. These people were the same,

calm and refined, loud and boisterous, caring and gentle people I had known in Jamestown, New York, but the language barrier was so profound, I simply could not communicate at all. I could say *"Buon Giorno,"* but that was about it. I realized that, though I had not gotten off a cruise ship or rented a villa by the beach, I was simply a voyeur, watching, but not participating in the lives of these people. I simply could not communicate with them at all. I could smile at a friendly face, but as soon as I spoke, a wall came between me and the speaker. Communication ended. These people drive cars, live in lovely or not so lovely houses, dress in western fashion, listen to American music, enjoy the food I enjoy, but I could not speak to them. How important it is for us to learn foreign languages!

Marina di Campo

Chapter 49

GIGLIO

From Elba, we sailed 35 miles to Giglio, an island right off the Italian coast, more recently made famous by the *Costa Concordia,* a cruise ship that ran aground on the shoals near the island. Of course, we were there long before that happened.

Again, we anchored in a little bay by a beach. We took a bus to the top of the hill where an ancient community was built some 400 meters above sea level. There are apartments and stores and narrow streets and restaurants, all the things needed to sustain a small community. As we walked through this fascinating city, built to protect its citizens from pirate attacks before the time of Columbus, a young lady asked us if we wanted to see a "cantina." We went inside a small room hung with hams beside jugs of wine and potatoes and onions in sacks. There was cheese on the shelves, spices, fruits and anything that could be preserved in its cool temperature. The hams were covered with thick layer of mold. There was a guitar in the corner. It was an amazing place that might sustain people in time of trouble. The girl could speak English and we grilled her about the town. Turned out she was Polish and knew little Italian. How ironic.

But there was another storm coming. It was called August. Somehow everybody seems to take August off in Europe. If we wanted to find storage for our boat, we had been told, we had better make arrangements before the first of August.

Chapter 50

FIUMICINO
AND
CONSTELLATION
NAUTICA

So we left the islands and headed for the Italian mainland. We stopped briefly at a huge marina in Rive di Traiano for fuel and there we found storage prices very high, so we continued to Fiumicino, where we understood more reasonable storage could be found. Finally, we had discovered the real Italy.

The chart showed "overfalls," a combination of fresh and salt water flowing into the sea at the mouth of the canal leading to Fiumicino. They turned out to be reasonably easy to maneuver through. We had to wait a few minutes for a foot bridge to open, but soon we found a place to moor the boat near the customs dock. We tied up and found ourselves in the middle of a small city. It looked unattractive and rough at first. (A small boat was sinking right in front of us.) We went for a walk. It was very warm. We went into a cafe where the waitress could not believe we would want iced coffee. She brought coffee and some ice, but would not combine them. There was an internet cafe, several restaurants, a bank, and a grocery store all within walking distance. *Triumph* and *Sugilite,* along with Kent on *Jack Iron,* whom we had met the previous summer, all were there.

That evening there would be a Miss Fiumicino contest in a park just a few hundred meters from the boat. Of course, we went, and, of course, it was wonderful. Loud music, pretty girls and handsome young men from 8 to 20 were strutting their stuff, along with the latest fashions, to the beat of pounding (American) rap music. Cars and motorcycles raced by the canal on the road just a short distance away. Pedestrians peered into the boat as they walked by. There were several marinas just up the canal from where we were docked. We would have to choose one and make arrangements to have the boat hauled. Our flight reservation were on the first of September.

We signed a contract for nine months of storage for *Tapestry* on the hard at Constellation Nautica Marina. It was not the original plan, but that is how things go. We learned by experience that all the marinas work the same way. They don't take reservations. They will reserve only when you show up in person with your boat. You must be there no later than the first week of August and then it is first come first served. We made it on July 31st. We got a good deal on the storage, but our boat would have to be hauled on the 8th. Unfortunately, our flight reservations were on September 1. What could we do in the mean time? We could explore Rome, and we could work on the boat.

On the first of August, we took the free bus to the airport and from there the subway to Rome. We found ourselves right at the Colosseum. We walked around for hours, exploring the huge structure and listening to tales of what happened within its walls. The stories were amazing. Animals were imported from Africa, lions, giraffes, zebras, and they were killed by gladiators. Gladiators fought each other; they fought Christians. The building was even flooded and used for sea battles. Eventually, the Roman people got tired of all the killing and didn't show up on Sundays.

From there we headed for the Forum. It is amazing to see the remains of so many huge historic buildings in that city. I could imagine Brutus stabbing Caesar. I could imagine all of Roman history. Everywhere there were towers and gates and rooms and walls and sometimes several columns standing alone or supporting a beautiful marble cornice. Most of the buildings were gone, but there were skeletal remains everywhere. It was wonderful. In spite of cautions by others, it was not terribly crowded nor impossibly hot. We got to see all that we wanted.

We walked across town to the tower of Marcus Aurelius, and then on to the Pantheon. This magnificent temple is not only a temple to the gods of Ancient Rome, but also a sundial. Unfortunately, hundreds of years ago some Pope took all the statues of the ancient Roman gods out and replaced them with paintings of the saints. Still, the building has the largest concrete dome in the world for a roof, and it is splendid. We had lunch near the fountain of Trevi, and then walked to the Spanish Steps, below which is the very exclusive area of Italian designer clothing boutiques. We browsed in the shops. There was even a Ferrari store.

We found a place in town that would sell us an electric windlass for our boat. The manual one we had on *Tapestry* had driven me to near distraction for the past several years. I regularly scraped the skin off my knees as I tried to turn the crank and hoist the heavy chain and anchor from the deep Mediterranean anchorages we frequented. It wold cost several thousand dollars, but they would deliver the unit to the boat. Dick, on *Triumph,* was an engineer, and he offered to help me install and wire the unit. We worked several days on the project, but when we were finished, we had a smooth running electric windlass on the foredeck that would allow Julie to hoist the anchor with a touch of a button. Of course, she would have to "spill the chain" in the chain locker as it came up, no small task, but much less than grinding the vertical mechanical winch we had used before. We were proud that we were able to save money by buying this Italian product in Italy. Then, a few months later, we were surprised to find it would have been several hundred dollars cheaper had we bought it back home from a discount catalog in New York.

We had culture shock while we were in Fiumicino as well. One night we were in a pleasant local restaurant when a group came in from a cruise ship. They were Americans, a dozen of them, and they had reserved a table near us. It was a quiet restaurant, but they talked loudly, laughing, animated. They pointed to their menus spoke loudly, and treated the waitress as though they were sure she couldn't understand. They ordered spaghetti, and wondered where the large spoon was, for twirling it, not an Italian tradition. One man, obviously upset, looked at his plate, slammed his fists holding knife and fork on the table and demanded, "Where's the meat?" The waitress was shocked; the pasta was as advertised, but the huge portions so common in the U.S. were not part of the Mediterranean diet. He pushed his plate away and fumed, grumbling and obviously displeased.

When the young waitress came to our table, she apologized for the noise and disruption, obviously very upset. I tried to apologize to her for the behavior of my countrymen. She just shook her head. "That's just the way it is," she said. I hung my head in shame.

Fiumicino

Chapter 51

FIRE!

We were in the garment district of Rome when Jan was the first to see the flames shooting from an apartment window, and soon fire brigades were on their way with people scurrying away from huge red fire trucks with their "he haw" sirens, going much too fast through the crowded streets. Streams of water poured from the truck as men lugged hoses to hydrants and added more and more water. Thick black smoke rolled from the building; it was mass confusion. The fire was a hot one and it took a while to put out.

We headed for the subway and there was a broken down train on the track where we wanted to go. Everyone was taken off the train we wanted, and the station was jam packed with people. After a few minutes another train came and we pushed our way on board with everyone else. It was simply a crush of bodies. When the train started to move, it lurched suddenly and a huge man standing right ahead of me lunged into me, pushing me into others. Jan said it, "Hank, do you have your wallet?" I was sure I did. I carried it in my side pocket, not the back one, but when I put my hand there, the wallet was gone. Jan had seen it go. I accosted the man ahead of me, but he just played dumb till the doors opened a second later and he got off the train. The four of us followed him. We were in an empty station. There was no one around. I yelled "Police," and grabbed him by the arm. Suddenly, it was clear he understood. He emptied all his pockets and then, to our horror, pulled his pants down to show he hadn't concealed my wallet inside. At that moment another train came. With that, he pulled his pants back up and, to prove his guilt, dashed for the open car door. Obviously he had passed the wallet off to someone else, got off the train as a decoy, and the wallet and his accomplice were safely on their way.

We did the police report, which took forever. The police couldn't speak enough English and we couldn't speak enough Italian to get anywhere. Fortunately Steve knew French well enough to get what happened across to the authorities. We lost two hundred euros, but we stopped the credit cards before they were used; we had a backup, and Steve's paying our twenty euro taxi fare back to the boat, saved what was left of an otherwise good day. Back at the marina, Kent from *Jack Iron* gave me a cheap plastic wallet filled with toilet paper. It was a splendid back pocket decoy and useful as bathrooms in Rome generally don't have any paper. He also suggested a thin chain to attach my real wallet to my belt. Good ideas!

Chapter 52

Loose Ends

Of course we had been in Morocco and had officially left the European Union with the boat. That meant the clock, or time allotted for us to be there without paying the VAT tax should have restarted. We tried to check on it while we were in Sardinia, but the customs officials there were unrealistic in their demands. They had wanted several copies of each page of our passports. For what? We decided to check with customs on the mainland. That's when we made our first mistake, we went in the afternoon.

The office of Customs was near the marina. We had our ships' papers and our passports and everything we needed. The waiting room of the office was empty and there were no chairs. We went to the window and explained how we wanted to be sure that, as we had taken the boat to Morocco, out of the EU, the clock should have stopped and then restarted when we checked back in to Spain. The lady at the window was pleasant enough, spoke English, and seemed to understand what we needed. We gave her our paperwork, she took ships papers and passports and she was gone. She insisted we were in the right place. "Sardinia is not Italy," she said. Hmmm. We waited. We waited. We stood on one foot, on the other. We rang the bell. Finally the lady reappeared. She wore a frown. Could we please come back the following day? One never is separated from one's passport, ever. But, we said we would be back in the morning. The next morning we returned and, after another hour's wait, we finally got our paper work showing we had indeed restarted the clock.

What was the problem? Friends suggested that one doesn't ever go to government offices in the afternoon. In Italy, as in France and Spain, lunch is often a kind of celebration; siesta follows, and somehow it is often difficult for those government employees to get much done after lunch. Hence, the wait. But the deed was done. We could stop the clock while the boat was on hard standing at the marina and have plenty of time to get to Turkey the following year.

Tapestry was finally on the hard. The owner of the yard used his crane to move her to a series of jack stands. It was a dicy maneuver, straining the old crane and making it groan, but he did it and she came through without a scratch. We waxed her topsides, greased her winches, changed oil in her various engines and prepared the water maker for winter. We were assured it would freeze there so we bought anti- freeze for the engines. Could we buy anti-freeze for the water system, you know, the potable kind? No. We cleaned and stored the sails, did our best to drain the water system, and did a million other little once-a-year odd jobs. It was a good thing, too, the Fiumicino canal lift bridge got stuck in the down position. The bridge had been destroyed at the end of the Second World War. The "new" bridge, now some 60 years old, had stripped a gear. Repair would take at least a month, perhaps much longer. They had to recast a huge gear, machine it, and then reinstall it. There were boats outside with flight and marina reservations that couldn't get in and there were boats inside that would like to get out, but couldn't. Every day there was speculation. Perhaps they would hire two cranes, disconnect the bridge and lift it so boats could get to where they needed to be, then drop it back for auto traffic; it was all speculation. We just hoped it would be fixed at the end of nine months when it was time for us to return. Meanwhile, helicopters hovered over the bridge from time to time. It was front page news.

And then, of course, there was the river itself. People, lots of people fished from the river at night. They had long bamboo poles, very long ones with bobbers with electric lights. They caught fish, of course. The amazing part was what floated past, especially after a rain. We saw bags of garbage, refuse of all kinds, even a television picture tube bob by on its way to the sea. The river was filthy, horribly polluted, but these people stayed up at night and fished. Were they ignorant, or really hungry? We never quite understood.

With that we boarded a plane at the nearby airport and were on our way back to Florida on the 12th of August. Julie would have a check up, and we would return to our more relaxed American schedule.

The Bridge

In Fiumicino there is a bridge
Broken and stuck in the
Down position.
Cars and walkers
Cruise happily through.
But trapped sailboats are
Stuck in dirty water.
Teased by beckoning winds
And the deep blue of the
Mediterranean Sea,
The bridge is the key;
Whether stuck up
Or stuck down,
Unless the bridge
Works properly,
The journey is
Impossible.

Language, too
Is a bridge,
When the bridge
Functions smoothly,
We can learn and grow
From our contact with
Other cultures.

Henry R. Danielson

When the bridge is broken
We are only tourists,
Peeping Toms,
Buying trinkets
And watching for oddities
In a silent movie.

H.R.D.

Chapter 53

Learning

So what did we learn? How had we grown? We had visited several countries friendly to the U.S. People were gracious, for the most part. We had gone on our own. We had no guides, took few tours. We read guide books, tried to learn a little of the language of each country, but we understood how Europeans valued language. They learned enough of each other's language to get along.

We found people in all the countries we visited exposing themselves on the beaches. They were naked. Some were beautiful, others unattractive, some young, others old. But we found no aggressive or erotic behavior. Did they use sunscreen? They didn't seem to. Sunscreen was available in pharmacies, but one had to ask for it.

Young people consumed alcohol with their families in public, which we found somehow liberating. Everybody seemed to drink quite a bit, but few people appeared intoxicated. There was crime, but few guns. When we were robbed, we were angered but there was no threat to our lives or the lives of our attackers. There was a level of civility here that we liked. These people were not sympathetic to war. They had experienced enough of it. British and German and French and Swiss and Italian people got along, laughed together and seemed to understand each other. We flew our American flag from the boat, a legal requirement, but really a technicality; we didn't have to. As soon as we opened our mouths, people knew where we came from. Still, we were tolerated, treated well.

For the most part we visited tourist venues in the islands and along the coasts. But we found we warmed to the people we met in more traditional settings even more than in the tourist sites. There was a genuine warmth toward Americans. People treated us with a kind of innocence. Everyone seemed to know something good about those who had emigrated to our country. In spite of some ugly Americans in our midst, we were made to feel welcome.

Part 3

Island People:

A Return to Italy

And East

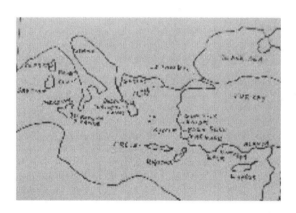

Chapter 54

Good News

Back home we had good news. Julie's cancer had not spread. All was good. We invited friends, Pat and her son Greg, and his wife Elizabeth. They would come with us for two weeks when we returned to Italy the following spring. Pat was an old sailing friend and her son and daughter-in-law were young and enthusiastic sailors as well. We could hardly wait.

When we arrived, however, the boat was not ready to be launched. It sat there, propped up with its name, *Tapestry*, Ashville, NY, prominently displayed on the transom for everyone, friend or foe, on the main street of Fiumicino, to see. It seems there was another festival and the owner was not there to run the crane. It would be two weeks. Unlike in Spain, we could sleep on the boat while it was on land. We would have to climb down the ladder to use the bathroom and we were, of course, very near Rome. So we made a change of plans.

We spent a few days in Rome, again exploring the ancient city with our friends, but then we were off to Florence and Sienna and finally to Venice. We rode trains and busses. We found our own hotels and restaurants. There were museums and churches, bridges and jewelry on display. The history of much of the world was laid out before us and we did what we could to find and absorb. We learned wherever we went that most people were kind and welcoming. We found small restaurants with delightful service and wonderful food. Out of the way places, enjoyed by the locals, were best. Our friends returned to Western New York from Venice, and we headed back toward the boat. Along the way we met our sailing friends, the Bishops and stopped in Cinque Terre.

Here were five cities scattered among the hills along the coast. They were connected by trails so that one could walk from one to the next and visit all five in a single afternoon.

There was a railroad, but no conventional roads between them. They were located on steep hillsides so enemy conquest was difficult. No one city was worth an invasion, and all five would be too spread out for an army to easily conquer. They were basically agricultural towns with small ports and buildings built into the hillsides. They are the stuff of artists, beautiful and remote. The walk from one to the next was memorable, vista after stunning vista.

Back in Fiumicino, the boat was about to be launched. We would need cash to pay for storage, so it seemed obvious we would simply use our credit card in a cash machine to get our money. Suddenly, the credit card wouldn't work. We found a bank and went inside. There was a guard with a rather obvious automatic weapon standing outside. He was intimidating, but we went in anyway. Inside, we had to place all our packages and belongings in a locker in an ante room before we could enter. We were all but searched. We waited in line for a cashier. She examined our card and then made a phone call. We were told to proceed to an office. In the office we were interviewed by a man in a brown suit. He didn't know much English, but I showed him the bill from the marina and he took our passports and our credit card and disappeared. Once again, we knew we shouldn't let anyone take our passports, but what could we say? Finally he came back and after more waiting, he gave us our money. That was it.

To celebrate, we headed for Ostia Antica. Rome is built inland from the coast, so the original port city was Ostia Antica. Like so many Mediterranean port cities such as Troy, it's port silted on the Tiber, the river changed course, and the city was no longer viable for trading ships and the transfer of goods. For that reason, the city of Fiumicino eventually took its place.

There was a story here, too. We found a bus to the ancient city and we entered anxious to see what it had to offer. Inside, we enjoyed walking through the streets. Tile floors of various buildings had been excavated and were much like they must have been several thousand years before. There were walls and rooms, much as one might find in Pompeii. There was an ancient market, places where people would eat and in all of them mosaics were still visible in the floors. It was late afternoon when we had finished and headed back for the marina. We saw a bus pull away from the curb just ahead of us and "Fiumicino" was written on the sign on the side. We almost caught it, but the driver pulled away, then slowed and finally stopped about a hundred yards ahead of us. We had tickets and we chased after the bus at full speed. When we finally got there, quite out of breath, the rear door opened and we squeezed in. The bus was really full, so it was a bit of a tight fit. I moved my way forward to validate our tickets in the machine on a post. As soon as I did so, fellow passengers, watching me, laughed! They watched me move forward through the crowded bus, and when I placed the ticket in the machine to validate it, they laughed. I didn't get it.

It wasn't until we got back to the marina that I learned the reason from a fellow sailor on *Vivache*. Kathleen was a friend who had sailed along with us, had studied in Italy, and taught us a little Italian. She said, "In Italy, even the nuns stiff the bus! That's why they laughed. Most people have tickets, but don't validate them and carry them for weeks at a time. If you get caught, the fine can be substantial, but there is little enforcement. You were an American, you didn't know better, you validated your ticket, so they laughed."

Back at the marina, we paid our bill, shook hands with the owner, got a surprising hug and kiss from his attractive young secretary, and eased out of the harbor, under the bridge, and back into the Mediterranean. We sailed south, to Anzio.

Chapter 55

ANZIO

What did I know about Anzio? My uncle Gus, my Dad's younger brother was in Anzio in the Second World War. He fought alongside Patton for much of the war and he fought in Anzio. I remember his telling about recurring dreams he had. He never bragged about the battles he fought in. He was in the artillery brigade, generally behind the front lines. Long after the war, he had recurring nightmares about that place.

While they were pinned down by German fire, several of his men brought back some German soldiers they had captured. Uncle Gus told his men to take them to the rear. Without their helmets he saw that they were blonde, young German boys, terrified, with tears in their blue eyes. He thought if he had a son, that son might look like one of them. They were hauled off to the rear. Later he learned they had all been shot. "Tried to escape," he was told. Recurring nightmares of that incident stayed with him for the rest of his life.

We anchored in the harbor and visited the town. There was a sporting goods store there, and we went inside. We thought a local fishing lure might do better than the ones we had brought from home. It was late afternoon and we hurried. The man behind the counter was surprisingly fluent in English. He said he used to live in New York. We told him we had sailed from New York. He wondered whether we could stay for a minute. He flipped the sign in the window to "closed" and then shared his story.

He and his wife had emigrated when he was a young man. They had gone to New York where they knew no one. He started a small business, selling fishing tackle, and before long his business grew, as did his family. He and his wife had several children. He bought a dry cleaning store and then a laundry. His businesses grew and he was successful. That is when his father, back in Anzio, became ill. He went back to see his father who was on his death bed and his father with his dying breath, made him promise to come home to Italy and never leave again. He was a good son; he obeyed his father's dying wish. He told us he had sold his American businesses and had a successful sporting goods store in Anzio. Sadly, he only wanted to return to New York where he had found real success. He and his family just wanted to go home, but after his promise to his father....

I don't know what made him want to confess to us, but suddenly I had a new understanding of Coleridge's *Rhyme of the Ancient Mariner,* the wedding guest compelled to tell his story and, of course, Uncle Gus. There was something eerie about it all.

It was dark when we motored our dinghy back to the boat. We had shared the story of a man who had found the American Dream and gave in to the will of his dying father, waking to an unpleasant reality. It was not a cheerful evening for us.

South of us was Naples. Unlike in Florida, Naples had a bad name. Friends had rented a car and driven to Naples and while they stopped in a restaurant, the car was stolen. "Mafia business," we were told. "Keep away from Naples." We did as instructed.

We did stop at Amalfi near the Isle of Capri and, after exploring that portion of the Amalfi Coast, we took a ferry to the Isle of Capri. We were told there was no place to moor there. Of course, when we arrived we found there was a pool of anchored sailboats just off the island's shore. They had used their dinghies to get to shore, as we would have. It didn't appear to be a problem. We explored and enjoyed the opulent and beautiful island, then ferried back to Amalfi and our boat.

Further south on the Vulcan Coast there were volcanos. Smoldering mountains reminded us of Montserrat in the Caribbean. We climbed a volcano in a place called Volcano.

Island People: Deep Water Dreams

People were walking through what appeared to be deep mud in the crater below us, leaving giant letters with their footprints. The word LENNA was spelled out. Interestingly, this was the name of a prominent family from Jamestown, where we grew up. People tromped in the mud beneath us in spite of warnings against possible hazards in this obviously hazardous place. We were happy to see the crater, observe the "Peace Pole" on site, and then return down the mountain and, after lunch, to our boat waiting in the bay. One can only look at the steaming mud in a volcanic crater for so long.

Chapter 56

MESSINA AND TAORMINA

The straits between the boot of Italy and the island of Sicily was our next stop. We crossed the straits and moored along the wall in Messina. The concrete wall we moored to was facing the sea and we were on the back side of it. Rough seas were breaking against the wall, causing thunderous noises and great chunks of water to tumble over the top and fall to the platform at the base of the wall just behind the boat. Spray was everywhere. Sometimes the tops of waves would crash on the boat. They weren't a hazard, but sitting in the cockpit was out of the question. We watched swordfish boats sail into the harbor in the afternoon. They had tall towers for lookouts aboard, making them very distinctive. A harpooner would spear the fish. We had never seen anything like them. The swordfish were considered a delicacy.

The next day we sailed the strait. Tidal flows in the area are extreme and, of course well predicted. Odysseus traveled this area and referred to Scilla and Charybdis. Scilla was actually a supposed monster that would snatch men from the decks of ships. It may have referred to powerful, hurricane force winds in the area that swept sailors into the sea. Charybdis was the great "sucker down." Whirlpools sometimes found in the straits, especially in Odysseus's time, were terrifying and potentially devastating to shipping. We avoided both in our passage, but we came to appreciate the powerful tides. The place had earned its reputation.

We crossed to Sicily and sailed down the coast to Taormina. We anchored with several other boats along the shore. The weather was calm and we were somewhat protected by several points of land. We could take the dinghy ashore to a small pier and then walk a short way to a bus stop where a regular bus would take us up winding switchbacks to the town at the top of the cliff. Needless to say, the vistas were beautiful, stunning. Everyone from Winston Churchill to John Steinbeck, Greta Garbo, and Oscar Wilde had loved the place. We had come for a reason. The town was as beautiful as we had imagined. In the distance was the huge volcano, Mount Etna, smoldering quietly.

What I remember most is the Greek/Roman theater that was there. We visited it and the guide pointed out that it had originally been a Greek theater on the hillside. Plays were performed in the theater and the gentle evening breezes from the sea carried the voices of the actors to the crowd seated above on the hillside. After the Roman conquest, the place changed. A wall was built between the stage and the sea and the edifice was changed from a theater to an arena. Rather than perform plays, duels between men and animals, and between gladiators, replaced the dramas. The sound wasn't carried so perfectly, but what did that matter?

We spent several days in Taormina and though we never walked, but bussed up to the city, we did walk down the steep hills. There were monuments along the road to people who had been killed in accidents along the way. One evening there was a trailer parked at the foot of the hill. It had "Polo Pronto" painted on the sides and through the plate glass window, one could see perhaps a dozen chickens rotating and roasting over a charcoal fire. The smell was overwhelming. We just couldn't resist. We bought one, complete with fries, took it back to the boat and devoured it. Delicious!

Another time I was just stepping onto the road by the bus stop when I heard a whirring sound. Two men in silver suits, mounted on silver BMW motorcycles sped past just inches from me. I was shocked; so fast, so near! These weren't thundering Harley's but quiet silver slashes in the summer afternoon; another side of Italy.

Henry R. Danielson

To the south was Etna, the huge active volcano famous metaphorically as the giant that hurled rocks at Odysseus. We would head west and sail near on our way to Siracusa. Taormina was such a special place, I couldn't help writing about it.

Taormina

We roll at anchor beneath a cliff
Where D.H. Lawrence extolled the
Beauty of Taormina, where ancient
Greeks built a magical theater and
Where Romans remodeled it,
Blocking out Etna, tearing up the
Orchestra pit and making it fit
For gladiator contests.

Here, not far from Scilla and Charybdis,
Monsters of the sea, the one eyed Cyclops
Hurled rocks at Odysseus and his men,
Sending them toward Ithaca and home.

Roaring trains greet us now as we row ashore,
Pull the dinghy onto a gravel beach, cross under
The tracks and up the ragged path to town where
Speedo Pollo promises us fresh hot chicken to go,
And motorcycles speed along a narrow road.

Meanwhile, every hundred years or so,
The one eyed monster, Etna, rears her ugly head,
And hurls rocks at those who lurk below.

H.R.D. 5/26/06

Island People: Deep Water Dreams

Domed Freight

Railroad cars roll by us
Here at Taormina. The track
Is right by the water;
Old freight cars with rounded
Roofs and just two wheels
On a side, rather than four.

They remind us of jerky films
With women in shawls and
Men in tight fitting suits boarding
Freight cars en route
To places we cannot forget.

Why do they keep them, these old cars?
Why not replace them with new?
History tries to teach us not to make the
Same mistake twice.
"Some of us never learn."
"About the Jews, you mean?"

"Yes, about the war."

        H.R.D.
        Anchored off Taormina
        5/26/06

Taormina Tribute

In *Tapestry* we roll below
Lovely Taormina.
It is a senseless rolling
In a calm sea.

Henry R. Danielson

Above us a lovely city lies on its rock
Looking over a timeless sea.
D.H. Lawrence, Goethe, and
Winston Churchill loved this place
For its cooling breezes, quiet
Simplicity and lovely view.

Today three cruise ships visited,
Jamming streets, crowding restaurants,
With waddling tired tourists
Who follow flags and raised
Umbrellas to see the Greek theater
Wrecked by the Romans and
Being improved by the Sicilians.
They bought tee shirts, ate spaghetti,
Saw all the right things,
And hurried back to their ship
Never having really seen
The lovely, quiet little town
That sits on its rock above the
Sparkling blue Mediterranean Sea.

In *Tapestry* we roll below
Lovely Taormina.
It is a senseless rolling
In a calm sea.

H.R.D.

Chapter 57

SIRACUSA
AND
RETURN TO ITALY

We anchored in the harbor of this ancient city, Siracusa. Archimedes lived and died here. He developed catapults and a system of mirrors that could be used to set fire to enemy ships in defense of the city. When one walks on the roads in Siracusa, one walks on the same roads Archimedes had walked on. There is something moving about that. Archimedes died in Siracusa. A soldier of an invading army forced his way into the great scholar's home while Archimedes was engrossed in his studies. Because he didn't rise at the command of the armed soldier, lost in thought as he was, the soldier killed him. What a shame for all of us. Actually, he was supposed to have been spared, but somehow that order didn't make it through the ranks.

Food prices in the local grocery were surprisingly high for us. They seemed almost twice what they were on the mainland. We were told it was the fault of the Mafia. Extortion was a regular part of doing business.

There was an American couple in a J-46 sailboat we met at a fuel dock. They told us the harrowing story of their stop in Catania. They had pulled into the harbor and purchased twelve hundred euros worth of fuel and then rented a car, left the boat at the marina, and drove to explore Mount Etna. When they got back to their boat, they found their tanks were empty. When they questioned the marina staff, no one had seen anything. Still, someone had pumped hundreds of gallons of fuel from their boat. Later, when they checked their credit card statement, they told us they found that according to their statement, the car they had rented had been involved in a minor accident and their security deposit was taken by the rental company. "Don't you dare go to Catania," they had said. We felt that was sound advice.

From Siracusa, we headed north, again stopping for a night in Taromina. From there we continued to the bottom of the boot of Italy to a marina along the sole of the boot. The marina was actually a series of floating docks that had been built and financed by the European Union, the stipulation being that it need be paid for by the Italians only when it was finished and earning money. We found the place and easily found a slip where we could moor the boat. Surprisingly, there was no fresh water and no electricity available. There were huge "inspection" holes in the decks, but the covers were missing. One could easily fall into them if not careful. The docks were not lighted at night. In addition, there were boats moored in the facility that had been left unattended for years. Some of them had sunk in their slips, others had simply been abandoned. Some were luxury yachts, others more modest. We learned from other sailors the story of the place. They said the money for the marina had come from the EU, and didn't have to be paid back until the marina was making money and self supporting. The powers that be in the area decided to never quite finish it. They would not connect the power or water or do any of the finishing touches. That way they wouldn't have to repay the loan. Visitors could dock there for free and keep their yachts there as long as they wanted. They would go ashore and spend money in the neighboring towns. Visitors would have plenty of money to spend as there were no fees, and they would stay, as there was no incentive to leave. They had not anticipated that those who had fallen on bad fortune, a death or illness, might leave their boats in the marina to disintegrate, and return to their home country, leaving the yacht to decompose and become an expensive eyesore.

Island People: Deep Water Dreams

Roccella Ionica

A medieval city on the sole of Italy
Roccella Ionica,
East of the Straits of Messina
West of the Bay of Squalls,
Its castle rises on rocky bluffs
Over a small Italian town.
Grocers sell fresh garden veggies,
Butchers cut chops from huge hunks of meat.
A perfumery, a pharmacy, a fish market,
Restaurants with colorful umbrellas
Crowd the public square;
No tourist town,
This is real Italy.

Tapestry waits weather in an
Abandoned marina. She groans
Against her lines, trapped by
Low pressure. Wind whistles
Through her rigging and her
Fenders squeal as she rubs
Sides with a French yacht;
Blue skies, black clouds,
Rain. We look to a rising
Barometer and raising
Sail.

H.R.D.
06/06/06

Delle Grazie Marina

It means "thank you" in Italian
And it is free

Henry R. Danielson

Docks for six hundred boats.
Finger piers, unusual in Europe.
A nice restaurant at the bottom of the dock,
And protection for all on
Italy's long and treacherous south coast.

It is we who should say *"Grazie,"*
Like Stintino in Sardinia,
Delle Grazie in
Roccella Ionica.
Protection from the storm,
Courtesy the European Union.
A beacon of light on a dark horizon,
"Grazie."

     HRD

Chapter 58

GREECE

We left the sole of the boot of Italy and headed for Greece. Along the way, we had an adventure of our own. I removed a radio from its place over the control panel in the pilothouse. I had to check the antenna and ground connections. Just as I was examining the wiring, the diesel engine below the floorboards began to sputter and then die. That had never happened before. I would have called Dick and Eileen aboard *Triumph*, as they were sailing with us, but the radio was dead and by the time I got the hand-held, they were out of range. I opened the floorboards to see what I could find in the engine compartment. The fuel filters looked clean, diesel engines don't rely on battery power, what could it be? Here we were off the boot of Italy drifting and rolling on a flat sea. There was no wind. What could it be? It was then I looked at the radio I had disconnected. I had set it on the control panel and it had shifted and its weight had triggered the "Stop Engine" switch. I moved the radio, touched the starter and the engine burst to life. So much for that. What a relief!

We arrived in Lefkas and took the boat to a proper marina. This one had set fees. Even though Greece is part of the EU, one has to officially check in with his boat. We would have to visit Customs, Immigration, the local police, in that order. Each would apply his stamp to the proper place in our passport or other papers.

As we moved from one government office to the next, we learned shops in the area were delightful. Unlike in Italy and Spain, Greek is foreign enough so the Greeks don't expect you to understand their language. They spoke English. We made an effort to learn a few Greek words and people smiled when we used them. We liked Greece already.

After our paperwork was finished, Julie and I rented a motor scooter to explore the island. We did. What more can I say? In one place a hill was so steep we had to stop and Julie had to get off and walk up the hill as I rode the scooter. There was little traffic. Though some roads were poorly paved, it was easy riding. Finally, we got totally lost. We stopped an old farmer who was mending his fence. We gave him our map, and asked how to get back to the marina. Not only did the gentleman not speak English, he didn't seem at all comfortable with the map. We managed to find our way back. It was an island, after all, and we left the cycle at the shop where we had rented it. The rental shop was closed for the afternoon, siesta, you know. So we just left it there with the key in the ignition. No problem.

Greece is old. I remember before we returned to our boat, walking to some ruins overlooking the sea. Huge rocks had been somehow cut and carefully set in place without mortar to form a defensive wall. It was so old, thousands of years! We climbed up and walked along to tops of the rocks. The Greeks insist they are concerned for your safety, but not responsible for it. The sense of connection with the ancient world there is moving. One slip and the fall over the side would surely be fatal. We were careful. What a moment!

We motored and sailed south from Lefkas and under the Antirrio Bridge, near Patros.

That bridge is the longest suspension bridge in the world. It crosses the Gulf of Corinth and is tall enough for shipping; no problem for us. Our first stop was the home of Odysseus, Ithaca.

Ithaca

The Island of Ithaca is too steep for horses to breed,
But it is the home of Odysseus
And, in his time, they used boats instead of horses
To get around to Vathi

Island People: Deep Water Dreams

A little harbor town, Vathi
Has a movie theater where teen-aged kids
Sit in the back row,
Make too much noise,
And are shushed by adults down front.

It is a clean town, Vathi.
Muted tones,
With white shuttered windows,
Potted plants, and restaurants
By the sea.
Where one can eat lamb,
Drink beer,
Be cooled by the breeze
And think of Odysseus
Coming home from Troy
To Penelope,
Telemachus, and Argus,
His faithful dog.

H.R.D.
06/06/o6

It was June 17th and we were in Trizonia when Julie and I celebrated our 39th Anniversary. We had dinner that night at Lizzie's Yacht Club.

Happy 39th Anniversary

At thirty-nine we're at our prime
Sailing the frothy sea,
We've worked a time,
And earned our dime,
Teaching kids what they can be.

Henry R. Danielson

We sail our boat
To spots remote,
Trizonia here today.
To castles we climb,
Researching time,
In our boat, *Tapestry*.

It's pretty neat,
It's quite a feat,
To be married for so long;
To still have fun,
To bike and run,
And sail and love and be!

Love to you,
Skip

The next day it was Missalonghi.

Missalonghi

A town in the Gulf of Corinth
With a free marina of old concrete at
The end of a three mile channel.
The land is low and houses on
Stilts greet the yachtsman as he approaches,
And the marina is grim, too, with skinny, hungry dogs
Who follow us to town.
Past vandalized tanks and aircraft in a little un-mowed park
With a broken fence.
An Ironic tribute to war.

It is the death place of Lord Byron, who came here to
Fight in the war.

Island People: Deep Water Dreams

A statue and museum reminds us
Of him.

But beyond formalities lie narrow streets lined with shaded
Cafes and restaurants where pork roasts and pops
On spits over red charcoal;
Where afternoon frappe's cool and sweet, are served in
Curved glasses, where a lively fountain sprays clear
Water into the afternoon sun, and where it
Is possible to escape from tourist Greece
To a place where young and old meet
And talk and drink and eat and live
And reveal Greek culture,
The reason we
Wanted to come to Greece
In the first
Place.

H.R.D.
06/18/06

The Lord Byron Museum captured our imaginations here, too. He was an English Romantic poet who died in Missolongi, fighting in a civil war. But it was the paintings that adorned the stairway of the museum that most moved us. Turks were the villains, armed with long knives, killing women and children. We were headed for Turkey. It didn't seem promising.

Chapter 59

DELPHI

Still in the Bay of Corinth, we stopped at Itea, the nearest port to Delphi, which is inland. Delphi is the famous place in ancient Greece where "Oracles" were able to forecast the outcomes of wars and decide whether marriages were a good idea or not. Itea had a wall where we could safely moor. We tied the boat up and a man came by and said we would have to report to the authorities in "the building with the yellow windows." One of the rules we had learned when we landed in Lefkas was that cities had the authority to charge fees, but that they would come to you; it was not necessary for the owner of the boat to go to them. Reluctantly, we left the boat and began our search for the building with the yellow windows. People on shore seemed to know what I meant and when we got there, there was a short line.

I walked up the narrow staircase at the top of which was a small office. Inside there was a cramped waiting room and an open door to an inner sanctum with an officer of some kind interviewing other cruisers.

"And how long will you be staying."

"Just one day"

"Will you be staying in town?"

"No, we'll take the bus to Delphi."

"That will be twelve euros."

"What!"

"Twelve euros, please!"

There was some rustling in a purse and then,

"Next!"

It was my turn and I moved to a spot across the desk from the officer as the Canadian couple, frowning, walked out the door and down the steps.

Just as I was fishing for my passport, a very large Australian man stepped in the doorway. He was red faced, clearly angry.

"If you charge this bloke," referring to me, "what you did that Canadian couple, my wife and I will take our boat and leave, right now. Do you understand? We'll leave right now and we will tell all our friends not to come here, ever!"

The officer looked at me, frowned and said "Ten euros!" With that the Australian, swore, grabbed his wife's arm and together they pounded down the steps out of the office. I was nonplussed. I reached for my wallet, found ten euros, gave it to the man and left.

The next day with Dick and Eileen from *Triumph* we took the first morning bus to Delphi. Right away we found the theater and Dick and Eileen and I walked to the top of the huge gently curved array of rock seats built on the hillside. The soft breeze and the rising morning air were perfect. Below, in the area at the bottom, the center of the stage, Julie whispered, "Take off your hats." and the three of us, at the very top, removed our hats together. It was simply a magic moment. The acoustics of the open theater were wonderful.

Delphi was where people went to learn truths from women called Oracles. It was the home of Apollo. These women had mysterious powers that enabled them to see truth. If you remember the play *Oedipus Rex*, by Sophocles, Oedipus came to Delphi where he learned he would kill his father and marry his mother. People from all over the world came to Delphi for the prophecies of the oracles. They paid large amounts of money for the information and pirates were often waiting to attack them and steal their money along the way. It was a dangerous journey. The process of learning one's fortune lasted a whole day and involved bathing in a special spring, animal sacrifice, inhaling smoke from burning laurel leaves as well as the Pythia's breathing intoxicating ethylene gasses from a cave, and then, the Pythia's babbling. The Pythia was the high priestess of the temple of Apollo. Other Priests would interpret the slurred speech to give it some kind of meaning.

The treasury, along with numerous other ruins is one of the remaining buildings at the site, along with a 177 meter playing field, surrounded by seating, where one of the first Olympics was held. There is also a museum that contains numerous artifacts excavated from the site. Delphi is still a center for world peace. It was well worth the visit.

Interestingly, long ago an earthquake caused a landslide that buried many artifacts and a sidewalk was built that covered many more. When the walk and the remains of the landslide were removed some years ago, the artifacts were recovered and the museum was opened.

We visited an impressive athletic venue and took the bus back to Itea in the evening.

We left the island of Trizonia at Itea on a Sunday morning, and we were quiet so we wouldn't interrupt the church services.

Grecian Sunday

Serpentine fences of stone climb hills,
Cover boulders and end at the sea or
Precipitous drop offs
So goats cannot find their
Way into terraced fields.

Blue skies and a deep blue
Aegean Sea are punctuated by arid islands
With stone houses
White chapels, blue
Domes and bells that say,
"Come to church
Come to church
Come to

Island People: Deep Water Dreams

Come to
Come to church."
On Sunday mornings.

As goats and old men
Move about
Watching sailors
Come and go
At abandoned marinas
And open air
Restaurants.

H.R.D.,
7/01/06

Chapter 60

THE CORINTH CANAL
NAOUSA, AMORGOS
AND
SYMI

From Itea, we headed for the Corinth Canal. What a wonderful surprise, Hundreds of dolphins, small ones, surrounded us. Unlike those we were familiar with in Florida, those that surface to breathe and then dive from sight, these little dolphins flung themselves into the air beside the boat as we sailed along. It was hilarious and simply delightful. Dolphins, Delphi. A delphinium is a flower named for a woman from Delphi. Wow. What a place.

The Bay of Corinth separates what was the famous city states of Athens and Sparta. We continued until we came to the Corinth Canal. In ancient times Greeks had wanted a canal to pass through the isthmus and under Emperor Nero, they had tried to dig one, but the labor was too intense. The land was unstable and there was concern that different heights of water at either end might create strong currents and make the passage unnavigable. It was not until the 1880's that the canal was actually dug.

The canal itself is about four miles long, seventy feet wide, and twenty feet deep. It is not large enough for modern shipping, but ideal for small boats like ours. The sides are still unstable and it needs to be maintained regularly to keep the canal from filling in.

Transit through the canal is carefully regulated. There is one-way traffic only. Boats go in one direction for a period of time, and then traffic is stopped and vessels heading in the opposite direction make their way. The canal saves over 400 miles of ocean travel, so for small boats it is very worthwhile.

Interestingly, at either end of the canal is a bridge that is submerged to allow passage, rather than being raised like a typical lift bridge. Passage through the canal was uneventful and, after the wait for opposing traffic, took less than an hour.

East of the canal, we continued on our way. Winds were strong and we found ourselves reefed much of the way. It was called the *Meltemi*, a strong wind from the north.

We sailed to Epihavros where we anchored and found we had internet. We made reservations home from Istanbul to Tampa for later in the summer. In Paros, I dropped the camera in the water at the pier. It slipped out of my shirt pocket. I dived in and retrieved it, then opened it and left it in the sun aboard the boat to dry out. The hot Greek sun did its job and when we got back, I replaced the battery and turned it on. It worked! Unfortunately, though the camera functioned properly, the salt water had done a number on the inside of the camera lens and, as I couldn't clean that side, it took the most amazing pictures. Of course, they weren't recognizable, just smears of color. I trashed the camera. It wasn't until I got back to the States I read about someone who had published a book of just such photos. What am I missing here?

While we were on Paros, we took a ferry to Naousa, a city that simply awed us with its stunning beauty.

Naousa

White boxes scattered on the hillside.
White boxes with dark windows and doors.
Houses and shops and narrow streets.
Breezy, clean narrow streets with
Everything painted white,
Not ivory, but bright white,
Glaring white set off by blue
Shutters and a sparkling blue sea.
There are shops here with white dresses

Henry R. Danielson

And colorful jewelry and
Sparkling windows and
Fresh fruit and vegetables
Against white walls.
There is a shimmering heat
And cold beer and
Frappe with sugar and milk.
Across the bay
People swim nude
Then dry tender parts
In the Mediterranean sun.
No tan lines here.
A little Grecian culture,
A bit of what it was
In the good old days,
Before Rome had its say.

H.R.D.
7/01/06

From Naousa, we headed to Amorgos.

It was in the entrance of the harbor that we saw her. She was an elegant J Class yacht that raced against Endeavor in the 1934 America's Cup Race. *Shamrock*, beautifully restored rested quietly on the still water. We passed her by and on the second of July, 2006, we entered the busy harbor at Amorgos. Comfortable restaurants surround the harbor and a village climbs the hill behind.

Blue and White

A hundred houses all pushed together
In the corner of a bay on a rocky island in the
Bright blue Aegean Sea.
All houses are white with blue trim.

Island People: Deep Water Dreams

Look closely and you will see
That they are individual buildings
With blue shutters and doors.
They are close together,
And between them are narrow
Streets offering shade from
The blistering sun,
Catching breezes, and
Holding small tables
With colorful clean cloths
Kept in place with stainless clips;
A tall bottle of cold water
Two glasses,
And two blue chairs.

HRD

We enjoyed fine protection on the island as meltemi winds
roared outside in the sea.

Fourth of July on Amorgos

There is no red, just white and blue
This Fourth of July on Amorgos Island.
Buildings are white cement with
Blue shutters of varying shades.
But there is green in palm
And conifer whose limbs shade
Colorful tables near the water's edge.
Buildings are stacked on the hillside
A kind of relief from the brown scrub behind them.
Stone fences zig and zag up the hills, keeping
Goats where they belong and isolating parched
Terraces where gardens used to grow.
Mycenaeans are buried here,

Henry R. Danielson

An ancient monastery climbs a rock wall,
But this afternoon we are on the boat
Rolling in strong wind, hoping anchor
And chain will suffice to hold us off
The rocky beach close behind.
It may be the quietest Fourth of July
Ever, for us, rolling on a blue harbor
With white caps, listening to the
Screaming of the wind.

> H.R.D.
> July 4, 2006
> Amorgos, Greece

We rented a car and explored the island. The hills were steep and the roads were narrow. There were memorials to loved ones lost along the road, perhaps run down, or involved in an auto accident. These weren't simple crosses, however. Often they were small memorials carefully encased, complete with a glass window, a lighted candle. Even though the loved one may have died decades before, the memorials were clean and maintained, the candles glowing. It was a touching side of faith, common in Greece, but rare in the rest of the world.

Hozovoiotissa Monastery was one of our goals on the island. It is eight stories high, but only five meters, or fifteen feet wide. Of course it is gleaming white. It clings to the side of a cliff and hangs over the sea. We drove to it, parked our car and walked to the foot of a long stairway that leads up to the entrance. One must be appropriately dressed to venture inside, and one must be invited. I had worn long pants that morning and a regular short sleeved shirt with a collar. Julie, Eileen and Dick had worn shorts. A priest appeared at the top of the stairs, moved from behind the door and signaled me to come up; not the others, just me. Perhaps it was something about the shorts or the uncovered heads of the women. Whatever, with some trepidation, I climbed the steps. At the top, I was warmly greeted by the priest. He asked about me, where I was from. I was introduced to others. I was offered whiskey, which, as I was driving on these narrow roads, I politely refused. There were prayers. I felt a strange warmth. There was genuine caring here. I sat at the table with these men of the Greek Orthodox faith. They offered bread and wine. They prayed in English, I'm sure for my benefit.

They were warm and sincere. When I told them that I had to leave, they graciously escorted me to the door and wished me well. I was truly moved. As I walked down the bright white stairs to the others, who had returned to the car, I was smitten by a thought. It was perhaps the only time I had been in a church building where there was no place for donations. No one had asked for money or for anything else for that matter. They didn't try to convert me either. They simply, warmly prayed for my well being. I was moved.

Back on *Tapestry*, we attached a small magnetic television antenna to the metal case of the SSB radio and with a portable tuner, converted the computer into a TV. We watched soccer, some preliminaries for the World Cup, on television. Next morning we raised anchor and eased out the entrance on our way to Symi.

Symi on the island of Nimos, is spectacular. There is no other way to describe it. Steep hillsides surround the lagoon where we entered. All around the shore are buildings. They are restaurants and shops of all kinds. Hundreds of yachts are tied to shore. Everyone uses Mediterranean moorings by dropping anchors in the center of the bay and backing to shore where passers by take lines and make them fast. Water in the center of the harbor is deep so adequate scope is important. Yachts lower *passerelles*, boarding planks, to the wall behind them. Sailors step off the transom onto the narrow board walkway and in a few steps are ashore. The boat is made secure and that's it. The sides of the valley at Symi are steep so roads going up the hill are often not roads at all, but stairways. Donkeys carry goods up the steps to buildings on the upper level. The area surrounding the harbor is filled with buildings in classical architecture. Shuttered windows are not just blue but red and blue and other colors as well.

When the island was liberated during the end of World War II, the German flyers who had been living there during the war and who escaped as the allies retook the island, returned in their planes to bomb the place where they had lived. The Greeks there are still mad.

As usual, we enjoyed the warmth of those in Symi. I remember I bought a suede leather jacket while I was there. Handmade, it was beautiful. Of course, the weather was warm that July, and late at night those who had been enjoying night life in the bars would walk along the harbor's edge. Music echoed along the streets in the open cafes and bars. We kept the aft cabin windows open hoping for the cool breeze, but with the fresh air was music and the noise of the street. I remember one passer by in the early morning hours, commenting to his wife. "*Tapestry*, Ashville, NY. Lived in New York all my life and never heard of any such place." And so it went. We dozed off eventually in the beautiful city.

From Symi, we would head for Turkey where we would be free of the constraints of the European Union. We would still have to abide by the limits of the Schengen Accord, but it would be easier than the EU We would have to leave the country every 90 days, but we could leave the boat without having to pay the VAT.

An old sail school buddy from the Chautauqua Lake Yacht Club, Bunny, had lived on a lovely yacht in Marmaris, Turkey, with her husband, Bill, for years. Her mom and my mother had played bridge together at our local yacht club in Lakewood when I was still a child. Bunny and her husband, Bill, had belonged to our yacht club back home, too. It would be great to see them.

Still, we didn't know much about Turkey. It was an Islamic country, after all. How would we be treated? What facilities would they have? Would anyone speak English? There were many questions. It looked as if we would find out the answers soon.

Hozovoiotissa Monastery

Chapter 61

MARMARIS, TURKEY

It was a short half-day sail from Symi to Marmaris. On the way in we passed a large ferry on foils speeding along. I called Marmaris Yacht Marine, where we intended to stay, on the radio, and received a competent reply in clear English. We were assigned a slip in what I saw was indeed a huge marina. A rubber boat met us at the marina entrance and we followed it to the slip where he guided us in and helped us tie up. There was electricity and water available. Wi-Fi was available everywhere, free and powerful. Clean, tiled showers and toilets were located on every dock. The place was immaculate. There were rules. Marine heads were not to be used in the marinas. Washing of clothes and the discharge of soap suds, including from washing of boat decks, was strictly prohibited and violators would face stiff fines. There was enforcement! Turkey?

Once we had secured the boat we walked the docks to shore where we checked in at the marina office. It was explained to us that, especially as it was our first time, we would hire a person to take care of Customs formalities for us. The price was reasonable, we agreed. To our amazement, we learned there would be hydroplane races off the marina in the harbor the following day. The marina would be able to haul and store the boat on land for 1150 euros. That was for a full year. We simply couldn't believe the place. They stored 1000 boats on shore and 400 at docks. They would haul and launch when we wanted them to. We could spend time at the docks or go off cruising and they would find a place for us upon our return to the marina. There was a lovely restaurant and pool overlooking the sea and a laundry where we could wash our clothes or have it done for us. The restaurant was elegant and beautifully appointed, therefore, expensive, but there was another option.

The worker's cafeteria was open to everyone and there one could enjoy delightful Turkish food on clean tables at very reasonable prices. One could even have a beer.

On Sunday, we visited with Gary and Sharon Groves on *Wingalot*. They had shipped their boat from the U.S. to Marmaris, and it still had fuel in the tanks purchased in the U.S. We enjoyed the hydroplane races with them from the comfortable cockpit of their boat. Bill and Bun Bailey, our old friends from the Chautauqua Lake Yacht Club, entertained us as on their lovely boat as well. What an amazing place.

We took the *dolmus*, bus, to town the following Monday. The little bus stopped up the hill from the marina and Julie and I squeezed in a back seat. As I didn't have correct change, and as there was no aisle to walk to the front, I was told to give my money to the person in front of me and s/he or she would hand it forward. I gave him a bill worth several times the fare and in a moment or so the person in front of me handed me the correct change. My money had gone from back to front through the hands of perhaps half a dozen people to the driver who had made change and passed the change back to me via the same six people. Perfect. Who were these people? Wow!

In town we found a city built around a medieval castle. There was a huge market where fresh produce and meat were available, and virtually everything could be found in stores along the streets of the town. My pulse did quicken a bit when a man on a motorcycle sped toward Julie and me in an old part of town. He wore a turban and had a propane tank strapped to his back along with two more tanks strapped, one either side, to his motorcycle. It was no problem, on his way to get them filled, no doubt. Islamic people were everywhere, and we even went to a mosque for lunch, where we had a delicious meal and *ayran*, a yogurt drink. The food was excellent. Of course, we could have gone to McDonalds, or K.F.C., but we chose the mosque. Oh….

Back on board *Tapestry* the upholstery had worn thin. We had been told Marmaris was a wonderful place to have such work done. At the recommendation of our friends, Bill and Bun, we contacted a man named Black Cloud, who came to measure the pilothouse of the boat for new cushions. They would be hand made in beige leather. He would purchase a hide and make and install the cushions himself. When we asked him about the origin of his name, he told us he had worked in Germany for Mercedes Benz as an upholsterer and, as they had trouble pronouncing his Turkish name, they nicknamed him Black Cloud. That was good enough for us.

We would pay him for the hide and then make a second payment for making the cushions when the materials arrived. Any additional final payment would be due when the work was finished the following year, when we returned to the boat in spring.

We had made our reservations to fly home to Florida from Istanbul. We would get to Istanbul by bus. Others assured us it would be a bus ride to remember.

Every day we were in the marina, we found something else to be amazed at. The travel-lifts, used for hauling and launching boats, were simply the largest I had ever seen. One was large enough to actually launch or haul and small ship or ferry. I could barely reach to top of its eight tires with my hand standing on tip toes. It was simply huge! There were several other smaller travel-lifts as well.

There was a strict procedure one followed when launching or hauling the boat. The owner of the yacht was responsible for deciding the date he wanted his boat launched the following year. That date was then clearly written on the rudder. It was the owner's responsibility to have his boat ready for launch on that date. The boats were then arranged in the yard in order of launch time. The time of day was up to the marina. It could be early morning or late at night, but when the travel lift appeared, the boat had better be ready to go, or additional charges would apply. The huge yard was an efficiently run, busy place.

Something else happened when we were there. We learned about the EMYR. The Eastern Mediterranean Yacht Rally left every year from Istanbul, sailed along the coast of Turkey to Cypress, Syria, Lebanon, Israel, and finally on to Egypt. There would be dances and dinners and parties along the way. Participants would meet government officials and be expected to dress with coat and tie for dinners at various sites. It was a big deal. We talked with our friends and decided we would sign up. Bill and Bun had done it previously and highly recommended it. Perhaps we could find friends from home who would want to do it with us. Why not?

Right on schedule, we were called to the haul out slip to have *Tapestry* hauled and placed in the yard in the order she would be launched the following spring. The workers on the lift were experienced and placed the straps right where they were supposed to be. Never mind the marks on the rail that identified where they should go; one of the men dove into the water. He carefully placed the forward strap just forward of the keel and the aft strap behind the keel, but clear of the propeller shaft. I was impressed. No one had ever done that on our boat before. I was a little surprised when logs standing on end were used to support the boat on land, but it was leveled and shimmed and the logs were securely strapped in place before the travel lift went off for its next load. We climbed aboard, the boat was secure; we felt confident it would be fine.

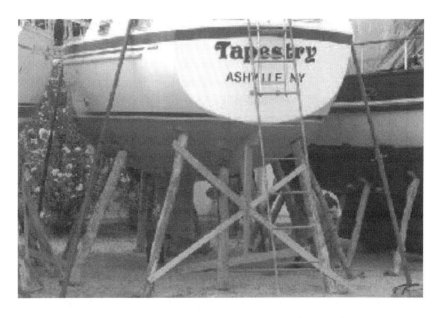

Tapestry on hard standing in Marmaris, Turkey

Chapter 62

ISTANBUL

The bus ride to Istanbul was an overnight run. We took the *dolmus* to Marmaris and then, after an excellent restaurant dinner, we boarded the modern bus. The ride was smooth though the roads were narrow and winding, rising on hills and dropping into vales. We were pleased and impressed with a breakfast of bread with black olive spread, a hard boiled egg and, of course, tea. Delightful! When we got to Istanbul, we got our first real surprise. We knew we were in the city and we gathered our things and got off the bus with other passengers. It was then that a young islamic lady turned to us. She shook her head. "Not here," she said. We asked the driver and when we told him we would stay in the Side (see da) Hotel, he assured us we would want to stay on the bus, cross the river and go to the European side. How had she known? How did that woman know we didn't want to be on the Asian side? Why should she care? That, we realized, was typical of Turkey. Our preconceived notions had been all wrong.

Our hotel was modest to say the least. The window in our room looked out on a brick wall. There was a small bath and a sink in the room. But it was clean, the double bed, comfortable, and it was all we needed. Of course, we were tired, but we had slept on the bus so we began our exploration of the city. We found the huge Blue Mosque and wandered inside. Topkapi Palace had been the home of the many wives of the sultans. On a tour there we viewed the lovely building along with the arm bone of John the Baptist.

Later we visited a rug shop where we assured the owner we just wanted to look around. He showed us rugs and more rugs, but we weren't about to buy. There was a young woman seated at a large wooden loom making a rug, thread by thread. It was colorful, delicate, ever so slowly being created. The articulate confident owner, seemed offended that we weren't ready to buy. We didn't understand the aggressive nature of rug salesmen in Turkey. He told us about Princes' Island, a place where we could visit. It had been home to the younger sons, princes, of the Sultan and his harem, those not in line to inherit the title of Sultan. It kept them isolated from the true prince so they would do him no harm. He had tickets to the island for sale, so we bought them.

It wasn't until later that day we learned the rug salesman had charged several times the official rate for tickets to Princes' island. When confronted, he bought back the tickets for which we had overpaid. We bought replacements from the travel agent at the official rate. We got on a ferry and went to the island. The island was a beautiful garden. There were no motor vehicles, just horse drawn carriages and lots of people walking from lovely place to place. Beautiful Ottoman buildings in near perfect condition reminded us somehow of Chautauqua Institution in Western New York, where colorful Victorian homes fill the pedestrian only community. We were truly drawn into the beauty of the island, so much so that we nearly missed our return boat. We ran back to the pier and were the last two to make it aboard before they closed the gate and sailed.

On the way back, we met a man from Iran with his wife. We sat at a table together, ate some food and drank tea. She was in full cover, with only a tiny slit for her eyes. We were able to have a bit of a conversation with them. He spoke English and she spoke through him. We peeked inside their world. We felt somehow welcome there, not quite what we had been led to expect back home in America.

In the evening we went to a Mosque in Sultanahmet, near our hotel. We enjoyed a fine dinner while we watched a whirling dervish. We had no idea. We were captivated by this lovely young lady as she spun round and round for many minutes. Why? "It gives the spinner a feeling of great joy, of being close to God," we were told. Later we rented a *hookah*, a water pipe. It had two tubes running from the bowl, which was filled with aromatic apple wood, but no tobacco. We smoked and enjoyed the aroma of the wood. It was nothing special, but the whole evening was very different than anything we had ever experienced before and it was very pleasant. Back at the hotel sleep came easily.

The following day we visited a giant Byzantine cistern built under the city in the sixth century. Corinthian columns, 336 of them, said to be from the Roman Forum, supported the city above. Back on the surface, there was an obelisk from ancient Egypt. The place was magic and everywhere we turned we found something new, well, very old, but new to us anyway.

Our dinner that evening was in a small restaurant with tables on the street. Our server was a Kurd. He shared with us the struggle his people had long endured with the Turkish Government. His English was easy to understand. It was obvious he was well educated. He told us the cooks in the restaurant were also Kurds. It was our introduction to Kurdish intolerance in Turkey.

And so, the following day, we boarded our first Turkish Airlines flight back to the U.S. What was this? There was ample legroom, free beer, delicious meals, caring hostesses. What a great flight.

Back home, Julie was well, life was good.

Henry R. Danielson

Part 4

ISLAND PEOPLE:

THE MIDDLE EAST,

EMYR

Chapter 63

Back to Turkey

It was the year 2007, and it was the 11th of April when we left Tampa Airport, bound, via London, for Istanbul and then to Dalaman, Turkey, where we would take a taxi to Marmaris. That was the year of the time change. For some reason the U.S. and Canada had extended Daylight Savings Time and everyone but our airline got it right. Somehow, though the changes were made public, it affected flight schedules. We arrived in London just as our flight to Istanbul was leaving. Fortunately, the airline found another flight for us that might just allow us to make the connecting flight to Dalaman.

The airport in Istanbul is an amazing hub and we somehow managed to make the connection. It was dark when we landed at Dalaman, found a cab and headed for Marmaris. The driver knew some English and we made our destination clear.

Riding in a taxi at night in Turkey was not something we were used to. First of all was the traffic. There was very little auto traffic, but there were pedestrians and bicycles, unlit, along the sides of the roads. Everyone seemed to be wearing dark clothing. It had to be dangerous. As we moved along the roads, the driver was very alert. Suddenly, the world lit up behind us. It was a police car making a routine check. The cab driver pulled over and a policeman approached the window. He talked with the driver, shone a light on us, and seemed to be satisfied. "Just a routine check," said our driver. "Checking for people moving illegally at night. Told him you were Americans returning to your boat in Marmaris." With that, the officer returned to his car and we pulled back onto the road.

At Yacht Marine, we were stopped at the gate by security, but a quick glance at us by the guard gave us admittance. It all seemed very casual. The driver took us to where the boat had been when we left, but it was no longer there. We unloaded our luggage, paid him, and then, as soon as he left, we began walking around. We found the boat nearby and then began a search for a ladder. There were occasional overhead lights in the huge yard, and we located a ladder which I was able to carry to the boat and lean against the side. It was well after eleven local time; the yard was deserted. We climbed up, unlocked the companionway and when we clicked on the light we were simply amazed. All the cushions in the pilothouse had been beautifully reupholstered in beige leather! They were snugly arranged on the seats and seat backs. Beautiful, just what we had wanted. But….how?

We had paid for the hide before we left, but the upholsterer, Black Cloud, was to get ahold of us by email and tell us the cost of the total job. We would send a cash transfer to him and then he would make the cushions. Trouble was, we had never heard from him. We thought the delay would put everything off for another year. Here it was, done. Had he trusted us? We were exhausted; Julie quickly made up our bunk in the aft cabin. We would sleep on it.

Next morning we enjoyed breakfast at the marina where we smiled at familiar faces. We asked at the office, Black Cloud? Where was his shop? Of course, that wasn't his real name. We didn't have a card or anything. Someone there recognized the name and gave us directions. We walked up the hill, caught the *dolmus,* or small bus, and headed for Marmaris. Sure enough, we found his shop. Inside there were children of all ages. Very small ones were playing with material, older ones were doing odd jobs and actually helping out. Black Cloud's adult son was there. He was working on a project, but he took time to say he wasn't at all worried about us paying for the work. He wondered whether we were happy with what they had done and if there was anything else we wanted. It dawned on me that the helm seat in the pilothouse had not been recovered and was the only part of the pilothouse with the old blue suede. He told us he would be at the yard later in the day and that they would do the seat with the leftover material at no additional cost. He'd bring the bill when he picked up the seat later in the day. On the way out, we saw the young man's car. On the outside it was a very small tired relic. But inside it glowed, upholstered in beautiful leather.

Our friends had suggested we also check out a small shop in town run by a man named Ali Ataba. They assured us that unlike the other rug salesmen we had encountered, Ali was not aggressive and would sell his goods at a fair price. We found his shop and looked at games, including chess sets and all kinds of locally made merchandise. Ali came in while we were there. We understood he was a Moslem. He prayed in the mosque. He spoke English clearly and appeared very Western. He was also a Kurd, and married to a Canadian woman. He showed us his rugs which were all clearly labeled. He didn't bargain. Prices were as marked. We told him the size of the pilothouse floor and he showed us several rugs that would fit. We picked one out, he wrapped it up and we took it home. We thought of him as a friend.

Another part of town we discovered a few days later was the sinai. That was where most of the craftsmen worked. Virtually anything could be repaired or fabricated there. Wrecked cars, beyond repair in our experience, were repaired like new in the sinai. Canvas and metal goods could be made there. Engine mechanics and electricians repaired the old and created new parts. They seemed to be all family businesses, much as Black Cloud's shop had been. The sinai was a vibrant part of town.

Back at the boat, we had things to do. We needed a new faucet for the galley sink, and we found a top quality one in town. We had purchased a GPS for the computer and we needed to install software so it would work with the chart plotter. We needed to varnish the teak, replace main halyard blocks.

Henry R. Danielson

We hired a man to paint the bottom. He carefully taped the waterline and his work was impeccable; the price was right. We waxed and polished the topsides ourselves. After replacing the zincs on the shaft, I removed the plugs from the feathering propeller, greased it and put it back together. Since we reassembled it when we bought the boat, it had worked perfectly for thousands of miles. We even had the gooseneck on the boom reinforced. As we would be traveling to places where parts might be hard to come by, we wanted to be ready. Three new 4D batteries finished the list.

Tapestry was ready, and though the date on her rudder had been painted over, right on time the travel lift appeared and she was eased into the beautiful waters of the Mediterranean. It took nearly three weeks to ready *Tapestry* for her next adventure, but by the first of May, she was set to go.

Chapter 64

BOZU BUKU

We finally pushed off and headed toward Istanbul where the rally would begin. We wouldn't sail the whole way to that huge city, but meet the rally at Bodrum. Our first stop was Bozu Buku (Broken Castle). It was just 27 miles from Marmaris, but an interesting stop with a restaurant.

We docked at the end of a "pier," which I would have called a twisty wooden dock. At the top of the pier was a restaurant. Beyond that was a hilltop citadel. In ancient times it had been a lookout. Built of huge carefully cut stones, the rocks were so close together one couldn't slip a dollar bill, or in our case, a Turkish note, between them. It covered acres. How men, without machines, cut and moved these huge rocks simply boggles the mind. We walked the wall and admired the fine workmanship until it was time to return to the restaurant for dinner. We had fish with green beans flavored with garlic. A friendly German shorthair pointer on the patio begged us to toss a stone. Rain poured down as we ate, but there was a roof over our heads and we stayed dry.

Bozu Buku

You can't slip a dollar bill
Between the cracks in the giant rocks
That make up the Ancient castle at Bozu Buku.
Acres of hillside surrounded by
Beautifully shaped rock walls with round turrets,
All built by ancient Greeks
With their hands and their backs.
Below the castle is a restaurant.

Henry R. Danielson

A leanto, really, a roof supported by poles,
With a cook shack behind.
Four tables with pink and blue covers,
Fresh fish, beans, salad and wine and a
German Short Haired Pointer with hazel eyes who
Brings a stone and waits patiently for you
To toss it across the floor.
"His name is George Bush," the waiter tells us with a wink,
"An animal, you know."
Out front is a dock winding and uneven where yachts
Moor for a fee, or for the price of a dinner.
Rain spatters on the roof as we eat fresh fish
And shiver in the cool damp evening.

A perfect little harbor, a magnificent fort.
Before the rain,
A girl in a rowboat
Selling scarves, jewelry and rugs.
Turkey in May.

    HRD.
    5/2/07

Chapter 65

KNIDOS GUMISILK AND TURGUT REIS

Next day we sailed and motored 35 miles, past Symi, and several other Greek Islands, to Knidos, where we anchored in a small bay. The city is very old. The Apostle Paul was aboard a ship that stopped in Knidos, on his way to Rome for trial. The city was already 300 years old then. Knidos is a truly beautiful ruin. It has been looted by most everyone who went there to study it for the past century and there is very little left. Still, it is moving to walk among broken columns that have looked down on a civilization three hundred years before Christ. One must purchase a ticket to visit the ruins. The cost in 2007 was 5 Turkish Lira, or about $4.00, U.S. The Turks don't accept having their precious bits of antiquity stolen, as has been done by many nations in the past, so one is warned never to pick anything up. You can look, you can touch, but don't put anything in your pocket! There are guards keeping an eye on tourists.

Knidos was home to a medical school that rivaled that of Kos. Sostratus, the architect of the lighthouse at Alexandria, one of the Seven Wonders of the Ancient World, was from Knidos. In its heyday, between 330 and 31 BCE, it was home to intellectuals of the ancient world. The first observatory may have been located there.

Wonderful Doric, Ionic, and Corinthian columns are standing and lying on the ground. They made the place magic. We were enthralled with a Temple of Aphrodite. In addition to a theater that sat thousands, there were mosaic floors and sundials that appeared much as they must have thousands of years ago.

The nude statue of Aphrodite is considered one of the most beautiful statues in the world. It was first carved by Praxiteles for the people of Kos. They rejected it, so it ended up in Knidos. Kos got the dressed version. The original nude has been stolen several times and reappeared, but currently seems to be gone for good. Still, the curved marble bases of numerous temples and monuments and theaters adorn the hillsides surrounding the small harbor. There are columns everywhere. The region was also noted for producing fine wines.

The harbor at Knidos has been famous for literally thousands of years. Amphora stamped with the symbol of that city, have been found in all parts of the ancient world. One of the unfortunate things the harbor is famous for is poor holding in a blow. Winds were calm, however, and by 7:30 the next morning we had raised anchor and were on our way

Winds piped up to the 20 to 25 knot range the following day and they were right on the nose. Julie and I huddled in the pilothouse as we pounded through large waves under power, the wiper pushing water from the windshield. We passed the Greek island of Kos and then turned into the port of Gumusluk, which is near the old city of Myndos. The harbor was known for its good holding which was fortunate as the wind continued to howl. Much of the ancient city is underwater. The people of this city used to drink wine mixed with sea water, and therefor were referred to as "brine drinkers." They claimed one could drink the water/wine solution without a hangover.   After the assassination of Caesar, Brutus and Cassius spent a year in Myndos. I don't think they went there on vacation, do you?

We would join the Eastern Mediterranean Yacht Rally at Turgut Reis, a lovely marina near the castle of Bodrum. When we arrived there, I called on the radio and received a reply in strong English. A pilot boat escorted us to our slip. There, we met Dave, our leader. He was on a yacht called *Mashona,* and he would guide us on our way. The marina was magnificent with beautifully tiled baths at every dock. Tile is a Turkish invention and the Turks know how to use it very well. There was another Nauticat 35 there as well. It was called *Fare Well* . Its German crew Gunther, Heidi, Erik and Ursula greeted us warmly. With bright varnish and glistening new canvas, she was beautiful. A young couple from New Zealand were aboard *Sunset Sam*, a 43 foot catamaran. They had three delightful children who we knew right away would add a happy feel to the rally.

Our first tour of the rally happened the following morning. We were off to Bodrum Castle. It was a medieval castle built and used by the crusaders in their quest for the holy land. The building was huge and impressive and our tour guide was articulate and very well informed. The castle is a historical monument and a maritime museum. There are English and Scottish coats of arms on the walls, left by the crusaders as they headed for the Holy Land. Though our guide was well schooled and had completed the four years of college history required to be a tour guide, she never mentioned the Crusades. The Crusades is a subject not popular among Moslems, and our guide acted as though they had never happened.

There were anchors and other ship's hardware on display, along with literally thousands of amphoras, used for shipping wine and grain and oils. More interesting, however, were the bottles and decanters and glassware from several hundred years before Christ. Beautifully displayed, it was truly unforgettable. Herodotus (485 to 425 B.C.) a scholar who has been called the father of history, was from Bodrum.

Afterward, our leader suggested we might visit a fish market where we could purchase a fresh fish, just brought in by a local fisherman. We could then take it across the street to a restaurant where they would cook it for us. We followed his advice. The meal was wonderful, and one of the cheapest meals we ever had in Turkey. After lunch, we walked to one of the seven wonders of the ancient world, the tomb of Mausolus.

Mausolus was a popular king of what was then Caria, part of the kingdom of Asia Minor. It was a tradition in those times for popular kings to have their riches buried with them. Grave robbers knew this and it became a huge problem. Kings would be buried, dug up and buried again in a different place. Mausolus, however, changed all that. He was buried in a huge edifice fifty meters high. It was public and guarded and his riches were entombed with him. Though it was public, it was also permanent and a real challenge to thieves. Of course, aside from a few columns in the dust, the monument to Mausolus is gone. It is in the British Museum. The Turks have little patience for robbers of graves, including, our guide told us, the British! Perhaps you have heard the term Mausoleum. The derivation of the word comes from the tomb of Mausolus. A gate near the City of Bodrum was being restored and it was the last stop on our tour. It is believed that Alexander the Great passed through that gate. We all walked through it as well.

Somehow, seeing and walking through such places makes history simply come alive. It certainly lends understanding and passion to what mankind has gone through on its way to the modern world.

Toward the end of our tour, someone asked whether Turkey was Asian or European. Our guide's answer was that it is neither. It is not European because it is Islamic. It is not Asian, because Turks drink alcohol. There are fine wines from Central Turkey and Efes is a popular beer. There is even a drink in Turkey made from alcohol and horse milk. It is ten times as expensive as Johnny Walker, our guide told us.

Our guide was a delightful young woman and she shared with us a contemporary custom relating to marriage in Turkey. She said when a young man wants to marry, he sticks a fork in a bowl of rice at dinner so that it sticks straight up. The family then suggests other families who have daughters that they might contact. When the family mentions the people the son has in mind, the family contacts them and arranges a dinner. The dinner is prepared by the young woman, and afterward there is coffee, Turkish coffee. If the coffee that is served the young man is thick and sweet with sugar, that means the girl agrees to marry him. If, on the other hand, it is bitter and unsweetened, it means he has to look for someone else. Marriage often happens to young Turkish men after they finish compulsory military service at twenty-two. The tour was wonderful and the insightful nuances provided by this young woman were something we would long remember. She was articulate, attractive by Western standards, and her head was uncovered.

We learned it was Ataturk, a Turkish leader after WWI who determined that women should not wear head scarfs in public places, and that Turks should enjoy alcohol, as was done in the West. Turkey was indeed a special place.

Chapter 66

THE EMYR

The Eastern Mediterranean Yacht Rally, as it is called, was really a delightful event. The rally is made up of yachts of varying sizes, eighty of them, which move from Istanbul, in the north, along the coast of Turkey to the island of Cypress, to Syria, Lebanon, Israel and finally on to Egypt. In those years it was an annual event and boats, mostly from Western nations, some from the US, more from the UK, France and Italy, made the journey. Everyone who went was thoroughly vetted and passport numbers were forwarded to all countries on the tour to streamline formalities. At every stop there were parties. Often government representatives were there to greet us. There were even more formal dinners and gatherings where the dress was "smart casual," which meant a coat and tie, for men and a dress and heels for women. There were tours that were part of the package and they took us to local landmarks and cultural sites along the way. We were excited. Julie's sister, Betsy, and her husband, David, would be coming from the States to join us. We would meet them in Kemer, a stop along the way. Of course, we would still be in Turkey.

I remember Port Gocek where we visited some fourth century BCE Lycian tombs. They were sunken into the sides of cliffs over the water and had been exposed. Further along, at Kekova Roads, there was a whole city half sunken along the water. Steps descended below the water surface, buildings that remained were half submerged. The water had not risen, but the land had sunk. Fascinating.

At Myra, we were in for a real surprise. We first visited an ancient theater and then walked to the town. There to greet us was a huge statue of Santa Clause! We heard the word "Coke" from the lips of some of our European friends. Indeed, they associated the statue with American ads in their periodicals for

Coca Cola. In reality, Myra was the home of Saint Nicholas. The church there was dedicated to him and the town had picked up on the name. At the church the story was told of this generous priest who had actually dropped goats down the chimneys of the very poor. Is that where the myth of Santa coming down the chimney to bring gifts to children comes from? They would have us think so. At any rate the tour of the church and town was impressive. There were stores in town where things Christmas were available and everyone wanted to have his or her picture taken with Santa. It was a good time.

The next day we visited Phaselis, an ancient Roman town with three harbors. There were the ruins of the town and the theater. Later that day, David and Betsy, Julie's sister arrived.

We had sent a taxi to the airport to pick them up, but the drivers at the airport weren't hearing of it. They charged a higher price than the locals, and weren't about to allow an outside cabbie to pick up anyone at the airport. Still, we enjoyed dinner with Betsy and David and the rest of the EMYR sailors in a delightful outdoor setting. Tables were set with white linen cloths and napkins. There were toasts and speeches and, after dinner was over, there was dancing. All of this in the shadow of magnificent mountains and the sparkling sea.

Chapter 67

ALANYA SURPRISE

We sailed from Kemer to Alanya, where we Med moored in an ancient harbor. Julie noticed there were rocks near our rudder, but we were made fast to shore and our anchor, off the bow, held us in place. The fleet literally filled the little harbor, but everyone made it in and all was well.

The next day we toured the local landmarks, The Red Tower, and the museum. Later we went to a trout farm along a roaring stream where we enjoyed lunch. The fish were kept in a pond that was also part of the stream. Food for the fish washed down from above and was eaten by the fish which were netted and cleaned and served very fresh in the restaurant. What a treat! Our bus took us back to the boat in time for us to prepare for another evening of dinner and dancing. The following day we would leave Alanya and head for Cypress, the island nation divided by Turkey and Greece. It would be a long sail.

It was the next morning when it happened. We had finished breakfast and the fleet was readying itself for departure. It was impressive how close we were to those huge rocks at the stern of the boat and I decided to dash down into our cabin and get the camera and snap a photo of them before we left. We had some time. I tried to get a picture, but the light was wrong, Somehow the pictures didn't capture the drama of the situation as I saw it. I thought maybe they would look better in the darkened cabin. I climbed down the five steps into the pilothouse, and swung around into the aft cabin.

Suddenly I was on the floor. I tried to get up, but I just found it very hard. My right leg didn't seem to move. I called to Julie who came to my assistance. She helped me onto the double bed. Try as I did, I couldn't seem to move my right leg at the knee at all. It wouldn't go forward or back. Pain? I wasn't in a lot of pain; there were twinges, but the leg below the knee simply wouldn't move. What would I do?

I lay on the bed. What now? Julie went on deck and called to a man on the boat next to us. He was a Frenchman and we knew he had been an EMT. He came over and looked at my leg. His first response was frank. "Well, Henry, it looks as if your sailing for this year is over. I believe you have a torn quadricep in your knee. You will need treatment right away. I will call an ambulance. I know you will be tempted to go back to the U.S. for treatment, but if it is as I expect, the muscle will begin pulling the torn tendon up your leg. You must have it fixed and the sooner the better. I suggest you see if you can have it treated here in Turkey."

With that grim news, he disappeared back to his boat. Within a minute, I could hear sirens. The ambulance was coming. All I could imagine was being laid in a room, a ward, full of cots filled with Moslem men. They would all get up to pray five times a day. I wouldn't be able to, so.. .... What would happen to me? What were hospitals like in Turkey, anyway? I had no idea.

Before long, the ambulance arrived. The attendants came into the cabin and placed an inflatable cast on my leg, but getting up the steps out of the rear cabin and up and out the companionway on a stretcher, seemed out of the question. They weren't strong English speakers, but as I was able and not in great pain, they helped me "scooch" up the steps. But then there was the *passerelle*. That was simply a 2x8 inch plank stretching from the stern of the boat to shore and held in place by lines or ropes. No way could they carry me over that narrow board or *passerelle* on a stretcher. Again, they wondered, could I slide myself or "scooch" over it?

Up until that moment, I had been okay with things. The young men were trying their hardest and with the language barrier and all.... But I did have an air filled cast on my leg. What if I fell from the *passerelle* and landed in the water? I could see that inflated cast holding my leg up like a huge bobber, and me dangling beneath it! But by then I had a life jacket on and, ever so slowly, much to the horror of the crowd that had gathered, I began to move my way, on my bottom, with both legs trailing behind me, across the water on the narrow plank. As soon as I got near enough shore, I was lifted to a stretcher and placed in the back of the ambulance.

What! There was a television crew there filming the departure of the fleet. Was I on television? Julie was in the ambulance with me as we raced through town, siren screaming and lights flashing. David and Betsy were back on the boat. The fleet departed. Our EMYR was over!

When the ambulance rolled into the emergency entrance to the hospital, we were pleasantly surprised. It was hardly the quonset hut I had expected, but a large, modern polished stone and glass building. As I was wheeled into the emergency room, a man walked up to me. "Hello, Henry. I am Doctor Ulius. I was a military doctor for years. I have treated many of this type of injury. You can expect a full recovery, but speed is of the essence, we must get started right away."

With that I was wheeled into another room where several nurses began preparing me for an MRI. Before long I was wheeled into a darkened room and my leg was moved into the tunnel-like screening device of the large machine. In the background, I could see several men behind a plate of glass, staring at a screen. Dr. Uluis was one of them and Julie was with them. The procedure took a while. Afterward, I was moved to an elevator and then to my room.

Room! Yes, room. It was a single room, too, and there was a window overlooking the city. There was a television, and a remote! It was air conditioned. The bed was a modern hospital bed. Better yet, it had its own bath, complete with toilet, sink and shower. What was this? The attendant who brought me to the room told me the doctor would be there shortly.

It was then I realized I needed to use the bathroom. The inflatable cast had been removed for the MRI. I sat up on the bed, dangled my leg. Perhaps I could hop on my good left leg to the bathroom. It was only a few feet and there were things to grasp along the way. I made it and back to the bed where I collapsed.

The door opened and Julie and Dr. Uluis appeared.

"You have completely severed your right quadricep tendon, Henry." He said. "The sooner we can surgically reattach it the easier the procedure will be. This is a private hospital. We will need assurance from your insurance provider that they will cover the cost of surgery and recovery. Who is that provider?"

I gave them the name of our insurance company in Western New York and the doctor disappeared from the room. A few minutes later he returned. "I called the number on your card. Unfortunately, it is very late at night there and I had to wait to get the information I needed. They said that they do not guarantee payment, but that they would pay depending on whether certain conditions were met.

I cannot run a hospital that way. If you give me your credit card, I will run a charge of a thousand dollars. If that goes through, we will begin with the surgery right away. Is that all right with you and your wife?"

Julie and I were stunned. Our credit card? How…?

We gave the doctor our credit card.

Very soon I found myself loaded on another gurney and being wheeled through the halls of the modern hospital toward surgery. My clothes were removed, I was dressed in a surgical gown, scrubbed, and wheeled into a large room where several men in white coats stood. It was explained to me that I would receive a spinal injection, and would be awake for the procedure. The anesthesiologist would keep tabs on me as the procedure progressed.

The large light over me shined down on my leg as several men bent over my knee. I stayed awake. There was a shield; I couldn't see what they were doing but I could feel they were doing something. There was no pain, but a tugging sensation on my knee from time to time. Finally a large plaster cast was placed over my leg and I was wheeled back to the room. The operation had gone much as planned. The doctor was sure that with proper rehabilitation, I could expect a full recovery.

Chapter 68

RECOVERY

After the surgery is when I began to learn a great deal more about medicine in this part of the Middle East. I was not in a regular government run hospital, but a "tourist hospital" that was there to take care of visitors like me. It was not government supported, but run for profit, by its owner, who in this case was Dr Ulius.

There was a cot next to my bed. It was for Julie if she wanted to stay there with me.

Whenever meals came, there were two, one for Julie, one for me. Of course, I wasn't critically ill and Julie wasn't staying at the hospital with me. Our boat was in a busy area and it had to be moved so the fishing fleet could take back their spaces. It was up to Julie to move the boat to another marina. Fortunately, she was capable, and David, my brother-in-law was able and willing to help. Sadly, for he and Betsy, they had come this great distance to tour the Middle East, but the tour simply would not happen for them. They would, they decided, have to return home with us. What a disappointment for them.

But for me, life went on in the hospital. There was a push button on my pillow which I could use to call for a nurse. If I touched the button, I couldn't count to ten before a young lady was at my side. She may or may not speak English, but she would not leave until my needs were met. These were young, very shy ladies who tried very hard to make my stay comfortable. If I wanted water or needed help getting to the bathroom, they were there for me.

I specifically remember the night after the surgery, there was an older Turkish woman who came into the room. She came to my bedside and said in a rather harsh voice,

"You pee?"

I shook my head and said, "No."

With that she leaned down and opened a small refrigerator next to the bed where she removed a liter of bottled water. She poured a glassful, placed it on the tray over my bed and said, "You drink!" This was not a question, but a command!

I drank the water. She refilled the glass and I drank that, too. Then she left the room. A while later she returned and asked the same question. Again, I had to admit no success. She produced another liter bottle and again said, "You drink."

Finally I was able to show her the container filled with urine. She smiled and said, "Good!"

And so it went. They got me up and I hobbled along on my cast. I was barely mobile and with my leg straight out I could only fit in a handicapped bathroom, of which there are very few in Turkey.

We made a plan. Julie and David would sail the boat to a large marina in Kemer, where we would have it stored. The ambulance would then take me to Kemer where there was a room available with a handicap accessible bathroom. Our friends, Bill and Bun Bailey would travel to Kemer by bus, and sail *Tapestry* back to Marmaris, where she would be hauled and stored for the winter. The four of us would fly home as soon as we could get reservations.

Of course, in the meantime I was there in my bed in the hospital. I had a book to read, but little else. One night I woke up in the middle of the night, and I couldn't get back to sleep. I clicked on the TV, but try as I did there was nothing on but soaps in rapid Turkish. I clicked along until I happened to come to a program about the Cannes Film Festival in France. Amazingly, the dialogue was in English. The story was about the festival and the famous people who come to the festival, many of them in their luxurious yachts. It went on to show rather voluptuous women swimming in the nude off these huge ships. Suddenly I felt pangs of guilt. What if one of those wonderful young nurses saw me watching this. What would she think? I turned off the tube and went back to sleep.

It was fully six days before I was released from the hospital. The doctor cut the cast so, should the plane lose pressure on the way home, the cast could be cut loose and my leg would be able to swell and compensate for reduced air pressure. I had never thought of that.

We had found a room in Kemer, Julie and David had delivered the boat there. Betsy and I would ride in an ambulance. That is a story in itself.

We got the bill for the whole ordeal when we left. It included the ambulance to the hospital, the MRI, the surgery, all medications, meals, six days in my private room, and finally the 40 mile ambulance ride to Kemer. The total was just under five thousand dollars. I couldn't believe it. Since we had already paid one thousand, I simply put the remaining four on the card. Done deal. Before I left Dr. Ulius handed me a CD in an envelope. "Give this to your rehabilitation doctor when you get home," he said. We shook hands, and that was it.

But the fun wasn't over yet. Betsy and I climbed into the back of the ambulance and an attractive young nurse, who probably was assigned to be with me, rode in the cab with the driver. We kept hearing sirens as we drove along and Betsy was sure there must have been a bad accident somewhere. It wasn't long before she figured out the sirens we were hearing were actually us. Our driver was showing off to the pretty young nurse, ringing the siren and flashing the lights whenever we came to an intersection. Some emergency!

Anyway, back in Kemer, once Bill and Bun picked up the boat, the four of us found our way to the airport where I was hurried through security and loaded aboard a box truck with a lift that hoisted me and an attendant to the rear door of the airplane where I was wheeled to my seat. I had to pay for two seats, but the flight attendants moved others so I had four seats across the center of the plane to stretch out on. Turkish Airlines simply could not have been more cooperative! Though there wasn't room to stretch my leg in front of me while seated, I could lie down comfortably across all four seats, watch TV or just sleep.

Chapter 69

REHABILITATION

Back home, we stayed a day or two with Betsy's daughter in Connecticut, and then drove back to Western New York.

Our rehabilitation was interesting. I went to a local surgeon who removed the cast from my leg and encouraged me to begin gently moving my knee. Life wasn't easy with the cast. I had to lower the top on our little convertible BMW, step into the car and then slide down into the seat. Julie could then raise the top and we could get on with our drive. Driving or operating the car itself was simply out of the question for me.

My first doctor's visit was interesting as well. He looked at my leg and wanted to assign me to a rehabilitation facility, but he explained, he was a bit reluctant. He didn't know just what had been done. How had the rupture been repaired? How had it been stitched, what had they used to stitch it? That is when I presented him with the CD Dr. Ulius had given me. My docotr looked at me, at the small disc and then said, "What is this?" I told him the doctor had given it to me and that it was for him. It had my name on it and the date of my injury along with the name of the hospital in Alanya. He was obviously concerned about using his office computer to load the disc. Was it Windows compatible? He asked me to come back the following day. He said he would make arrangements for me at a local rehabilitation clinic.

When I returned the following day, he said he was simply amazed at what he had found. The disc had my original MRI, a photo of my knee before the surgery and photos of the procedure as it progressed. It provided answers to all of his questions. He had never seen anything like it.

At rehab, I was placed on several machines and gradually began to exercise. The nurse there suggested several things we could do at home to speed the process. There was a wastebasket in the bedroom at home and Julie would place it on its side under my knee and ask me to straighten my leg out with the basket under the joint. That hurt, but there was no getting out of bed in the morning until that was done. We had a small box in the kitchen we had used years before to help my mother get into our Honda van. I could practice stepping onto that. Up and down, up and down. Ouch.

However, it was the second visit to rehab where I found what I believed to be the answer. It was a stationary bicycle. As the doctor tenderly moved my leg, I asked him if I could try the stationary bike in the corner of the facility. He thought it would be great if I could use my good leg to move the pedals and my injured leg would, well, get moved up and down. It worked. At first, I found myself just allowing my right leg to be bent and moved, but then I began to apply a little pressure.

Next thing I knew, back home, I was trying to ride my bike, slowly, around the yard. Then I found, if I could borrow my brother-in-law, David's bike in Lakewood, I could pedal that around Lakewood on somewhat level streets pretty much avoiding stress. I felt I was on the road to recovery. Heaven help me if I fell, but somehow the exercise really made my leg feel better. With my doctor's permission, I found I could drive again. Hills were no longer so impossible on the bike, and before long, I found myself riding all the way to Lakewood and back from our home in Ashville. I still remember riding up the long driveway to the house the first time. Yes, it hurt a little, but it convinced me this episode had passed.

We had bicycled for years in Ashville and even in Florida. We had owned mountain bikes and hybrids. How wonderful. Bicycling seemed to have been the answer to the cure for my injury. Would there be more bicycling in our future?

We still had the boat in Marmaris, thanks to Bill and Bun who had put it away for us. Would we ever do that EMYR Rally? David and Betsy were not interested in going again. Who would want to go with us?

We went back to Florida in the fall where I was determined to continue bicycling and building up my leg. There was a club there. I had bicycled casually in Florida for years, but from time to time I would be overtaken by groups of riders, some of them women, who were strong and, try as I would, I just couldn't catch them. On Manasota Beach one day, I stopped and visited with a lady in lycra. I asked about their club. "Get yourself a bicycle and a pair of shoes and join us." was her enthusiastic reply. Apparently she didn't think my hybrid bike was up to her standard. And what could be wrong with my shoes? These people rode road bikes, the ones with the skinny tires, and they wore shoes that clipped into the pedals. It was true, it was difficult for me to keep up with them. Maybe they had something. But I would have to get a much better bike before I could ride with them. And shoes with clips? I'd have to learn to unclip before I put my foot down. I really didn't want to fall on my repaired leg. Hmmm.

It was Halloween, the last day in October when Julie and I got resettled in to our Florida home. My leg was healed and I could finally walk without a limp, drive and shift easily, and function much as I had before the fall. I thought it was the bicycling that really made me heal.

We went to a bicycle shop, Bicycles International, in Venice, that day and asked about a quality road bike. They showed me a Raleigh Competition. It was a demonstrator, and had some miles on it; the dealer assured me, fewer than a hundred. I took it for a ride and, somehow, it fit me perfectly. It was Halloween, the bike was carbon fiber and orange and black; perfect for Halloween. That was the beginning of the next chapter. I bought the bike and at the counter was more information about the Coastal Cruiser's Bicycle Club. There was a ride every Tuesday.

His name was Barry, and he was the leader. I will not soon forget than morning. I joined several dozen other riders at the head of the Pioneer Trail, south of Englewood and we glided over trails and roads for about 25 miles. There was a guy named Hank on the ride, too. He seemed a little concerned another Hank might be joining the club. It was all good. When the official ride was over, Barry and I went for another short loop. He assured me that the Cruisers was the right place for Julie and me.

A few days later Julie bought a road bike as well. We joined the club and bicycling became part of our Florida lives. It was all good.

But, of course, the boat was still in Marmaris. Would we again sign up for that EMYR cruise and challenge the Middle East? We were sure we would. Though Betsy and David didn't want to go again, we learned other friends, Bruce and Joan were eager to join us. We had to do this thing. The Middle East was calling, Cypress, Syria, Lebanon, Israel, Egypt and, of course, Turkey, and we had to answer.

Glossary

Almanac: an annual publication of celestial and trigonometric tables. With the aid of a sextant and an accurate clock, it enables a navigator to find his position several times a day in clear weather.

Afterguy: a line running from a whisker or spinnaker pole aft, usually to a winch.

Anchor light: A white masthead light. A boat at anchor must show an all around white light at night.

Athwartships: at right angles to the keel.

Automatic (safety) lights: are attached to life vests (jackets), horseshoe floats, man overboard poles, and other rescue gear. They turn on automatically when in the water.

Automatic Bilge Pump: an electric bilge pump activated by a float switch in the bilge.

Autopilot: steers a vessel on either a selected compass heading or on a heading relative to the wind.

Autopilot servo: applies force to the rudder so that the autopilot can steer the boat.

Bailer: one who empties water from a vessel or a device that does the same.

Batten: a strip of wood or plastic used to give shape to a sail, especially a mainsail.

Bay of Fundy: A stretch of water between New Brunswick and Nova Scotia known for extremely high tides and strong currents.

Beam's ends: when a vessel is on her side she may be on her beam's ends, meaning on her deck beams which run athwartships.

Bearing: a line of position from the ship to a fixed object.

Below: the area beneath the deck. Used in place of "downstairs."

Bilge: the area at the very bottom of a vessel inside the hull where keel bolts are located and where water and dirt collect.

Block: a pulley on a sailboat.

Boom: a horizontal spar attached to a mast at the base of a sail.

Boson's chair: a scat used to secure a crewman so he/she can be hauled up the mast.

Bottom paint: toxic paint used to inhibit marine growth on the underside of a hull.

Buss: a metal strip to which electrical cables of similar polarity are attached.

Casters: small wheels that allow a heavy item to move and swivel to allow it to move in any direction.

Chandlery: a place where boating goods are sold.

Charter boats: boats that can be rented.

Cleat: a device used to secure lines on a vessel.

Coast Guard Approved: the U.S. Coast Guard places its approval on some nautical goods.

Coaming: trim around the edge of a cockpit intended to keep water out.

Companionway: an opening in the aft bulkhead of a cabin where one enters to descend into the cabin. Companionways are generally sealed with watertight boards to keep water out of the cabin in rain or extreme conditions.

Cockpit: that part of a sailing boat where people sit. On modern yachts it is self-draining so any water that comes into the cockpit drains safely away.

Cockpit remote (radio): enables persons in the cockpit of a yacht to hear, select channels and transmit messages over the vhf radio from the cockpit rather than having to enter the cabin.

Courtesy flags: are flags flown from the starboard spreader of sailing yachts after checking into a foreign country. They are usually, but not always, the national flag of that country.

Crest: the top of the wave. Sometimes the part that "breaks" or forms a white-cap.

Crotch straps: straps attached to life vests that pass between ones legs so the vest or jacket cannot slip off over the head. They are seldom found on American vests, but required in the U.K.

Crowned: curved. Decks are sometimes crowned so that water will drain away.

Dinghy: a small boat used to serve a larger boat and stored aboard the larger vessel.

Davits: block and tackle arrangement used to lift, suspend and lower a small boat on a ship or yacht. On a yacht they generally support the small boat over the stern.

Dock cart: a small cart used to carry goods from shore to a boat moored to a dock.

Dock ornament: a slang term for a boat used to impress others rather than for its intended purpose of sailing or cruising.

Dolly: a device used to help move heavy objects.

Dorades: specially made vents that allow air, but not water to flow from outside into the cabin below.

Drag anchor: an anchor may drag or slip over the bottom if not adequately set.

Drogue: a sea anchor, sometimes in the shape of a parachute, which is dragged to slow a yacht in strong winds.

DSC radio: a marine vhf (very high frequency) radio that can be used to alert nearby ships of the position of a vessel in distress in an emergency. It also can be programmed to transmit the position of the caller to a friend without revealing that position to boaters at large.

Electric winches: devices that use electric motors to provide power to trim or raise sails.

Emergency flares: alert other vessels to the position of a vessel in distress. They are required on pleasure boats and must be updated regularly.

Emergency steering: a manual steering system attached directly to the rudder post to be used in the event of steering system failure.

E.P.I.R.B.: Emergency Position Indicating and Reporting Beacon, a device which sends an emergency signal via satellite if a ship is lost or the crew in mortal danger.

Exhaust flange: a metal thru-hull device which allows cooling water and exhaust to flow from the engine to the sea.

Fall off: to move the boat so that the wind is more abeam and less toward the bow.

Feathering propeller: a propeller that collapses while the yacht is under sail so that it offers less resistance as the boat passes through the water.

Fender: a soft shock absorber attached to the hull of a boat or hung off the side of the boat to protect it from piers or other boats.

Fin keel: a short weighted keel which begins aft of the bow and ends forward of the rudder of a sailing boat. It is generally associated with modern performance sailboats.

Fire blanket: a fireproof blanket used to smother small fires, especially in the galley. Standard equipment in Europe but seldom available in the U.S.

Floorboards: decking above the bottom of a vessel to enable walking on a flat surface rather than the curved hull of the ship or boat.

Foreguy: a line leading from a whisker pole forward to the deck of the boat.

Fresh water flush: an automatic system on watermakers which rinses the membrane with fresh water after each use and at regular intervals, often weekly.

Gaff: a spar used to support the top of the mainsail on older sailboats.

Gale Sail: a patented sail which slips over the furled jib for use in extreme weather.

Galley: the kitchen on a vessel.

Genoa: a large jib which comes behind the mast and overlaps the mainsail.

Gimbals: devices that keep things level at sea. Stoves, and oil lamps are often gimbaled.

Glow plug: an electrical device that provides heat to the combustion chamber of a diesel engine for starting purposes.

G.P.S.: Global Positioning System. a navigation system using information from satellites to determine ship position.

Halyard: a line used to raise a sail up the mast. Yachts may have a main halyard, a jib halyard, a spinnaker halyard, etc.

Harness: a device worn by crew aboard boats, attached to a jackline enabling them to move forward and aft but securing them to the boat. Used mostly at night or in bad weather.
Hatch: a usually watertight door through the deck of a vessel.
Heel: the angle measured from level that a boat "tips" to port or starboard.
Helm: the device used to steer a yacht. It may be a tiller attached directly to the rudder or a wheel. The helm is what steers the boat, the helmsman does the steering.
Head: the toilet or bathroom on a boat.
High lift muffler: is a marine muffler that allows water to flow from the engine of a yacht into the sea but not from the sea into the engine.
High water alarm: a float switch located above the normal safe water level in the bilge and connected to an alarm.
Holding: refers to the suitability of the sea bottom for anchoring. Good holding or poor holding indicating a risk factor in anchoring.
Hook: slang for anchor.
Horseshoe buoy: in the shape of a horseshoe, it replaced the more traditional life ring. It can embrace crew who have fallen overboard and keep them afloat without their having to hold on.
House bank: a bank of batteries intended to provide power to everything but the engine on a yacht, including lighting, communication, refrigeration, navigation, etc.
ICOM: a Japanese manufacturer of high quality marine and amateur radios.
In-boom furling mainsail: a mainsail that rolls into the boom. This rig allows the mainsail to carry traditional battens and to be infinitely reefed.
Jackline: a strap or wire which runs fore and aft on a yacht and is well secured. Crew attach harness lines to this strong point so that they can move forward or aft without feat of falling or being washed off the ship.
Jib fairleads: run fore and aft on the deck and can be adjusted to flatten or add shape to the jib.

Knockdown: when a sailing yacht is driven onto its side by an extreme gust of wind.

LCD lights: liquid crystal diodes produce pure bright light using little current and not requiring colored glass to create the appropriate color.

Leeward: the side of a vessel away from the wind.

Lee cloth: a sheet of canvas attached to the outside of a bunk to keep the sleeper from falling out when the boat heels.

Life raft: a small automatically inflated raft used to support the crew if a yacht sinks, catches fire, or suffers some other emergency. Rafts have to be inspected regularly to meet requirements of offshore racing and cruising organizations.

Lifesling: a floating device thrown from a yacht when a crewman falls overboard. It is dragged past the person in distress so that he can grab it and be pulled back to the boat.

Line: a term used to describe a rope with one end attached to a boat or ship.

Line honors: used to describe the first boat over the starting line in a sailboat race.

Link 10 Battery Monitor: a device that monitors battery condition on a yacht. It measures voltage, amperage drain and rate of charge and confirms whether the battery bank is gaining or losing energy.

Man overboard pole: a long stick with a weighted float on the bottom and a flag on the top used to help locate an overboard crewman in rough water.

Manual bilge pump: a pump activated by a crew member by means of a pump handle, used in emergencies to replace or supplement the electric pump.

Marine surveyor: one who examines yachts to see that they measure up to requirements of the American Bureau of Yacht Standards for insurance and resale purposes.

Membrane: part of a watermaker through which only fresh water can pass.

Masthead: The top of the mast.

Mooring: (n) An anchor attached to a chain and a float. Moorings are often for rent in places where anchoring is not permitted or is not practical. Some moorings are private. (v) the act of making a boat fast. Ie. He is mooring his boat to the dock.

Motor Charger: a small diesel engine which drives a powerful alternator to generate D.C. electricity for the sole purpose of charging batteries without running the main ship engine.

Overflow (expansion) tank: Marine engines, like automobile engines, have a small plastic tank into which excess coolant flows as the engine heats up and the coolant expands.

Passerelle: a boarding ramp suspended from the stern of a vessel to a pier. Used to facilitate Med. mooring.

PFD: Personal Flotation Device. A device used to keep one afloat. Commonly called a life jacket.

Pilothouse: a room in a vessel with forward facing ports from which a ship or yacht can be steered while keeping the helmsman sheltered from the weather.

Plow anchor: in the shape of a plow it buries itself in the seabed.

Port: the left side of a ship facing forward. A window on a boat. A harbor.

Preventer: A line leading from the end of the main boom forward to where it is secured to prevent jibing. The preventer must be released when coming about.

Racor water separator: a specific but very common fuel filter for marine diesels.

Radar reflector: a device that reflects radar signals back to the sender to help see the target ship. Often made of aluminum plates at right angles to each other, they are to be suspended from the rigging in the "rain catch" position to be most effective.

Radio net: an opportunity for boats to check in by radio at a predetermined time to request assistance, discuss concerns about the weather or other matters.

Reach: a point of sail with the boat roughly at right angles to the direction of the wind.

Reefing line: used to shorten a sail as wind increases.

Henry R. Danielson

Rhumb line: The course of a vessel from its present position to its destination, regardless of wind direction.

Rudder post: a strong member extending upward from the rudder to which the steering arm or quadrant is attached.

Safety at Sea Seminar: a seminar sponsored by various marine manufacturers and publishers to provide sailors with an opportunity to learn safe boating techniques from experienced seamen.

Scope: the ratio of anchor chain to water depth for safe mooring of a vessel. With an "all chain" rode, a length of chain five to seven times the depth of the water is thought to be safe. Insufficient scope frequently leads to boats breaking free and washing ashore.

Sextant: a device used to measure the altitude of heavenly bodies from the horizon for navigation purposes It is called a sextant because it measures 60 degrees, or $1/6^{th}$ of a circle.

Sheet: a line used to trim a sail.

Shore power: Alternating current electricity supplied from shore rather than the boat's electrical system.

Shortening sail: a means of reducing the size of sails so they produce less power and reduce heel. Same as reefing sails.

Shrink wrap: plastic tubing used around electrical connections that when heated shrinks to seal out moisture and contamination. A plastic film used to cover boats in the off- season.

Shrouds: wires that support the mast from the sides of the vessel. They are adjusted by turnbuckles.

Single Side Band/Ham radio: used for long distance communication at sea. Some SSB radios also cover ham or amateur frequencies and can be used for amateur communication as well if the user is properly licensed.

Signal flags: A set of flags with the coded alphabet, numbers 1 – 9 and several "repeaters" included. Originally used to communicate, they are used mostly for decoration today, a means of dressing ship.

Skeg rudder: a rudder hinged to a support attached to the bottom of the boat. A spade rudder is attached only to the rudder post. An attached rudder is hinged to the aft end of the keel.

Slip: a parking space for a boat at a dock. Sometimes called a well.

Smart regulator: controls amperage sent to a battery bank by the alternator. Smart regulators control the amount and timing of charge so that they extend battery life.

Stanchions: vertical metal posts along the deck of a boat used to support vinyl coated cables. These "lifelines" are helpful, but not always reliable.

Storm trysail: a very small heavy sail used to replace the mainsail in extreme conditions.

Sole: refers to a floor in a yacht. Cabin soles are often hardwood and varnished.

Spring line: a line leading fore or aft from a boat to pier. It keeps the boat parallel to the dock while helping to absorb shock from wind and waves.

Spinnaker: a light often colorful nylon sail used when sailing before the wind.

Stern: the back or aft end of a boat or ship. Astern is a direction related to the back of the ship.

Starboard: the right side of the ship facing forward. The side of the ship where the steering board or rudder was on ancient ships. Hence ships were docked with the left side toward the port or harbor.

Starting battery: an isolated battery dedicated to starting the engines. Should this battery fail, the house bank can often be used as a back up.

Stays: wires, similar to shrouds, used to support a mast fore and aft on a sailing vessel.

Stern ladder: a ladder used to enable one to climb from the water or a dinghy onto the boat.

Throwable device: a boat cushion, life ring or life preserver of some kind that can be thrown to someone overboard at sea. One is required on each boat in U.S. waters.

Thru-hull: a fitting on a yacht which allows water to pass from the boat to the sea or from the sea into the boat. Boats have thru-hulls for engine water intakes, sink drains, etc. Each thru-hull is generally protected by a valve that can close it if necessary.

Topping lift: a line which supports a pole or boom from the mast.

Traveler: a track athwart ships to which the main sheet is attached. It can be adjusted to increase or reduce twist in the sail.

Tricolor light: a white, green and red light attached to the top of a mast so that a yacht needs to power only one bulb rather than three while sailing at night at sea. It makes a vessel more visible to ships especially in rough weather.

Turnbuckle: a screw device used to lengthen or shorten wire.

Watermaker: a device that removes fresh water from sea water. It uses mechanical power to force sea water through a membrane. Using a process called "reverse osmosis," it makes drinkable fresh water from the sea.

Watch schedule: as boats must be manned at all times, a schedule determines who is responsible at any time.

Water key: In some Caribbean marinas water is metered. A key and lock is provided so that others cannot use the tap assigned to one's boat.

Weather radio: a service sponsored by N.O.A.A. Weather radio provides weather broadcasts 24/7 to all navigable waters in the U.S. It is not available in Europe.

Well-found: a term used to describe a boat that is seaworthy.

Whisker pole: a pole used to hold a jib out when going down wind.

Windlass: a powerful winch used to raise anchors on ships and yachts. In the past they were often manually powered but today most are electric or hydraulic.

Trough: the valley between waves at sea.

United States Power Squadrons: a boating fraternity dedicated to boating education and safety.

Weather: refers to the windward side of a sailboat. When one is passed to weather s/he is passed on the windward rather than the leeward side.

Winches: mechanical devices used to trim lines aboard a sailing boat. Traditionally, operated by a crank or winch handle, more recently electric motors have been fitted to reduce effort.

Acknowledgements

I would like to thank those who have helped me with this book. Julie, of course, is my inspiration. When I wanted to sail places, it was Julie who figured out how we could make it happen. Whenever there was hardship, her determination helped pull us through. Even when she was ill, she wouldn't hold us back. What more could one want?

Several people read and commented on the book before it was published. Gigi Gresson, a friend from the Venice Sail Squadron was the first, followed by my cousin and faithful friend, Bill Dwinelle. His mechanical corrections and thoughtful comments were valuable indeed. Our good friend Tom McCreight helped us with final corrections.

Mostly, though, were the people we encountered wherever we went. They were warm and caring people. They worked hard to please us and helped to make our voyages successful. Whether it was Hastings in the Virgin Islands, Filipe in Marin, or countless others along the way, we need to thank them all. They were wonderful, hard working people and they knew what they were doing. Dr. Ulius in Alanya, Turkey, took me to his hospital and treated me professionally and respectfully for a very low price, allowing me to still ride my bicycle 100 miles in a day in my mid 70's. He was a wonderful, compassionate physician who used modern methods to help me recover from my severed quadricep tendon.

Wherever we went we found helpful, compassionate people. That is not the way the world has been portrayed to us. Julie and I have come to believe that the people of this world are far more loving, understanding and helpful than they have been portrayed by our government and media. With that, I would say a very warm "Thank you" to all of the people who served us, helped us, and showed us how they live.

About the Author

Born near the shores of Chautauqua Lake in Western New York, Hank Danielson was close to the water from the start. He and his dad began fishing from their small boat while Hank was still in kindergarten. At the age of ten he got his first sailboat, an 8 foot Clearwater Pram, that he learned to sail and race at the Chautauqua Lake Yacht Club. He met his future wife, Julie, in 8th grade. She, too was a sailor and had learned on a similar boat. In his teens, Hank and his father built a seventeen foot plywood outboard cruiser in the family garage. They built the boat from scratch and labored several years on the project. Once launched, *Poly Ester,* named for the very contemporary plastic coating she was sheathed in, proved to be a seaworthy boat that provided years of enjoyment. After college at Grove City, Pennsylvania, and S.U.N.Y. Brockport, respectively, Hank and Julie were married and he began a career as a buyer for a Pittsburgh Department Store. Julie's invitation to the Peace Corps led the couple to accept and teach on a remote island in Malawi, Central Africa. Later both were teachers in Western New York, where they earned masters degrees in their various fields. They bought a boat before a house, and they spent their summers sailing. First it was Lake Ontario, then Erie and Huron, finally Superior and Michigan. They made their home energy efficient, heated with wood and solar, lived close to the bone and on their 25th anniversary, sailed their 31 foot sailboat *Trilogy* to Bermuda. Julie, a childhood polio survivor, overcame breast cancer in 1988.

Retirement found them buying a second home in Florida, moving their boat there and exploring first the Bahamas, and then, after purchasing a 35 foot Nauticat pilothouse sailboat they named *Tapestry*, they set out for the Caribbean where they continued to delve into the culture of these magnificent islands. From the Caribbean, they crossed the Atlantic via Bermuda and the Azores, with the Atlantic Rally for Cruisers, and that took them to the south coast of England, and across the Bay of Biscay to Spain. After sailing the coast of Portugal, they stored the boat in Rota, Spain

Back home, a second bout with cancer caused Julie to suffer a mastectomy, radiation and chemotherapy. Undaunted, she continued to exercise and keep her spirits up and by the following spring she and Hank returned to their boat to explore the Mediterranean. From Gibraltar they moved to Morocco, the south coast of Spain, the Balearic Islands, Sardinia, Corsica, Italy, Sicily, Greece and on to Turkey. From there they explored the Middle East, including The Turkish Coast, Cyprus, Syria, Lebanon, Israel, and Egypt. That was, of course, in 2008, before the uprisings in Syria and Egypt. Back in Turkey, *Tapestry* continued to explore the Greek Islands, bathing the Danielson's in both ancient and modern Greek culture. Finally, they headed north, through the Dardanelles, the sea of Marmara, the Bosporus and finally after an exploration of Istanbul, the Turkish coast of the Black Sea.

Back in Marmaris, they placed the boat on the market. At home in Ashville, Julie was again diagnosed with cancer, this time cancer of the esophagus. No one was optimistic. But Julie was her usual strong and resilient self. The boat sold, and after six weeks of 200 mile commutes for treatment at Moffett Cancer Hospital in Tampa, Hank and Julie prevailed and celebrated her success with a hundred mile bicycle ride on the Withalacoochee trail in Inverness, Florida.

Today, the Danielson's still ride regularly with the Coastal Cruisers Bicycle Club in Englewood, Florida, where he is president, sail their Rhodes 19, and spend summers in Western New York. There they also teach sailing, bike and sail their Precision 16.5. Life has treated them well. They feel blessed.

September, 2018

Made in the USA
Columbia, SC
19 November 2018